The Nature of Ásatrú

The Norroena Society Presents

The Nature of Ásatrú

✦

An Overview of the Ideals and Philosophy of the Indigenous Religion of Northern Europe.

MARK PURYEAR

iUniverse, Inc.
New York Lincoln Shanghai

The Nature of Ásatrú
An Overview of the Ideals and Philosophy of the Indigenous Religion of Northern Europe.

iUniverse books may be ordered through booksellers or by contacting:

iUniverse
2021 Pine Lake Road, Suite 100
Lincoln, NE 68512
www.iuniverse.com
1-800-Authors (1-800-288-4677)

Cover art donated by Damon Keiffer.

ISBN-13: 978-0-595-38964-3 (pbk)
ISBN-13: 978-0-595-83348-1 (ebk)
ISBN-10: 0-595-38964-3 (pbk)
ISBN-10: 0-595-83348-9 (ebk)

Printed in the United States of America

This book is dedicated to the men and women of the Ásatrú nation, past and present, who have fought and worked for the continued survival of our sacred path.

To my wife, Katia Puryear: without you this work would not have been possible. I am so grateful to have you in my life and thank the gods and goddesses every day for bringing us together.

Special thanks to: William P. Reaves, Sharron Puryear, Les Puryear, Anthony Upshaw, Hengest, Osred, Adam, Else Christensen, Æinvargr and Thorstein Gudjonsson.

"Hearts in the Past, Minds on the Present, Eyes on the Future".

The Norroena Society Motto.

Contents

Introduction to
The Norroena Society

We at The Norroena Society are dedicated to the thorough and proper investigation of the ancestral traditions of Northern Europe as well as the promotion of our results and expansion of the Ásatrú faith. By keeping our hearts on the past, our minds in the present, and our eyes on the future we feel that we can maintain a strong institution of higher learning based upon a logical and spiritual understanding of our path.

Our society is made up of loyal men and women who work as a synergistic whole to bring you a well researched and purely heathen body of customary beliefs. It is our mission to record, for the most part, rather than interpret the traditions of our ancestral path and we feel that we have the means to do so correctly. Interpretation is for the individual; it is up to each and every one of us to find the logic within our beliefs that fits one's own way without violating our laws.

Because of the conflicts we Ásatrúar have faced over the last few hundred years we are left with some burning questions which many of us feel must be answered; questions such as: how much of our lore was corrupted by the Christians who passed it on to us? What can we do to restore it to its former glory for us today? And is there anything we have left out of our religious lives?

We are going to do everything in our power to answer all of these questions and give our people a new light to see the gods with, for we know that we can and will solve the problems that have plagued us. All of us in the nation of our faith can contribute in this quest, so long as we work together, keep our minds open to necessary changes, and listen to the voices of reason.

One enigma we each must ponder is how a sacred tradition originates and what constitutes its sacredness. Generally when we think of something very old, we recall the familiar adage—"if it was good enough for our ancestors, it's good enough for us". Such reasoning is fine as long as we do not forget about the powers we hold within ourselves. We are all capable of hearing the voices of the inspiring gods and goddesses. We need only to recognize these moments of divine intervention, when we're inspired by their presence, and to use what they give to us when they come. Inspiration is the power to keep a religion growing, if care is taken to not disrespect the foundations already laid within it. Without this true form of divine providence our movement would only retain archaic philosophies and exist as an anachronistic society, if it were to exist at all.

The ancient ways, before their transliteration and "interpretation" by Christians, existed as a living communicative interrelationship between our people and the gods above. In respect for this and the ancient path that developed from it we work for what we believe to be the closest shadow of these ideals and customs by using the investigative methodologies of the pioneers of theological research into Teutonic lore: Jacob Grimm, Rasmus Anderson, Dr. Viktor Rydberg, and others. We allow our inspirations to guide us, but will not use the word 'inspiration' or 'intuition' as an excuse to betray the works of these men by making up just anything without having evidence to back up our claims. Occasionally we may make some logical speculations but these will be few and far between and based upon sound conclusions in our investigations.

The point of our work is to use our powers of intellect and inspiration, the gifts of the gods, to rebuild our faith in the patterns set down by our ancestors, while, as I have said, keeping our minds in the present and our eyes on the future. We shall use tradition as our foundation, but inspiration will show us the way. We have, as a movement, made much advancement in the past few decades but there is still much to be done. Only as a nation, united in our faith and in our blood, shall we rebuild our sacred legacy.

There are many who believe that we have reached a stopping point in the recreation of the religious traditions of the North, that we have already picked up the charred remains and have cleaned them up as much as possible. We of The Norroena Society do not believe this is so, that in many ways we have just begun to scratch the surface! We look at the documents from the global Odinic community and we mainly see the study of yesterday's Ásatrú, filtered through the Christian pen, practiced today. The early traditions of our faith are certainly very important to us, but it is time that we make our religious evolution just as important, if not more important, than the ancient customs we hold so dear.

In order for us to commit ourselves to such an ideal, we must have a direction, a map to point us toward our goals. We have found in our researches twelve fundamentals which form the physical culture of any pagan faith. At one point or another every single one of the heathen religions have recognized them. Ours is no exception. They are: Pantheon, Lore/Theology, Ritual/Prayer, Nature, Music, Dance, Magic, Diet, Law, Folk/Ancestry, Combat, and Arts and Crafts. Using this map we shall create a series of texts that shall fully manifest each fundamental. This will be the hierology that we of The Norroena Society shall use in our practice of the Ásatrú religion, so each text will be religiously applicable. We shall also publish books on some of our investigations that are not directly related to a fundamental, but which benefited the work put into several of them. In each fundamental concept there is an entire field of thought and practice to stimulate the mind and continue the cultural advancement of our people, as well as our faith. If we let but one of them go unnoticed, we will have dropped an important element of our heritage into the abyss that opened in the Dark Ages, and will thus cause its extinction. Those of us who have love for our folk and for our gods and goddesses, certainly do not want to see that happen.

With every one of the fundamentals there are projects The Norroena Society will undergo so that we shall not only write about them, but will also experience them. The results will see to their growth and survival and our recording will insure that they are never corrupted or lost again. We understand the diligence and dedication that it will take to reach the goal of a fully manifested heathen cultural body and we gladly accept the challenges ahead of us. Together we shall raise up the banner of the gods in its full glory and let their light shine once again upon our world!

—The Norroena Society

Introduction

What is Ásatrú? It is commonly defined as the indigenous religion of the Northern European peoples, namely the Teutonic branch of the Indo-European family. The word "Ásatrú" is translated "Faith in the Aesir", the Aesir being the highest clan or tribe of our deities. This belief was once celebrated as the primary religion by people as far east as Russia, as far west as America and as far north as Iceland. Relics of its existence have dated as far back as pre-historic times, making it the heritage of anyone of Nordic descent. It is a religion that reveres nature and ancestry, and values honor and nobility. We worship many gods and goddesses, each a representative of natural forces as well as the ideals we aspire to. All across the world Ásatrú has re-awakened after centuries of slumber. Its profound philosophy challenges us to live life to its fullest and to continue to better ourselves. This is combined with a straightforward system of ethics and morals, all of which has appealed to people of all walks of life, many of whom seek to reclaim their sacred birthright.

I have been an "Ásatrúar" (practitioner of Ásatrú) for almost 20 years now, so I have seen just about all of the biases and misconceptions surrounding it. Although many of these are primarily derived from religious bigotry, much of the prejudice against the faith is due to a lack of understanding the true ideals behind it. A particular picture has been painted of the history of the ancient Teutons, especially the Scandinavians, so we are here to challenge this false imagery. I hope that, with the creation of this book I will be able to clear up many of the problems concerning what is to us a sacred way of life, while, at the same time, teaching the general philosophic ideology that it is built upon.

I will now explain what will be made clear as this work progresses, what Ásatrú is not. It is not "devil worship". We fully understand and accept the concept of good and evil and choose to work for what is good and right. There are no cults of Loki or Aurboda (our male and female representatives of corruption and evil); those who will try to include them into our pantheon have clearly not read our records carefully. We do not partake in human sacrifices and we do not believe in the harming of innocents. Animal sacrifice may be practiced by some groups, which is perfectly acceptable, since it is well understood that sacrifice was merely a means of sanctifying one's food before it was slaughtered. This is similar to the

Jewish method of koshering animals. Of course, some religious groups will always see us as "devil worshippers" because we do not worship their god, but we cannot concern ourselves with such religious intolerance.

Ásatrú is not a religion of violence, strife, and war. It is true that there is a warrior aspect to Ásatrú, but certainly, as all people, we prefer peace to war, love over hate, and harmony over discord, as did our ancestors. We are simply not hypocrites when it comes to the use of force. Some of the most warlike nations in the world are ruled by followers of religions that claim to be peaceful and pacifist. Physical confrontation is sometimes inevitable, but always must be a last resort. What few realize is that the ideals of honorable combat or chivalry, where rules are imposed to maintain our humanity when we are at our least humane, have their foundation in the tenets and social mandates that Ásatrú is built upon.

Ásatrú is not a "Viking" religion. Even though the most famous practitioners of the faith were the Vikings, their era represents a short time span in the long existence of our religion, which has lasted for thousands of years. Because of biased representations of the Vikings initiated by the church, it has been reported by some that Ásatrúar support rape and pillaging. Nothing could be further from the truth, and it is irresponsible of so-called 'educated' people to base their conclusions on what they see on television or in the movies. In many ancient Ásatrú societies rape was considered as bad or worse than murder and it was often punishable by death. Ancient laws tell us specifically that rape was never considered acceptable by our ancestors, nor was thievery for that matter. We cannot deny that the Vikings attacked and robbed churches in their time. This is historical fact. In their defense the so-called "Viking Age" must be looked at, for the most part, as a sort of war between the natives of Northern Europe and its Christian invaders, since it coincides with the violent introduction of Christianity into this region. Under Roman decrees the church was heavily taxing areas it controlled while non-Christian "heathens" were brutally attacked, tortured, and murdered for practicing their ancestral ways. In response, the Vikings raided monasteries and the Christian villages near them, taking back what belonged to the natives there in the first place! Even so, there isn't any reason why Ásatrúar today would consider pillaging of any sort, just as a Christian today, in most cases, wouldn't stone someone to death for committing "deadly sins".

Ásatrú is not a "racist" religion. It is an ethnic religion, and there is an emphasis on heritage and ancestry, but this must not be misconstrued as racism. There are some hate groups out there who have perverted the ideals of our beliefs to meet their political agenda, but few religions are exempt from this. The Ku Klux Klan claims to be based on Christian teachings and Muslims all over the world try to separate themselves from the terrorists that threaten our safety. In considering the folkish values of Ásatrú, the best comparisons would be those of Native Americans, Hindus and followers of the Oriental Shinto religion. All of these faiths represent an entire culture embodied by the ethnicity and nationality of their adherents. This does not imply any sort of hatred or disrespect towards other peoples or cultures. In fact, I have often found that respect for others and their cultures is much greater when one first learns to love themselves and their own.

Ásatrú is not an exercise in anachronism. There are some out there who like to play "dress up" when attending ceremonies or festivals, which is fine, as long as it is not seen as the primary purpose in our observances. I believe that our ancestors were very progressive, with a sense of fashion and technology that continued to evolve throughout the ages. They did not wear clothes that befit a bygone era, and there aren't any records describing such a tendency. Of course, pageantry was known, as was mummery, so we wouldn't reject the idea of dressing up, it's the purpose behind it that is important. We must be progressive and creative, not simply relying on the past for our practices. There is even evidence that the priesthood of ancient times had changing styles in their mode of dress for ceremonial purposes. The point is that our religion is an evolving ideal that advances with the ages and continues to move forward in our modern era. To focus mainly on the past is missing the point, since it is clear that our people have always forged ahead with the latest advancements in our civilizations. Although honoring our past is important, it should not keep us from looking towards the future. Our motto should be: "Hearts in the past, minds on the present, eyes on the future".

Ásatrú is not dogmatic. Although certain methods of reconstruction are being developed which may help to bring this faith to a state similar to that which it had before its corruption by Christianity, it can never be stated that there is only "one true path to the gods". How people interpret our traditions is up to them. I think that most Ásatrúar appreciate this independence, this ability to live one's spiritual life free from the mandates of a dictatorial hierarchy. No one can claim to be an "authority" on our path, since we have the freedom to accept or reject any idea or tradition, so long as we remain within the boundaries of the overall principles. No two Ásatrúar will think alike, as it should be. Many of the ideas presented in this book may be subject to scrutiny, for my views may not be the same as those of others. But my aim here is solely to help people understand the basic concepts of Ásatrú, in hopes of re-kindling the ancient fire in the hearts of our folk as we shine new light on this ancestral belief.

Now that we have examined what Ásatrú is not, I'll continue explaining what it is. To me, it is a connection to life, to the living universe, which in itself is a truly empowering concept. Our gods and goddesses are our earliest ancestors, representing a continually evolving network of existence that spans throughout all of nature, with all of us taking part. I am the son of my fathers and the father of my sons, a part of a line, a bloodline that is metaphysically significant and will continue to be for all time. The deities of our pantheon are an ancient source of inspiration who have always been there driving our people forward. Their stories give us something to aspire to, their wisdom guides us in all that we do. Even if we ignore them they are still there, and their blood still pumps in our veins. Even if we look at foreign cults for spiritual fulfillment, they are still there, watching over us as parents to their children. They give us our honor and our courage, our talents and our strengths, for we will always be one with them, as long as we exist.

There are various interpretations of our myths regarding the existence of our gods and goddesses. Some see them as personifications of natural forces; others view them as paradigms, or models to live our lives by. Still others consider them to be actual beings living on another world or plane of existence. The latter are divided into two categories: the spiritualists and the materialists. The spiritualists maintain that the gods and goddesses are ethereal beings living on another plane or dimension of reality. The materialists claim that these deities, products of evolution, are actual living beings who reside on another world somewhere in our universe. Most people use logic and science to validate their respective beliefs, since many choose to accept a worldview they consider to be based on intelligence and a true desire for understanding. Anyone new to the faith must first seek out and find the interpretation that makes the most sense to them, so they may see the gods and goddesses in a way that inspires them and helps them to find the spiritual path that suits them.

People today grow so sick of "religion", and with good reason. Religion without spirituality quickly stagnates so all that remains is an addiction to the mob. Religious groups try to feed this addiction by building huge places of worship and filling them with thousands of people, most of whom merely pay lip service to the belief out of fear of "eternal damnation". Then you have thousands of sects to choose from and each sect thinks all the other sects are doomed to this "eternal damnation", so, at the very least, there is constant bickering among them. Who needs that?

The fact is that spiritual decay comes from a lack of a cultural identity for the belief itself. Why is this? It is because indigenous religions were formed from the very core of our ancestral soul. They developed as we evolved through countless eons and are ingrained into the very fiber of our being. In ancient times the word 'religion' did not exist, nor were there any distinctions between different beliefs, other than the cultural identity. A person's religion was reflected by their very existence; by the way they looked and where they came from, for religion was culture! The faith was expressed in their laws, in their diet, in their modes of transportation, in all that they did and in every aspect of their lives. Ancient, organic religions encompass every facet of the human experience, and Ásatrú does this with a bold and direct approach. The god or goddess of love exists because love is a part of the human experience, as is war, agriculture, wealth, etc. Without such strong connections to the lives of our people and our ancestry a religion must have powerful tenets of subjugation to keep its followers humbled and silent.

Christianity was forced upon Northern Europe with centuries of warfare, inquisitions and political manipulations. Even with the immense power of the Roman Empire behind it, it still took over 500 years to convert all of the northern nations, and they never realized their goal of wiping out the ancient religions entirely. This book is living proof of that, as is the entire Ásatrú nation as it stands today. We mustn't resent modern Christians for this, for most do not even know about it and just want to live their lives as good people under the standards they were raised by. You may read essays and books from the Ásatrú community and think that many of us are vehemently anti-Christian. For the most part, when we are discussing the past atrocities committed by the church our words are not intended as blanket statements against all Christians, but are instead aimed at helping people to better understand the truth of what happened. In our search for the truth and our desire to uncover it we hope to show our folk, those who will listen, that we can be religious without all of the negative emotions usually associated with this. We will not proselytize, for our aim is to teach, not preach.

Because of the attempt to completely destroy these ancient beliefs, many of our traditions have been left in shattered pieces collected by monks in the Middle Ages. Their reason for collecting the fragments was partly due to nationalism and partly to a propaganda method used by the church to explain why Europe had been heathen for thousands of years, contradicting the biblical idea that the Christian god had always ruled over our world. The concept of the propaganda was that our gods and goddesses were ancient kings and queens who tricked our ancestors into worshipping them, for they were powerful magicians who became demons after their deaths.

We are fortunate that such collections were made at all, for we could have lost all records of our faith forever. However, these records are greatly mutilated and tainted by Christian and Classical influence, so we have much work to do in reconstructing the religion. It is our duty to do this—to rebuild and re-establish the ancient customs in the best way imaginable. In doing so we are effectively re-creating an entire culture from the ground up. Because Ásatrú is an organic religion, grown from the social strata of Northern Europe, all aspects of the ancient culture must be rebuilt in order to fully embrace the Teutonic religious way of life. The separation of religion from culture has even caused Ásatrúar today to overlook many facets of our belief. Focusing on rituals and runes shows that the sacred way of life has been contained within temple walls for far too long. Now we must begin to see the sacred in all that we do, for we are a part of the world around us!

Our method of reconstruction must involve every single aspect of living culture. Such a basis, built upon "The Twelve Fundamentals", will allow us to turn over every stone and find all of the information we need for our revival, our Ásatrú Renaissance! These fundamentals are Lore/Theology, Pantheon, Nature, Diet, Law, Music, Dance, Combat, Ritual and Prayer, Folk and Ancestry, Arts and Crafts, and Magic. Every ancient civilization has manifested these fundamentals in one way or another. I have found them to be a potent tool in developing a foundation for our research so that we may reach our goal of a renewed faith. In order for us to have a religious revival we must have a cultural revival, for to the practitioner of an indigenous religion, they are one and the same.

I have no doubt that Ásatrú can bring many answers for our people in their search for spiritual fulfillment. Anything that can be found elsewhere is no farther than your own front door, so to speak. As we build communities and develop projects to serve our folk, more people will realize the power of our collective unconscious, and will find significance in their individual life. You are significant. You are valid. You are important. No matter what or who you are you belong to a family, a genetic line that is the lifeblood of your folk, celebrated through your cultural heritage. Once you recognize this perhaps you may consider taking your place among those proud men and women who honor their gods and goddesses, their ancestors, and their lands. Thank you.

1

The Gods and Goddesses

"For the fourteenth I know,
If I have to name the gods,
Aesir and Álfar,
In the society of men,
I know them all well,
This few can do unskilled."

—*Ódin, Hávamál 160*

At the core of every faith are the deities that are worshipped or honored. Worship, in our view, denotes a reverence through celebration and respect. We pay tribute to our gods and goddesses as the parents of our folk, choosing to face them with bold and noble spirits. We will not submit ourselves before the divine, nor do we see them as our "masters", for we are kinsmen, related through an ancient bloodline with origins reaching back to the dawn of humanity. Their stories still live with us and speak to us as they did to our ancestors millennia ago. This continued survival is a testament to the strength and power of the folk-will, expressed through the vitality of the ancient customs themselves.

Each deity in our pantheon has a specific duty or attribute within their family or clan. These attributes manifest to us as focal points for specific prayers or lessons we can learn from their lore. In all respects the gods and goddesses represent the higher ideal of mankind, which we must strive for as creatures of evolution. No matter who you are or what your station is in life you can and should always strive to be something better. That is the ultimate purpose of our existence, and the ultimate goal for Ásatrúar. To evolve mentally, physically, and spiritually is the entire foundation of our religious motives. When we read the ancient tales we allow them to inspire us to reach for the divine, bringing us closer to our beloved gods and goddesses in this life and the next.

The following is a list of some of the major deities of our faith. The primary focus here is to explain the philosophical ideology centered around the pantheon, so this list is by no means complete. I will give a brief explanation of their nature, followed by the lessons they teach us within the lore associated with them. Simply serving as an introduction to our concept of divinity, this should begin the quest of familiarizing yourself with all of the gods and goddesses known to us. In your own discoveries you may find new lessons, and new bits of wisdom that will affect you in some way. Read their stories in the *Eddas* and elsewhere, and then see how they speak to you.

The Gods

The masculine paradigm of the ancient Teutons was unique among the peoples of the time in that it represents a balanced approach to the very image of manliness. Northern Europeans have always stood apart in their definition of masculinity, seeing it as a combination of heroism and benevolence. Machismo was utterly foreign to this ideal, since our ancestors placed a strong emphasis on nobility. The Teutonic hero was as kind as he was brave, a theme seen repeatedly in the myths and folklore. Nevertheless, it was manliness that was admired and always has been admired by our people. Rather than adapting feminine modes of behavior, our model supports the idea that men should be proud of their gender, and that women should value and respect them for this. Understanding, then living up to the ideal of manhood as displayed by our gods and heroes will help our folk in reclaiming their cultural identity. It could even begin a new appreciation for true family values; when men act like men—as providers, protectors and teachers, their roles as fathers should be highly acclaimed. For this model, we look to the gods to guide us on our path.

ÓDIN: Our highest god, known by many different names, is the All-Father: lord of the winds, god of wisdom, of ancient secrets and untold powers. With his brothers, Vili and Vé, Ódin created our people and our world. The reason he is worshipped as the highest god is because he represents the perfect balance of higher life. He is a warrior, willing to fight for what is right and honorable. He is a king, a noble and valiant leader of gods and men, always placing others' needs before his own. He is a magician, wise and intelligent, always seeking new knowledge and learning new secrets. Finally, he is a lover, kind and benevolent, gentle and caring. From a psychological perspective, this is the ideal of the well-rounded man.

From Ódin, we see the life of struggle for improvement directly, as stories of his adventures describe toil and sacrifices made to gain wisdom and experience. He hung on the World Tree, Yggdrasil, for nine nights without food or drink, wounded by his spear. Then he later gave his eye—all so he could continue to better himself for the sake of the worlds and his beloved children. He travels all the realms of existence in search of new ways to evolve, to continue learning the secrets of the universe, so that we may gain from his teachings.

Ódin's search for wisdom is not based simply on self-aggrandizement or personal accomplishment. The quest for the higher self is never subject to narcissism, which contradicts the very concept. When Ódin journeys through the worlds he does so in the service of his folk: the eternal student is also the great teacher. All that he does he does for us, so that we in turn shall help those around us.

THÓR: Ódin's son is the mighty champion of the gods, the most powerful warrior in all the worlds, and the protector of Midgard (another name for earth). In his own way, Thór represents an inner balance as well, for he is seen as both the fierce combatant and the loving friend. In one instant his menacing gaze could strike fear into the heart of almost any creature. In the next, his hearty laugh and warm disposition could move even the sternest of souls. His is the most ancient, most profound image of the Nordic warrior, which has lived through the age of Vikings, the era of knights, the time of musketeers, onward to today's soldiers. The Nordic warrior is not known for his savagery, but for his nobility. He will aid the weak, protect the downtrodden, and even pay tribute to a fallen foe. It is true that gods of war are worshipped in the Ásatrú faith, but without them and their creed, combat would have been a much more brutal activity than it is today.

Thór protects those who cannot protect themselves, always fighting with honor for honor's sake. His powerful hammer has become the emblem of our religion. This mighty weapon he uses, on the one hand, to destroy the forces of chaos, then on the other, to sanctify all sorts of things with his divine force. Stronger than all of the gods, Thór teaches us to respect power, both within ourselves and within others. We must use our strengths wisely and beneficially, refraining from the destructive paths of tyranny and malevolence. Simply because one has power does not mean they should abuse it.

Of course, the model of Thór is a heroic one, so he inspires us to be courageous as well as bold, and to always be vigilant against the forces of chaos that could do us harm. It is our duty to our people to fight against tyrants, bullies and criminals, a duty that Thór holds in the highest esteem.

BALDUR: Where Thór stands above all the other gods in strength, Baldur does so in kindness. He is the most beloved deity in our pantheon, the god who won the hearts of all creatures with his loving spirit. Although he too is a warrior, he has the most forgiving, most conciliatory disposition than all other beings. He teaches us to always consider physical force as a last resort, to display cooperation and compromise in the face of conflict. I believe that Baldur is considered "the most beloved god" because he represents the highest ideals of civilization—compassion and kindness, which in turn should be considered the greatest virtues within our religious philosophy. It is easy for a warrior to forget their humanity in the face of an enemy, easy to give in to anger and rage when frustrated by an opponent. It is the paradigm of Baldur that keeps our hearts in check when we might lose control of ourselves.

To make peace, to forgive, to express love to others, these are all ideas associated with Baldur. All living things, even those among the forces of chaos, adore him for this. Only Loki and Aurboda were hateful enough to lack sympathy for his death, which Loki ultimately caused. Baldur is our god of justice as settler of disputes, promoter of harmony. His son, Forseti, inherited this position from his father after he was slain. The peacemaker is a duty well-loved by all, for everyone prefers peace and harmony over conflict and strife. He is also god of summer, that most joyous season when the warmth of the sun reigns supreme, when ancient tribal assemblies were held as part of the celebrations of this happiest time of the year.

FREY: He is the god of fertility and virility. His status among the gods includes all aspects of male sexuality and reproduction. Often depicted naked, with an erect phallus, Frey is the incarnation of vigorous sexual strength. As a representative of the creative energies he rules over the harvest, the nature-artists known as Álfar, and the cycles of life. He reminds us that we are still natural beings, as much a part of the world around us as any other creature. It is foolish of us to try to separate ourselves from nature, to think we are somehow above it or to think that it is there for us to exploit in any way we choose. As natural beings we should never be ashamed of our sexuality, for it is as much a part of our existence as breathing.

We should not confuse Frey's role as the god of sexuality and fertility with that of a god of hedonism. There is no Nordic equivalent to Bacchus or

Dionysus, no orgiastic cults associated with our ancient faith. Although we do not subscribe to puritanical suppression of natural sexual urges, our people have always recognized a personal responsibility towards honor and dignity in our affairs between men and women. Such responsibilities, which will be discussed in detail later, are a part of Frey's role as well.

Frey's lesson is to embrace our human nature, as well as to accept certain limitations. Eastern religions have taught us to reject the most valuable aspects of life! There is nothing wrong or shameful about sexuality, only in acts that bring harm to you, to others, or to your family and folk. We must cast off the shackles of artificial doctrines that would deny us one of our most basic needs! Without a natural, healthy sexual idealism for the folk perversions arise that leave many trapped in the self-imposed lifestyles of degenerate behavior. Even among the most "free-thinking" people there is still a need for some shred of respectability, which is innate within us all.

NJÖRD: Father of Frey and Freyja, he is the god of wealth, prosperity, and commerce. As stated before, Ásatrú recognizes and celebrates all aspects of the human experience. Because of this there is no disdain towards wealth or the wealthy found in our traditions. In fact, almost every ancient tale from Northern Europe glorifies the noble class in one way or another. Why is this? Because Ásatrú religion is based on the natural evolutionary competition where all must strive and struggle to be the best they can be. With such a philosophy must be combined the strict mandates of generosity and hospitality that were the hallmarks of Nordic civilization.

Today, a lot of emphasis is placed on equality among all, which isn't necessarily a bad thing in most cases. We simply must not take this too far and forget that we are supposed to work towards excellence, to essentially become better than others. Such a desire to rise above should not be combined with guilt for our achievements, for we earned them and deserve rewards for them.

Often times we can recognize nobility through actions more than wealth, for anyone can be noble. If we toil for our improvement eventually we will succeed, for those who will continue to move forward in spite of difficulty or opposition will always profit from this. Njörd teaches us to work hard, persevere, educate ourselves and try to be as successful as we can be, so we can become benefactors among our folk. This shouldn't be regarded as some sort of "cult" philosophy, where we would want to siphon money from other Ásatrúar. It is simply a decree that success, coupled with generosity is honorable, even encouraged within our ancient customs. We do not see money as "the root of all evil", but we do not accept greed in any of its forms. Such a vice is known in our ancient records to incur the wrath of the gods, since those who are miserly care little for the needs of their family and folk.

HÖDUR: He is probably the most misunderstood of all the gods, and is indeed the most unlucky. The idea that he was ever believed to be blind is a concept developed in the Christian era from a misconception, and is thus false and should be ignored. He was actually a brave warrior, a renowned hunter and an avid sportsman, none of which he could have achieved without sight. The lore tells us that Loki tricked Hödur into killing his own brother, Baldur. This act condemned him to die, in turn. Some have taken his slaying of Baldur, along with his supposed blindness, as a sign that he was some sort of dark god, worshipped by the sinister among our ancestors. However, such thinking defies what we know from our sources and undermines the tragedy of this, the saddest of tales.

From his youth to the moment of his death, Hödur had to deal with one misfortune after another, telling us that even gods can have bad luck. But Hödur accepts his fate, even in the end when he had to die at the hand of his other brother, Ódin's newborn son, Váli. Thus, Hödur's lesson is that no matter who we are we are bound to face adversity at some point in our lifetime. The amount of misfortune one faces is no measure of a man; it is rather *how* he faces them that is important. Because of Hödur's noble spirit in the face of struggle he shall return with Baldur after Ragnarök, the great conflagration, to rebuild the worlds.

TÝR: The most well known story concerning Týr is the binding of the Fenris wolf, Loki's monstrous son who became so large and savage, threatened the world order. Many interpret this binding as the restraining of chaotic forces by those of order and goodness. In order for the wolf to be bound, Týr had to sacrifice his right hand so that the honor of the gods would not be forsaken as they tricked the wolf into letting them fetter him. Therefore, Týr is viewed as a martyr-god, who gave up his sword hand to protect the worlds. As the god of war such a sacrifice was indeed significant, for lack of the sword hand is a great loss for one in combat.

From this, it is obvious that Týr's lesson is one of bravery and a willingness to do whatever it takes for the safety of one's people. It takes a supreme amount of love and loyalty for one to give up life or limb for those they are devoted to. Anyone who would make the ultimate sacrifice should be honored and revered by their folk as true heroes, given a place among ancestors before them who have done the same. Peace cannot be maintained without warriors, which is why it is the war god who must bind the wolf. An admiration for heroism is a sign of true appreciation for those who would fight and die for their land and people. Such sacrifices must not just be left up to soldiers either, for any of us can play our part in the welfare of our nations. We simply must be bold enough to do so.

HEIMDALL: Once, Heimdall, the guardian of the worlds, came to Midgard to bless our genetic lines with his essence and to bring culture to our people. It is believed that all of our earliest industries and technologies came to us from the gods through Heimdall. He taught our ancestors how to pray, how to grow crops, how to make and use fire, how to bake, to craft and forge, spin and weave, read and write, and gave them the knowledge of the runes—ancient secrets and symbols used in various ways.

As the great Teutonic culture-bringer, Heimdall teaches us the sanctity of our heritage. There is nothing more valuable, more sacred than the ancestral ways and genetic inheritance passed down to us through countless ages. Not only do they connect us to who we are, they give us our place in eternity, as the middle point between that which has been and that which will be. Patriotism doesn't even come close in matters of importance, for borders come and go, while our cultural, ethnic birthright is eternal! How can we take pride in being American or Canadian or German or English, etc. if we cannot first be proud of who we are genetically? Geographic distinctions are man-made and artificial, whereas our bloodline was given to us by nature, and for us Ásatrúar, by the gods and goddesses of our people! This heritage, above all else, is what makes us special. We should not allow the perversion of this natural tendency towards our own folk, which has manifested, for some, as ignorant bigotry, turn us away from a legacy that has existed for centuries, which we should be proud of.

In celebrating our ancient faith we honor Heimdall as the god who taught it to us in the first place. As he established the earliest customs, so must we continue teaching them to our children, encouraging them to teach it to their children, and so on. An understanding of the importance of the cultural identity may bring new life into the hearts of many who feel lost in the cultureless morass of self-centered consumerism.

ULL: Originally, he was one of the Álfar, lesser demigods in close relations to the higher deities. His mother is Sif and his father is Egil-Örvandil, both well-respected members of the Álfar clans. Through a series of adventures with his half-brother, Svipdag, Ull managed to build an outstanding reputation of heroism, leading to his adoption among the major gods. At one point, during a period when Ódin was exiled from Ásgard, Ull was elected to act in his stead as the high-est god. Fortune continued to smile on his family as Svipdag married Freyja, thus becoming a higher god himself, and Sif, after Egil died, married Thór, thus mak-ing her a goddess.

Ull's life story tells us that nothing is unachievable for those willing to strive and struggle. He inspires us to reach for our dreams, to never settle for second best, and to never lose sight of our goals. Sometimes the road of ambition is a long, difficult path to follow, but in the end its rewards are tremendous. If a young demigod can attain the position of highest of all the gods, certainly we can achieve anything we set our minds to. As with Ull, we only need the support of others, a strong heart, and an opportunity and we can do anything!

The Goddesses

As the gods epitomize the ideals of manly virtue, the goddesses exemplify all that can be expressed through feminine nobility. Beauty, motherhood, sensuality, nurturing, all that women are and can be is represented through the female divine principle. Since there are no goddesses among the patriarchal, monotheist reli-gions, this principle has long been missing from the lives of many. The ancient Northern Europeans maintained a profound respect for goddesses and women that was unparalleled anywhere else. No other cultures in the world put more of an emphasis on honoring women than the Teutons and Celts, a national charac-teristic well documented by foreign observers. In fact, Europeans are the only ones known to have had established matriarchies, where queens ruled. Even today, the only countries that fully embrace the concept of women's rights are either European or are strongly influenced by European values. The goddesses inspire our women to be strong, independent, and noble, without compromising their femininity. They are to be vital members of our Ásatrú nation, standing beside our men as equals, valued for their roles among our people.

FRIGGA: The wife of Ódin and queen of Ásgard, she is identical to Jord or Ner-thus, our Mother Earth. This title is connected to both her husband's creation of Midgard and her clan's position in the pantheon, for she is one of the Vanir, the nature deities. She is our All-Mother, Ódin's female counterpart representing motherhood, childbirth, and the revered roles of women in the home. She is the incarnation of the female creative force, highly honored by our folk. Where Ódin is Father Sky, she is our bounteous earth, bringing forth the rewards of life and plenty for those who will work for them. Instead of being given reign over the earth and its creatures, the gods gave us Midgard as a house, one which we are responsible for, as it takes care of us. Frigga is a domestic goddess of the earth, and of the hearth, which can, in a way, be viewed as synonymous.

Frigga's lesson commands respect for her powers of creation. With soaring populations and rampant industrialism we have abused our earth for far too long. It is our duty as Ásatrúar, as people living on this planet, to do our part in protecting our environment. Our faith originates in a strong connection to the land and to the forces of nature. Religion and nature must never be separated, for we must never believe that we are somehow above natural law. With all of our money, with all of our technology, we are still children of Mother Earth, whose powers we have only begun to understand. The balance of her ecosystems is fragile and sacred, not to be toyed with by the selfish or greedy. Those who will treat her with respect, who will toil for her gifts, may reap the rewards of her bounty without raping her.

FREYJA: She is our goddess of love, fertility, fecundity, and female sexuality—the counterpart to her brother, Frey. Like Frigga, she represents motherhood and childbirth, the woman's powers of creation. The most beautiful of all the goddesses, women pray to her for help in all matters. She is married to Óð-Svipdag, and once traveled all the worlds searching for him when he was in exile. Her tears, the tears of a woman's love, became gold, serving as compensation for an insult her husband had made against the gods.

Before the coming of Christianity our women had the freedom to live their lives in any way they chose. Some even became warriors, joining men in battle on land or at sea. Still others became mighty rulers. At the same time, traditional female roles were admired by all, having an equally important status as men's duties. No matter what her class, the housewife, named after Freyja (*Húsfreyja*, G. *Hausfrau*) was highly respected in her home and community. She wore the keys to the house around her waist as a symbol of her authority. From this, a competition of sorts would have existed, where women would work to have the most well kept home in their tribe or clan. There was nothing subservient about the position at all, until foreign belief systems were introduced, diminishing the place of the "lady of the house" considerably.

Freyja teaches women to love who they are and for men to love them for it. In order for a man to have respect for a woman, she must first have respect for herself. For feminists to condemn or devalue traditional roles for women is to betray some of the most valued aspects of femininity, essentially giving in to the patriarchal view that these roles are not as important as men's. Women are natural caretakers and nurturers, so the idea of motherhood should be considered the most significant for women in our society. But this does not mean that we would chain our women to the idea, just as we wouldn't hold our men to any preconceived notion about what should be important to them. There is power in promotion, and it is important for us to promote the idea of family and kinship to all our people.

Remember, the same forces that enslaved women enslaved all of us, men and women, to their crude doctrine. Reactionary disgust towards an intrusive, foreign paradigm is natural, but should not get in the way of our developing a positive, productive outlook towards these traditional roles. New trends must be created and promoted where natural roles are respected and valued by everyone, while at the same time continuing the work for women's freedom and equality. The first man and woman created by the gods were formed from intertwined trees, and given gifts that made them equals in the eyes of our deities. If all aspects of femininity are not given equal value, those women who do not meet current standards, who choose to adopt traditional roles, are not treated with as much respect, essentially, as their more "progressive" constituents. Such a devaluation is part of the reason European populations are steadily declining, leading us towards our extinction.

NANNA: Daughter of the moon-god, Máni, she is Baldur's devoted wife. The love she has for her husband exceeds any love ever known. When she saw him being carried to his funeral pyre, after he had been slain, she immediately died from a broken heart. Now, she lives with him in the Underworld, preparing the children of the renewal for their duties after Ragnarök. Her eternal love reaches even beyond the boundaries of life. It is generally accepted that, from her devotion to her husband, Nanna represents fidelity and loyalty. However, her name means "The Brave", which denotes her feminine strength as well. Her loyalty could never be confused with submission, even though Christian doctrine interprets this as such. We can therefore consider her to be the goddess of the marriage of equals as well. Modern Europeans are only reclaiming their heritage when reestablishing the idea of equality between husband and wife, where we are partners in our relationships.

Nanna's death not only represents her devotion as a wife, it also signifies how much Baldur deserved such affection. We should strive to love our spouses, or mates with all the passion we can muster, while continuously earning their passionate love. Imagine how strong a love must be for a wife to actually die from seeing her dead husband. If we only earn a fraction of such faithfulness, we could build relationships to last a lifetime!

SKADI: If there is any doubt about the existence of the ancient model of the strong Nordic woman, one only needs to read the lore on Skadi. She is the mighty goddess of the hunt, who seems to manifest all of the freedoms women held in ancient Northern Europe. She was allowed to choose her own husband (which was unheard of elsewhere at the time), hunts the wild mountain ranges near Thrymheim, her home, and once even challenged all of the gods and goddesses of Ásgard! Early nobles proudly traced their ancestry through her, and it is thought that Scandinavia (Skadinauja) was named after her.

She is the daughter of Völund-Thjázi, and was enraged when she learned that the gods had killed him. She suited herself with arms and armor, walked up the Bifröst Bridge to Ásgard, and demanded compensation for the slaying. In doing so she was following the sacred duties of kinship, which commands that we seek reparation for any harms done to our family or ourselves. Obviously, given her attire, she was well prepared to fight, which surely would have led to her death. But the gods and goddesses chose to make amends by allowing her to choose a husband among them by the sight of his feet, which in effect would give her the rank of an Ásynja, or goddess of the Aesir. Also, she was made to laugh by Loki, alleviating her sorrow, and Völund was honored by having his eyes cast up into the heavens by Thór, where they become stars.

When Skadi made her choice of a husband, thinking that she had spotted the feet of Baldur, who she wanted, it was Njörd who became her spouse. Even in her marriage to him she exemplifies her independent nature. Her home is in the mountains, which Njörd cannot stand to reside in; his home is near the ocean, which she cannot bear. So they live separately, although they are presumably still married.

Loki played a major role in the death of her father, a fact that Skadi never forgets. In the end, after Loki is banished from Ásgard for his treachery and bound by the entrails of his own son, she is the one who places the serpent over his face, which will drip burning venom on his face until Ragnarök, causing him much pain and suffering. In all respects Skadi is the embodiment of the strong, free-willed woman, standing equal to many of the gods in might and bravery.

URD: There is a late tradition where Loki's half-black, half-pale daughter rules the Underworld under the name Hel. The idea is based on a Christian misconception developed to make the Teutonic eschatology and cosmology match that of the Bible. His daughter's real name is Leikin, who only watches over the realm of the damned as Hel's servant. The true Hel is, in fact, our goddess of fate, of that-which-is, the benevolent deity concerned with matters of life and death, Urd. She is the highest of the Norns, powerful maidens directly linked to all sentient beings as their guardians or the creators of their destiny. Her sisters, Verdandi and Skuld, help her weave the web of *Wyrd*, a symbol of synchronicity and the relationship between all life in the universe.

To our ancestors, no power was greater than that of fate. It is possible that it was personified as a mighty deity (Metod) worshipped by the gods and goddesses, with Urd as his representative. Today there are many caught up in the ideals of individualism, who do not believe in fate simply because they feel they can control their own destiny. Such a belief is based on a lack of understanding of what fate is. All we can "control" in life is our own choices, how we choose to live and deal with what life has to offer. Everything else is fate. Let's consider an example:

You see a carrot lying on a table, then decide you want to eat the carrot, so you move towards it. Here you are controlling your choice, your decision that you want that carrot. But then, I run up, grab the carrot and take off with it. Of course you could say I'm just being boorish, but nevertheless, you do not have the carrot, even though it was your decision to get it. This is fate. You cannot control your destiny because you cannot control your environment or those around you. This is why, in Ásatrú, the concept is represented by a web, with each thread, a thread of fate, signifying the life of an individual. When two threads meet this is the overlapping of two lives: our relationships with one another. As we live out our existence Urd creates our threads of fate from her sacred well, feeds them to her sister Verdandi who weaves them into web, the lives or fates of others, then Skuld cuts them, deciding our time to die, then to be reborn in the next world.

Urd's lesson is to accept life on life's terms. We may not be able to control our environment, but we can control how we deal with it. We will make our decisions, trying to make the best of any situation, and hope that Fortune will shine down on our endeavors. No matter what the outcome we must face our ups and downs with dignity. Most problems human beings face are based on our perception of how things should be, rather than how they are. Developing an acceptance of what happens is a mark of the highly evolved person. This is not to say that we do not try to fix wrongs, or that we live passively, waiting for fate to lead the way, it is simply a decree that things happen for a reason. This is why Urd is not the goddess of that-which-was or the "past" as it is commonly defined, but rather of that-which-is, the way things are and the circumstances that have led up to them. When bad things happen we learn from our mistakes, or demand compensation when we are wronged, or fight against those who oppress us. Fixating on the past changes nothing.

SIF: Although the most noteworthy story about Sif is Loki's cutting of her hair, which led to the great artists' competition, it is not here that we look for the wisdom of her lore. There is a tale where she appears under a different name, Kraka, where she is the stepmother of Svipdag-Erik. Freyja was once betrayed by her maidservant, Aurboda, and placed in the hands of the Jötuns, the children of Chaos. There she was guarded by a large clan of powerful Jötun warriors under the leadership of Beli, a mighty chieftain. Sif enticed her stepson to rescue the goddess, which was indeed a perilous quest. So perilous, in fact, that Svipdag believed his stepmother was trying to lead him to his death. But Sif knew the decrees of the Norns well, and knew that Svipdag would achieve his goals. When Ull, her son, decided to join in the adventure, she asked Svipdag to watch over his brother, which he readily agreed to do. This began what could be called the greatest hero-saga known in the Teutonic lore. Ull gained the greatest of glories, as we have seen, and Svipdag, also known as Ód, became Freyja's husband and a god himself.

From this story we can see Sif's lesson as one of shrewd, stern wisdom, where one may have to go against the wishes of those they love or care for, for the greater good. Svipdag believed she had malicious intent in her urges for the adventures he would face because he felt that they were beyond his abilities. But Sif knew better, and did what she felt was right for her stepson. Sometimes we have to do what's best, even if it isn't necessarily popular. Had she not been bold enough to incite Svipdag, he would have missed out on the highest honors. Those who will stand their ground on such matters, no matter what stands in their way, are the people we want as leaders among our folk.

GRÓA: Sif is Svipdag's stepmother, Gróa is his mother, they were both wives of Egil-Örvandil. When Svipdag suspected ill-will in Sif's demands that he seek out Freyja, he went to his mother's grave to call upon her aid. Before her death, she had told her son to visit her cairn if he was ever in need of her help. Rather than supporting Svipdag's suspicions against Sif, she sang songs over him that would strengthen his heart and his abilities, so he would be victorious.

In another story, Gróa sang songs of healing over Thór to help him remove a piece of Hrungnir's hone that got lodged into his skull when they dueled. During the adventure, Thór came across Gróa's husband, who had been missing. When he tells Gróa of this she is so happy she forgets the chants needed to heal him. So the hone remains in Thór's head to this day.

Gróa is the selfless goddess willing to help those in need. Though this could probably be said of any of the gods or goddesses, it is she who stands out in such matters, it is she who Thór goes to for assistance above all others. She teaches us to always be ready to give aid when it is needed, as well as accept assistance ourselves. Not even the gods are so stubborn or arrogant to think that they can do anything and everything by themselves. Whenever they need help, they are quick to ask for it, and are always willing to give it in return. This is the very idea of a tribe, or clan, or family, or community—when one drops the load, the other picks it up. Such a concept was once imperative for the survival of any group of people, for without a communal effort many tasks are simply not possible.

IDUN: She is the goddess of youth, whose golden apples rejuvenate the gods and keep them immortal. The best-known tale about her is when she was taken by Völund-Thjázi, then subsequently "rescued" by Loki, who had been involved in her kidnapping in the first place. There is evidence in our records that tells us that Idun was Völund's sister, as well as his lover. Such incestuous relationships are common in the ancient lore, but have always, even by our ancestors, been treated as a unique, and somewhat shocking trait of the divine. One source states that incest of this kind is found only among the Vanir and Álfar, but is expressly forbidden among the Aesir. Perhaps it was considered necessary to keep the divine blood within their family, although it is more likely that this is a relic of the earliest symbolism when they were viewed merely as forces of nature.

Some sources tell us that when Idun was in exile with Völund she changed her appearance, as well as her disposition. She began to delight in guile, to take on the same characteristics as her vengeful lover, who hated the gods for rejecting his gifts in the artists' competition between Ívaldi's and Mímir's sons (Völund, Egil, and Slagfin versus Sindri and Brokk). This loving, beautiful goddess became an evil witch, a myrk-rider as they were known. She began to take part in acts meant to destroy the gods' creations, which she had previously promoted. Namely, this was the first Fimbulwinter, an Ice Age that would annihilate all life. While she was gone from Ásgard the destructive powers began to dominate as the gods and goddesses grew old. Fortunately this Fimbulwinter was reversed before it was too late, but a second, final great Ice Age is prophesied to occur right before Ragnarök, which will signal the end of the world.

Several factors came into play which caused the first Fimbulwinter to end: Völund-Thjázi, who had been conjuring the terrible ice storms, was killed; all of the captive deities of vegetation were returned to their rightful places, and new powers arose to fend off the forces of Chaos. But how was Idun allowed to regain her status after she had helped in an attempt to destroy creation? Obviously she has atoned for this in some way, which is her lesson to us. In our lives, we will make some bad choices or wrong decisions, some more than others. This is just a simple fact of life. Our gods and goddesses do not expect us to be perfect, nor do they expect us to grovel before them when we make a mistake. When we err, we should do our best to make up for it, then try not to do it again, it is as simple as that. There is no crime that cannot be placated for, no transgression that cannot be repaired. Sometimes one might even be made to pay for a crime with their life. In ancient times, the idea of capital punishment was based on the concept that, by taking one's life, they had suffered for their infraction and could therefore face the possibility of being rewarded with a blessed afterlife. However, even murder could be recompensed by means other than execution. Most likely, it simply depended on the status of the victim and/or the demands of their family.

NÁT: (Night) She has been called "The Mother of the Gods", which designates her position in her family rather than any sort of royal title. Her bloodline reaches into all of the divine clans—Aesir, Vanir, Álfar and the Jötuns. With Delling she had the son Dag, a high Álf prince, lord of the day; with Anar-Fjörgynn (Hoenir), she had Frigga, a Vanir-goddess who married Ódin and had the Aesir sons Thór, Baldur, and Hödur; with Naglfari-Máni, she had Njörd, the Vanir-prince who sired Frey, Freyja and several other goddesses with his sister, Frigga. Nát herself is a *dís* (goddess) of the higher Jötun clan (which will be explained below) that was spawned from Ymir's, the Chaos being's, arms. Thus, all of the most ancient tribes have some relation to her.

Above all, Nát is a representative of order as our patroness of night. Our ancestors actually reckoned time by nights, rather than by days, for Night is Day's mother, and thus preceeds him. She teaches us to work for the order, the universal order that flows in its natural progression, opposing the chaos that would bring all things to ruin. In all of existence everything moves through the never-ending cycle of birth, life, death, and rebirth. All of nature exists in some way or another as an adaptation to this cycle, as a part of the process of evolution. We can further our development by understanding and working for the natural order, constantly toiling in the face of adversity. By living our lives honorably, focusing always on bettering ourselves, we can use these ideals to our advantage, while paying tribute to Mother Night.

All of the gods and goddesses have some sort of benefit to present to us in one way or another. Some of their lessons are easy to find, while others are more obscure. We have a long way to go in piecing together the ancient fragments left to us from our lore. You can be sure that all of the above information has been well researched and can be verified. I simply want to give these ancient archetypes a proper introduction without going into a lot of detail or representing all kinds of complicated research. However, these stories are valid and should be recognized for their worth to our people. Our goal is to have a restored *Edda* that will have all of our ancient tales given in their proper form (at least as close as we can get to it) so everyone will know and understand the full body of our lore.

The Divine Clans

Besides personal descriptions of each deity, it is important to describe the purpose behind each of the divine families, as they are understood in our religion. Each clan has a role to play in the natural order, and each work more or less harmoniously with the others towards maintaining it. Without one clan the others would be lost, for each meet a particular need within creation. The needs met are related to the dispositions of the deities involved, as we shall see.

AESIR: The Aesir have the role of protecting the worlds, which is why all of them are warriors or gods of war. This is also why they are honored as the highest deities, for they represent the perfect ideal of heroism, which all men have admired since the dawn of time. Many Vanir deities were adopted into the Ása-clan as they began to take on more warlike aspects, though they still maintained their status as Vana-gods or goddesses. The fact is, we need protectors more than anything. It may not seem like it in our modern world, but without heroes defending our people from threats, both foreign and domestic, our entire idea of civilization would break down. As much as we long for a peaceful world, there will always be crime and war. If we do not have those that are prepared to fight against criminals or foreign enemies we are certainly vulnerable to attack. Soldiers, policemen, even firefighters play the same roles as the Aesir in protecting our folk, and should be honored as such.

VANIR: The second highest group of gods and goddesses are the regulators of the natural order, who see to it that all of the processes of creation are maintained. The cycles of time, rising and setting of the sun and moon, the ebb and flow of the ocean, the growth of crops, all of these occur under the authority of the Vanir. Thus they are our nature-deities, as well as representatives of love and peace, more so than they are gods and goddesses of war. Of course, in the Aesir and Vanir clans the attributes of war-deities and nature-deities are interchangeable, some simply stand out more than others. The Vanir will certainly fight to protect the order if need be, and the Aesir may represent some forces of nature, but in normal circumstances these are the duties they perform.

The Vanir teach us to revere nature in its many forms. Ásatrúar do not look for "miracles" in burning bushes or divine magic, we see the power of nature for what it is, as the miracle that it is. When we stand in awe of the sunrise, when we are moved by a mountain landscape, when we find joy in the forests or ravines or oceans we are experiencing the religious inspiration of the Vanir.

ÁLFAR: They are the great nature-artists who, under the patronage of Frey as their leader, are in charge of the actual work required to keep the natural order going. They decorate the worlds with vegetation and create wondrous artifacts for the gods and goddesses, to aid them in their duties. The gods may have created Midgard, but it was the Álfar who adorned it with flowers and birds and all sorts of living things. To me, these Teutonic demigods represent the scientific basis of our faith, for they seem to be the earliest conception of men and women of higher learning. Some of their inventions, such as chess games that play by themselves or flying machines are technologies that we take for granted today. All of our stories can be interpreted through science: from the creation of life by fire (energy) and ice (matter), to the evolutionary theories on the possibilities of gods actually existing, to the renewal of life from destruction (Ragnarök).

Some of the Álfar, such as Delling, Dag, and Sunna work particularly in the duties of bringing light to the worlds, and as such are called Ljósálfar, the Light-Elves. Others, known as the Svartálfar, Swarthy-Elves, and Dökkalfar, Dark-Elves, may be designated thus because they are pictured as living in deep, underground realms where they mine for ores to make their creations with. Or, these may have moral implications surrounding certain rebellions against the gods. All of the Álfar teach us the value of hard work, of the importance for us all to do our part in the duties needed to keep our civilizations moving forward, with respect to our earth and the universe around us.

JÖTUNS: There are two divisions of the Jötun clan: one monstrous and evil, the other noble and good. Both were descended from Ymir—the former through Thrudgelmir who was born of his father's feet, the latter through Mímir and

Bestla who were born under his arms. The idea is that the arms were considered more noble appendages than the feet.

Many benevolent characters came from the higher Jötun clan, including Nát (Mímir's daughter), the Norns, Gríd, Gunnlöd, Aegir, Sigyn, etc. We cannot simply dismiss the Jötuns as entirely evil or chaotic. Their roles always seem to have something to do with the primal age of creation, when all the worlds and all life were coming into being. Indeed, all Jötuns represent, in some way or another, the primordial past.

Tales of giants who lived on the earth before men came to replace them have been told in almost every civilization, almost every religion in the world. Even the Bible has its story of David and Goliath. It is likely that these stories represent the actual invasion of homo sapiens as they overcame their predecessors, earlier forms of humanity such as Neanderthals. I will not consider here exactly who these ancestors were, I will only point out that this is yet another example of when myth and science overlap.

There is a certain degree of personal empowerment that accompanies a relationship with divinity, a feeling known by religious people for centuries. No other faith will have a more profound impact on your life or your spirit than the one developed through your own heritage, by your own folk. Ásatrú is based entirely on the improvement of the self and of the folk. Our gods and goddesses are out there, watching down on us, trying to help us as we take each step towards joining them in our next life. We only need to hear their voices again and to embrace them as our ancestors did so long ago. Once they have become an important part in all of our lives we may begin to work towards reclaiming our sacred birthright, then we will start the path towards our destiny.

2

Wyrd

"A cowardly man
thinks he will live forever
if he avoids the fight;
but old age will
give him no peace,
though spears may spare him."

—Óðin, Hávámal 16

"To his friend
a man should be a friend,
and requite gifts with gifts;
laughter with laughter
men should receive,
but leasing with lying."

—Óðin, Hávámal 42

Probably the highest philosophical ideal within the ancient Teutonic beliefs was that of fate or *Wyrd*. It was looked upon as an entity, so to speak, prevalent in all of nature, to which all are subject. Life and death, freedom or enslavement, happiness or sorrow, everything is somehow connected to *Wyrd*, which, by the way, is also a variant of "Urd", our goddess of fate.

In our ancient tales, there lies the prophecy of Ragnarök, the end of the ages, where our world will be destroyed in a great conflagration, to make way for a new existence. When the gods know the great battle has arrived they will calmly equip themselves for combat, then advance onto the battlefield. They go calmly because they understand and trust in the wisdom of *Wyrd*. They will know that their time has come to fight and die for a better tomorrow. Rather than being bogged down by emotions, such as fear or anxiety, they accept their fate and do what must be done.

In one of our sources, Freyja tells us "Salvation awaits the free, at last they shall see me again. Though, him alone may I recognize as free who is no slave of another nor of his own impulses." This relates to the above quoted *Hávamál* strophe (16), which tells us that we must not be ruled by fear, but rather to accept what is. We are all going to die one day; this is a fact, no denying it. Strength, true strength comes in accepting this and dealing with it boldly, without emotion.

This is not to say that we should reject our emotions or strive for stoicism, we just need to keep our impulses in check and not let them become our masters. When something bad happens it is easy to get angry, blame the universe, kick and scream and complain, but this is futile. It gets us nowhere. Fate is neither positive nor negative, it just is. Everything we do or get involved with can have good or bad consequences, sometimes even both. When we realize that the world does not revolve around us and that not everything will go our way, we can begin to accept our position in the grand design of *Wyrd*.

Everything is a choice; we make choices every day in our dealings with events and the paths we will take. We cannot determine what happens outside of ourselves, we can only select the best means of handling situations as they come to us. When we are ruled by emotions our choices are as well, which will lead to disaster more often than not. You have to condition yourself to make decisions rationally, to have the courage to look past fear, sorrow, anger or hate and do what you know is right, objectively and effectively. Rather than emotion, let your conscience be your guide, it will rarely steer you wrong.

Örlög

It is the foremost concept of ethics and morality in our religion. It is the central ideal for our entire belief system regarding our interactions with others and the world around us. Denoting the precepts of karma, fate, balance, and our relationship with the divine, *örlög* is indeed important to us.

When the gods were first bringing order to the Nine Worlds, the Norns were in the process of creating the first laws from the wisdom of Urd's well. From this, *örlög* was created. In German, the word is *urlagnen,* meaning "the original laws". These are natural laws with several facets embodying the unified form of primordial decree. *Örlög* represents the unity, synergy, and synchronicity of the universe through which such ideas as destiny, action and reaction, consequence and compensation are manifested in our daily lives.

In consideration of this, we must look at the Web of *Wyrd*, which is very much related to this belief. The "threads of fate" that make up the web are actually "threads of *örlög*", *örlögthaettir.* Beyond the lifelines of each human being personified by these threads, there is the concept of how the gods and goddesses watch over and keep track of their followers. We must remember that there is no belief in Ásatrú of any sort of omniscient, omnipresent, or omnipotent deity. The gods and goddesses are connected to us through a system of messengers and spies who relate to them our deeds, and will be with us when we die to stand witness for us as we are judged at the *Thing* (Legal Assembly) of the dead. She (always a she) is our protector, our guide, our benefactor, known as the *hamingja, fylgja* or *gipte*. She is a lesser Norn in the service of Urd and is assigned to us at birth. In this vast system of guardian "spirits", as they may be called, lays the key to the gods' vigilant watch over their people. In this capacity, these women manifest each thread of Wyrd's (Urd's) Web in both the experiences they share with their chosen one and in the network they represent.

The messengers themselves are connected by the web that Urd and her sisters weave, for they measure out the fates of all beings. The *örlög*-threads are personifications of destiny, the proverbial line which one walks throughout his life. Do you want to know the meaning of life? It is to find YOUR meaning in life, to find the purpose of your existence; why you are here, what you are supposed to accomplish while you are on Midgard. Such questions may be easier to answer once you have crossed a few other threads, i.e. after you have gained more experience and have dealt with others in various ways. These experiences add up to form the kernel of our personality, how we view the world, and how we view ourselves. Once we have gained a clear perspective of who we are, we may begin to feel like we were meant to do or be something. This may happen sooner for some than for others, but no matter when it happens it will give meaning to your life and will seem, to you, to fulfill your destiny!

Our ancestors believed that the *hamingja* watches over us and regulates our course on the paths of order. Of course, we are free to make our own choices, but one may find all the forces of nature opposing their purposes once they have acted maliciously or have committed disgraceful acts. This is our guardian in action, a servant of karmic responses. On the other hand, she would reward those who have acted in accordance with our sacred laws. None of this is as rigid as it may seem. The choices we make have a wide range of possible outcomes, just as the reactions others may have to them, and just as we would react to their choices.

Örlög does not dictate every single detail of our lives; rather it manifests itself within the idea of cause and effect. In the universal order all life is mandated by a perpetual balance between actions that take place and the reactions that result from them. When an imbalance occurs by the violation of natural law, what we know is right or wrong, we have an obligation to correct this. When we do not, compensation will be made somehow, as we have pointed out with the *hamingja*.

To put this in better perspective, let's not look at it from a "universal" point of view, but rather apply it to our everyday lives. Say you enter a room full of people, that you have had a particularly bad day, and do not want to talk to anyone. Someone comes up to you, seeing you're upset and they try to cheer you up. In your bad mood, you say something mean or derogatory to them, hoping they will go away. This person leaves you, now angry as well, and perhaps tells others how you have treated them. At this point, a simple apology could remedy the situation, but say you leave things the way they are. This single hateful act could seriously effect how others look at you and may end up falling on your head. The person might just get some friends together and meet you outside to rough you up, or they might know someone important to you and tell them about your attitude. Like ripples in a pond, our actions spread out all around us as we affect our environment.

From this, we can see that we are the ones who direct the course of our lives by the choices we make, *örlög* merely determines if those choices will have positive or negative results. Our universe is made up of billions and billions of forces, all vying for a place in the great order of life. In order to continue living for this perfect ideal, we must constantly work towards harmony with all life around us, while at the same time working as implements of *örlög* in making sure that those around us do not violate our people, our families or ourselves. Foolish, selfish, and ignorant decisions are generally what lead to disorder, which is why the ancients believed that evil came through carelessness and stupidity. The message from the gods is "self lead thou thy way thyself", but one must always be prepared to face the consequences of bad decisions, which we are all bound to make.

To have a calling in life is important for us all because it gives many of the tools we need to be successful: goals, focus, and a sense of purpose and fulfillment when a job is well done. Parents, mentors, and guides should all strive to help their children or protégés find something they can truly be passionate about. When such things are prevalent in one's life it is quite difficult to fall into self-destructive patterns. Such a belief was so prevalent in our ancestors' beliefs that stories exist describing people who died immediately after fulfilling their destiny. To find your place in the world, especially when individualism and lack of tribal communities has left so many feeling isolated, is a truly important achievement, one we must all work towards.

The Norns

The Norns signify those aspects of *Wyrd* that relate to who we are individually, which will lead us to the paths we shall follow. Urd represents the most basic principle: birth and potential through the gifts we are given by our *hamingja*, or *gipte*, "gift giver". These are our innate talents, physical attributes, our health, and our luck. Symbolically, these gifts come to us soon after we are conceived, which takes place when fruits of fertility are picked from the World-Tree and sent to the maternal womb, sanctified by the god of childbirth, Hoenir. Frigga and Freyja see to it that the fruits are properly delivered and the *hamingja* is right for the child, since she will care for it from that moment on. The World-Tree represents the connection between all things, so the fruits signify our genetic inheritance, which has been proven to play a major role in our development. The *hamingja* herself represents a personal relationship with the divine, connected to us for as long as we exist.

Verdandi, Urd's sister, presides over life and evolution—what Hindus call *Dharma*. This is the actual progression of the individual, as the goddess feeds the *örlög*-threads Urd pulls from her well into the vast web. She thus presides over what is right and what is wrong. What is right and good will further a being's evolution, while charging their environment and those around them with positive energy. What is wrong leads towards degeneracy, contaminating everything it comes into contact with as the entire web (microcosm and macrocosm) is affected. According to the belief, those who would willingly follow the path of destruction could lose their *hamingja* forever, resulting in great misfortune, violent death, and a damned afterlife.

Skuld, the third Norn and Urd's youngest sister, represents death and consequence, the results of our actions. She does not "punish" those who have made bad choices and who have been declared by Verdandi to do so. In fact, the idea of "crime and punishment" is utterly foreign to the Teutonic creed. Justice, as we know it, focuses on finding ways to make criminals suffer for their infractions of the law. From this, state and federal laws have been created by governments all over the world, which defy the true purposes behind them. Other than protecting citizens from personal injury to themselves or their property, special interest groups have been allowed to legislate their morality based on this Roman standard of law. In Northern Europe, government was used as a means of maintaining peace by settling disputes between individuals and seeing to it that a balance was kept within society. The idea was not to punish crime, which is an abstraction, but rather to renew harmony by fixing the problems that kept individuals in conflict. At the foundation of this is the payment of compensation for harm done to another, the act of making true amends, which could come in the form of a fine or a service rendered, but could also involve more severe forms of recompense, even death! This form of settlement was sacred, watched over by Skuld, who will make sure that the debt that is owed will be paid.

Urd helps us to find our purpose, Verdandi motivates the actions needed for this, and Skuld handles the conclusions met by these actions. This continuing cycle may be repeated thousands of times during the course of our lives. It is important for us to understand that, in this cycle, we are but vessels of nature, creatures of divine origin who are as much a part of the universal order as anything else. The power of fate is a neutral design that neither works for us nor against us. Sometimes bad things happen to good people, while the vile may see great fortune. Fretting over such lots is missing the point. We face hardship for a reason, for without it we are weakened and dependent on those around us. By accepting the reality of how things are and how we affect the world around us, we gain a perspective that strengthens us to the point of being able to handle almost any situation.

The Universal Struggle

Because of what has been said here about action and reaction, we can begin to understand the concepts of good and evil within our faith. The universe exists in a constant struggle between positive and negative forces, chaos versus order if you will. Therefore, in order to meet with positive results, one must contribute positive actions and thoughts. Positive actions create positive results, negative actions create negative results. This is a law as concrete and natural as any of the laws of physics. So, when life begins to become difficult, as it most certainly will at one point or another, we accept it and try to move forward with a joyous disposition. Disaster will strike, suffering will take place, and we won't always be able to correct it. But, if we meet it with detachment and accept it as a necessary and natural phenomenon, we can meet life's downside with a strong heart. We can't stop bad things from happening, but we can control how we react to them.

Just as bad things can happen to us without warning, we too will bring harm to others, whether it be physically or emotionally. Sometimes we may even violate our relationship with the gods and goddesses. These can be simple infractions that lead to minor misfortunes (the *hamingja* is said to be responsible for the stumbles we sometimes take) or they can be horrible crimes that demand reparation. We Ásatrúar will not beg for forgiveness when we make mistakes, for our moral system is based upon balance, not subservience. We correct our errors with action, choosing to pay for our crimes, rather than merely using words to make up for them.

It may be that the notion of compensation for crime has its origin in religious beliefs regarding punishment for the damned after death. A disgraceful act, what some might call a "sin", was known as a "*nid*", and the person who committed it a "*niding*". If you compensate for your *nid* you are cleansed of it, but the individual you are compensating must feel that some effort is being put into this, so there must be some sort of sincerity involved. Those who do not cleanse themselves of their shame will have it cleansed for them in the afterlife, as it is believed by many cultures. Even if a state must handle a crime you have committed, you should accept your punishment with nobility, for our ancestors tell us "one ought not to bewail the punishment that befell one's desserts".

Maintaining Balance

Everyone has a duty to protect themselves and their family. Even today most people accept this as an undeniable fact. In ancient times such an obligation was taken very seriously, to the point where taking blood-revenge was considered one of the holiest laws. As civilization progressed, the act of blood-revenge was replaced with that of *weregild*, a form of payment made to appease the family of a person one had slain. We can still apply this tradition by the laws of our lands, making sure that we diligently seek justice against those who have harmed one of our family members. There may even come a time when you will have to physically defend your kindred, so it is also your duty to be prepared for such an event. Our laws are built upon a foundation of recompense, which at one time saturated every aspect of Nordic life. Each individual had what was known as an "honor-price", which was paid when one injured or killed him or her, or if a woman was taken against her will. The idea of some form of retribution being attained for any injustice, even down to the smallest insult, maintained a peaceful way of life for those not in the business of war. To keep balance, to pay one's debt to another for whatever infraction, held up the values of honor and nobility without resorting to the Draconian measures of law used by many civilizations, even today. Compensating another is not meant as punishment, it re-establishes amity between the two parties, or their family.

To recompense one we have wronged gives us the power to neutralize the forces of vengeance [whether they be physical, mental or spiritual] that would cause us harm if we did not do this in some way or another. There are several ancient traditions concerning the divine intervention manifested when *nids* are left unavenged, including the order of the Teutonic Erinnyes (Furies), goddess of retribution, known as the Heiptir. The Moon-God is said to be lord over them, which would put him in relation with Skuld as the deities involved in such matters. It is up to us, ultimately, to make sure that we put in what we expect to get back.

Not only are those who do harm and who have no desire to correct their mistakes dishonored, but those who have been wronged and do not demand justice are shamed as well. Our ancestors saw it as a sign of weakness if one did not try to seek some form of retribution for a wrong caused by another. It was even more damaging if the former took the latter as a friend without seeking amends first. This is probably because the ancients knew well the nature of man: if retribution is not sought for and gained quickly and immediately then a grudge could develop and grow like an infected wound, then the later troubles this could cause would be far worse than if the situation had been rectified. On the other hand, we are warned not to take hasty vengeance against our kinsmen. One can easily see how delicate this balance of order is, and only those with a strong sense of honor and integrity will remain true to the virtuous path.

Gift for Gift

We have discussed the element of compensation that lies within the law of *örlög*, of that which we give returning to us. Stemming from this is another concept, which forms the core principle of our traditions regarding our relationships with others: the ideal of reciprocity, of giving gift for gift. This custom is inherent within all types of friendships, including those that we share with the gods and goddesses. As stated, the most highly valued ideal within Ásatrú is that of balance, which must be appreciated in both positive and negative circumstances. The gods tell us to repay a gift for a gift, and a lie for a lie, i.e. that we will return what we are given, be it kindness or treachery. At first, of course, we should always try to be gracious and amicable, so that we may be met with the same. One will quickly learn how much easier life becomes when we live benevolently, free of guile or deceit.

The most celebrated form of this tradition lies in our method of worship, when we sacrifice to our gods and goddesses. The word "sacrifice" may be perceived as controversial by some, as it can call to mind images of brutally slain pets for 'shock value', or the killing of virgins in bizarre blood rituals. Although there may be some disturbed individuals out there who might find such vulgar displays intriguing, they have no place in our ancient religion. To sacrifice simply means "to make sacred" for the purpose of offerings to the divine. It is true that our ancestors practiced human sacrifice at one time, as did all other peoples, but these were almost always condemned criminals or prisoners of war. In the rare case when a voluntary sacrifice occurred it was meant to fulfill an individual's desire to join a loved one in the afterlife or to save the tribe or clan from starvation. In times of famine one might have offered their life for their people, the ultimate sacrifice that would have been beneficial in two ways: it would have acted as a means to get the gods to bring forth a bountiful harvest, and it would have eliminated another mouth to feed. An admiration for such acts would have been no different than the respect paid for martyrdom that is still prevalent today. In any case, we consider human sacrifice to be a relic of our barbaric past, as it is considered by almost every culture on earth. Even before the coming of Christianity such practices began to be regarded as archaic and unnecessary.

This leaves two forms of sacrifice that are used in our faith today: the mead offering and the food offering. Similar to the Soma of the Hindus and the Nectar of the Greeks, Mead is considered to be the most sacred substance to us. It is the holy drink of the gods, the morning dew. The froth from the bits of the celestial steeds which falls onto the fields of Midgard, allowing us to partake in its power and inspiration. This is how the mead comes to us: the three subterranean fountains (Urd's Well, Mímir's Well and Hvergelmir) feed Yggdrasil with the purest and holiest form of the liquid, nourishing the tree with its powers of strength, wisdom and resilience. These powers go through the roots, into the branches, then the leaves of the tree, which are then eaten by the horses of the gods. The most noteworthy of these is Hrímfaxi, who is ridden by Nát (Night) each time she crosses the sky. Nát, identical to Ostara as the goddess who greets the dawn, reaches the eastern end of heaven, where she meets Delling, her husband and god of the dawn. When this happens, the froth formed on Hrímfaxi's bit rains down onto the earth as morning dew. This dew is collected by bees, who make honey from which we make our holy mead. It is specifically stated in our lore that some gods and goddesses, including Ódin, should primarily be honored with offerings of mead, accompanied by toasts, since this is all they are sustained by.

Animal sacrifices are a bit more controversial than the mead offering. It is in keeping with the traditions of our faith that we may slaughter animals as gifts to our gods and goddesses. However, this should not be considered a savage act. Sacrificing animals, in its true from, has always represented a solemn practice of preparing them for a sacred meal, similar to the Jewish rite of koshering. We will never kill an animal just to kill it, since such an act would violate our standards of respect for the flora and fauna of our planet. An animal intended for a feast would be slaughtered reverently, quickly, and with as little pain as possible, then every part of the animal would be used for some purpose. In fact, this is why many prefer to prepare their food in such a way. Considering the deplorable conditions animals face in industrial farms, as well as possible health problems due to chemicals and steroids injected into them, taking the initiative in killing them ourselves is actually the smarter and more humane choice, as long as one follows the right procedures. For us, it is simply a matter of having our meat sanctified before we consume it and offer it to our gods and goddesses. Of course, one can choose to buy food that has already been packaged to send to them, but we must always remember, at some point someone had to kill the animal for the meat that we eat.

Methods of Sacrifice

So how and why do we sacrifice? There are several ways to give a gift to our deities, each having a relation to a specific element. This is proper, since the elements were the very first natural implements used in the worship of the divine, for each element is believed to have a particular connection to the powers.

For the element of air there is the custom of "leaving out", where mead in a bowl or a portion of the feast may be left in the open. It was thought that spirits of the land or gods in animal form would then come to partake in the meal.

For the fire element, sacred flames would be kindled using the bore method or the friction-fire (also called "the need-fire") made from the friction of two pieces of wood. Often times a specially made 'bow' would be used in this process, which is supposed to imitate the motion of the great World-Mill, from which the need-fire originated. Once the flames were raised, the portion of the meal offered to the gods would be thrown into the fire, where it was carried up to the heavens by the smoke and cinders.

Drowning the offering or pouring the mead into a holy body of water served for the water element. Our ancestors believed that all waters flow from the fountain Hvergelmir, in the Underworld. Because of this a sacrifice thrown into a lake or river or ocean could eventually make it to Ásgard's river, since through Hvergelmir all water is ultimately connected. Just as they flow from the subterranean well, every ocean and stream eventually returns its mother, its source.

For the earth element, mead would be poured onto the ground or food buried. Entering into the womb of Mother Earth, just as when a person is buried after death, allows the inner-essence of the object to descend to the Underworld where it will be accepted by the gods. For this reason, the ancients would have many of their life's possessions buried with them after they died, as a sign of how well they were respected by their kinsmen, serving as a testament to their honor before the judgment of the gods in the afterlife.

Although other forms of slaughter existed, it seems that the most revered among the ancient Indo-Europeans (Teutons and Hindus) was beheading. This is probably due to the fact that it was considered to be painless and humane, which is certainly debatable. Even in the early part of the 19th century, when the guillotine was introduced as a less barbaric form of execution (versus hanging and burning at the stake), beheading was thought to be less brutal. Many farmers still use this as a means of killing animals for food.

The Purpose of Sacrifice

Sacrifice is never viewed as a form of humility on our part. There is even evidence that the gods sacrifice to one another. The reason for this is that we believe such offerings empower the divine, which allows them to perform magnificent feats, usually to our benefit. When Ódin, in *Hávamál*, hangs himself on the World-Tree he does so as a sacrifice to himself, which then gives him the strength to perform the grueling deed. In return for this power, the gods and goddesses grant our wishes or help us in our struggles. That this does not always happen is due to the powers of fate, which cannot be denied. This may sound like a cop-out, and indeed there are stories where heroes would get angry at Ódin for not giving them victory in battle, but someone has to lose in order for someone to win; such is fate. So, because of this, their reciprocation does not end there. Where fate must have its way our deities give us the fortitude to meet its decrees valiantly and with dignity. In the end, balance will always be achieved, for this is the rule of *örlög* and its concept of reciprocity, even if we do not immediately recognize its effects.

The gods warn us against too much sacrificing, because a gift must always be repaid, so those who offer too much will be seen as greedy for divine favors. This will most definitely turn fortune against you. In all respects, we must view our relationship with the divine as a friendship like we would have with people here on Midgard. A bond must be maintained with generosity, mutual respect, and praise. As long as we continue to value our connection with the gods and goddesses, we will thrive under their watchful care. The more of us who offer and pray to them, the stronger their union will be with our people. One who lives far away must feel welcome in your land or country in order to feel comfortable in your home.

The exchange of gifts must never be taken lightly, for it is a sacred act that unites two individuals in their relationship. For this reason, gift exchanges have become common in all sorts of observances, where we gather to celebrate occasions as well as our love for one another. Such exchanges may occur at weddings, to bind husband and wife; in the workplace, to show employers and their workers how much they value one another; and even in diplomatic affairs, when countries wish to form alliances. The connection or obligation made through the act of giving was used by ancient chieftains in keeping their subjects loyal, while in turn showing the folk the noble nature of their leader. He might offer them a gift of some sort, and they would then pledge their allegiance to him. When a gift is received it falls on the receiver to give something in return, even if this is simply one's gratitude. If this cannot happen, and if one cannot return the things that are presented to them, they are indebted to the givers for their generosity.

In a faith such as ours, where munificence is considered one of the greatest virtues, there must be principles attached to this that would protect charitable men and women from being taken advantage of. After all, we can romanticize the ancients all we want, but the truth is that there have always been thieves, liars, and predators who would try to take all that we have. On the other hand, we must not misconstrue the "gift for gift" ideal as an excuse to not be helpful for the less fortunate. The concept is not based on a strict expectation, that every time we give something to someone we must have something in return. This custom is based upon the maintaining of friendships and relationships, which should be formed from reciprocity. At the same time, we should not begrudge our offerings, creating demands or expectations for every act of generosity. The gods condemn such as well. A bond between two people can only be kept strong if both parties work towards that end, otherwise one person, at least, will not have the motivation needed to want to continue the relationship, for they will have become less valued, given a less respected role that saps their energy. This is a tried and true fact of life. But when it comes to helping those in need, it is our religious duty to give aid whenever and wherever we can without any thought of return.

I would like to relate a story that is relevant to this, which comes down to us from one of our sources:

An ancient land had been ravaged by war, and from the remnants of war came famine. Desperate people often revert to disreputable means to get food. Three such persons had each stolen a sack of corn from different owners, and all three were caught. The first owner took the thief before the local authorities, and for this the priestesses of their land said that he had done right. The second owner took the corn from the thief and let him go in peace, which the priestesses agreed to as well. But the third owner went to the thief's house, where he saw how need had stricken his home. So, he went back to his place, and then returned with a wagon full of goods, which drove poverty away from the man's hearth. Because of this extremely noble act of charity the owner was extolled by the priestesses, who held much sway in that land. They recorded his name in a sacred book of revered ancestors, declared him free of any transgressions, and told of his deed far and wide.

Such an admiration for unselfish acts is known throughout our literature. Although this virtue will be discussed in further detail later on, it is important to differentiate the "gift for a gift" tradition with our ethics of generosity. In doing so, one will need to use wisdom in determining when they are being liberal and when they are being taken advantage of. It is a fundamental precept of our sacred path that we avoid subservient positions that would siphon our power and strength. Of course, in any group there will be leaders and followers, but it is important for a balance to be maintained that will elevate the sense of self-worth for everyone involved. This balance is maintained, as we have seen, with the idea of reciprocal relationships.

3

Morality

"Never find joy in evil,
but let good bring you pleasure."

—Óðin, Hávamál 128.

"Vices and Virtues
the sons of men bear
mingled in their breasts,
no one is so good
that no failing attends him,
nor so bad as to be good for nothing."

—Óðin, Hávamál 133.

Most of us tend to look at religious morals as restrictive tenets mandating much, if not all of how a person lives their life. Eastern traditions abound in rules as declarations that piety is to be manifested through suffering and abstention. Because of the severity of these beliefs, followers of mainstream faiths, all of which have Oriental origins, consider "pagan" religions such as Ásatrú to be lacking a system of morality. To them, the ascetic lifestyle is ideal, as is surrendering yourself to a strict code of religious decrees where everything one does is dictated. There are over 600 Mosaic laws alone, making up the body of restrictions set in Middle Eastern religions. Some continue to search their holy books to find and distort any passage they can to limit yet more actions. These systems are so extensive it would be impossible for anyone to maintain a strict adherence to every statute imposed by Biblical writings, so many of them are ignored by the followers. Because of this, they feel like they will never be good enough for their god, living in guilt and hoping that he will give them mercy or "grace".

There is nothing wrong with asceticism, or spiritual discipline, which indeed has its place within Ásatrú. However, the indigenous religions of Northern Europe never recognized the need to punish one's self before their pantheons. Morality was strongly influenced by the ideals of honor, of what we know deep inside of us as right and wrong. Because, essentially, native religions are merely one aspect grown from the broader cultural spectrum, there were few distinctions between social law and religious law. Our ancestors relied upon the nobility of their fellow countrymen, expecting a certain standard to be valued within their interactions and disputes. For this reason, religious edicts were simple and to the point, demanding wisdom in their interpretation and application in everyday life. Bear in mind though that the Teutonic people were and are extremely ethical, with revered concepts of right and wrong, good and evil, as well as a retributive eschatology. Even Roman historians made note of the chaste nature of the ancient Germanic tribes.

Freedom

Probably what would be respected most within our view of morality is our devotion to the concepts of freedom and independence, which form the basis of Western democracy. No one within our faith has the right, divine or otherwise, to try to tell others how they should live, nor should they judge him or her by our ethical standards. This is one of the privileges of ethnic, esoteric religions, for we do not feel that it is our place to proselytize or try to force our opinions on anyone, including other Ásatrúar. When religions, especially those that are not natural expressions of the folk-will, legislate their morality the only end result can be tyranny, as the theocratic state has proven time and again. We will teach others, make information about our faith available, we might even speak publicly about it every now and then, to a willing audience of course. But make no mistake—our ideals reject the belief that one has to "spread the word" by preaching or the condemnation of those who do not think like us. There is a wealth of wisdom, power and fulfillment in the path that we follow, one that can enrich lives on so many levels. That it has survived so long in the hearts of our people is proof of its validity. But those who do not choose our path are not to be devalued or disrespected, for the choice is theirs alone to make.

The only time I can think that Ásatrú morality could affect those who do not worship our gods and goddesses would be in our relationships, through our adherence of the precepts of *örlög*. Any way that we deal with anyone must be considered through the edicts of nobility as represented by this belief system. We cannot force someone to be honorable, but we can demand that we be treated with respect and will repay any treatment we are given in kind. Even enemies, even *nidings* are to be met with noble behavior, for actions towards them reflect upon us, and those who will treat a *nid* with a *nid* are no better than the individual they seek to harm.

We are polytheists, meaning that we believe in many deities, many races of deities, each representing the various nations in the world and perhaps elsewhere. As there is no "one god", there is no one path to the divine, no single "road to redemption", leaving all others to be damned for eternity. There is also no such thing as a "chosen people" who are supposed to be destined to become 'masters' over all others by their god. Originally, the doctrines of the many gods were held by all peoples, until monotheism spread through every land, oppressing all cultures it came into contact with. To say there is only one god in a world of many, at the time this was developing, is a testament to the antagonistic nature of this ideal; it simply cannot have manifested without conflict, war and tyranny.

It goes without saying that Ásatrú *as a faith* strongly opposes oppression in any of its forms. We would be free, would fight for that freedom, and would *never* take it away from others. The entire focus within our institutions of legal concepts remains, as it always has been, upon catering to the independent nature of the Teutonic spirit. It is our duty, to ourselves and to the world around us to work for our rights, to earn them in the struggles against any force, friend or foe, which would take them away from us. As ancient tribal law evolved into the more complex systems that would ultimately forge the way for our modern foundations of government, there is no doubt that our folk-will expresses itself through a need for liberty and self-reliance.

The Roman Paradigm

Although Christianity is the form most of us recognize as the force that predominated Europe for centuries, the faith itself is not entirely to blame for the atrocities committed by the church. In fact, the key to understanding this may help many people, Christians and non-Christians alike, to figure out exactly what went wrong. How could the teachings of a supposed "loving" god be used to justify the brutal slaughter of thousands and thousands of people? Why is there such a contrast between what is taught in the New Testament of the Bible and what we know in our history of Orthodox Christianity? To answer these questions all one has to do is study the rise and fall of the Roman Empire. Even before Constantine adopted the Christ-faith as the state religion of Rome, the empire had been stretching its tentacles out to invade the rest of the known world. Already Europe was being poisoned by what I call "The Roman Paradigm", which saturated every nation they invaded.

Early Northern Europeans developed their civilizations with a fierce adherence to their values of personal sovereignty. Almost every aspect of their cultural expressions manifested their reliance upon this ideal. It was because of this independent nature that the Roman Empire was able to invade, then dominate almost all European lands, for it represented a united front against nations of divided clans. Like the cunning Loki, the Romans manipulated Germanic tribes against one another while brainwashing many into desiring Roman favor and adopting Roman customs and habits. This invasion, which would later serve as the catalyst for the forced conversion to Christianity, changed the mindset of our people dramatically. No longer would liberty and personal freedom remain at the forefront of the Nordic philosophy. Self-reliance would be replaced by servitude for some, and for others by a strong desire to conquer, conquer, conquer. The old Viking passion for traveling and adventure would be used to spread European empires across the globe without any concern for the sovereignty, ecosystems, or cultural boundaries of foreign nations.

A good example of the difference between the Teutonic and Roman paradigms can be delineated by how America was colonized. When the Icelanders first came to "The New World", which they called "Vinland", they built small settlements away from the indigenous tribes. Attempts were made to explore the land, but conflicts with Native Americans caused the Vikings to cease their activities and abandon their efforts. These were Nordic men and women who had not yet been infected by the ideals of Roman imperialism, allowing them to live conterminously with the natives.

Now fast-forward a few hundred years to when the Italians and Spaniards, fully indoctrinated by Roman Catholicism, made their way to America. Almost immediately after their arrival, fleets of soldiers and explorers poured into massive colonies, like locusts plaguing the land, as they threatened wildlife wherever they landed. The "Indians", as they called them, were either converted or killed as their homeland was rapidly stolen from them. Their treatment was no different from that of European "heathens" not long before. Eventually, like many other nations, America would be conquered by the "White Man"—a designation often used by displaced races to explain their disdain towards this bloody history.

What many fail to realize, when they complain about the past oppression their people have faced, is that Europe was the first of all lands to have been taken over by this cancer that would spread over the entire earth. We must look at these invasions as part of a timeline that began with the might of the Roman Empire and continued as a legacy of tyranny that would affect almost every civilization. The Nordic obsession with exploration once led our folk from one end of the globe to the other without any sort of imposition of our way of life. Then, under the Roman paradigm, we would become the great culture-killers, which began with our very own. In embracing our Teutonic heritage we not only wish to reclaim our birthright, we also want to cleanse ourselves and our people of the stain left by the Roman Empire once and for all.

The Helthing

As was stated in Chapter 2, Ásatrú morality is based upon setting right that which has been wronged, of restoring peace and order, or bringing balance back into place. Since religious beliefs and social realities often co-existed among the ancients, ideals in regard to the eschatology and judgment of *nidings* in the after-life reflected the same tenets used here on Midgard. As such, there is a *Thing*, a legal assembly that judges the dead to determine whether they are worthy of bliss or damnation. The gods gather every day at the Thing, near Urd's fountain, to decide if the deceased should be allowed access into Valhalla or Urd's fields of bliss (the actual Hel) or if they should be condemned to Niflhel to suffer at the hands of demons. Because of its location and the fact that Urd-Hel, our goddess of fate, presides over these assemblies, it is only right that we dub this the "Helthing".

The purpose of the Helthing is to see to it that people live with honor and in accordance with the decrees of the Norns, the creators of law. We must not look at this as some sort of "fire and brimstone" creed where we must use fear to keep followers in line. There is no demand that one fears our beloved deities, or that we are already condemned "sinners" who will only be granted access into paradise by their divine grace. Our ancestors saw the court of the dead as judging very leniently when it came to certain human faults and frailties. Getting drunk or having sex with a strange person (so long as you do not violate the sacred ties of matrimony) isn't going to damn you for all eternity. Even Ódin has faced situations where he was "very drunk" and has met with embarrassing circumstances with women, all of which he speaks of openly and with much humor.

The facts remains, that our gods and goddesses, with all their wisdom, fully understand human nature and would apply this knowledge in their judgment of us. Many of the decrees passed down to us are more or less guidelines or words of advice we can use for success and empowerment. One of these, which I personally value greatly, is that we should not take ourselves too seriously and should understand that life is meant to be a joyous experience, even when we face adversity. It is so easy to alienate ourselves from others when we lose our sense of humor, a fact none of us should forget.

The Runelaw

I began experimenting with the runes as a system of Ódinic law several years ago, after noticing references to the possibility of such a system in the *Eddas* and the rune poems. At first, because I figured that this idea might be a bit controversial, I wanted to wait until I could devote all of my work on the Law Fundamental of Ásatrú culture, so I could present all of my finds and theories. However, even though some might wish to debate the presentation of these religious tenets, I doubt anyone will disagree with their content, since most of them can be found directly in the *Eddas*, so it seems necessary to introduce them as part of our morality. For those interested I will say this: in compiling these laws I have used the Eddas, sagas, histories and several ancient law texts to find common themes matching those known within runic lore. They seem to be a part of "The Runes of Eternity and Runes of Earthly Life" taught by Rig-Heimdall at the dawn of Teutonic civilization. I can promise here that I will illuminate these in another text.

Fehu

Be neither a thief nor a miser.

Uruz

That which we send out shall return to us, so do no harm and work for the order. When we err, we make amends. When we are wronged, we seek reparation.

Thurisaz

Be courageous and bold and never shrink from a challenge. In our lives, we face the decrees of the Norns with a strong and valiant heart.

Ansuz

Journey on the paths of power with respect and devotion for our gods and goddesses and the ideals, institutions, and traditions that represent their divine might.

Raido

One must be careful when traveling about, retaining the standards of nobility and using wisdom in unfamiliar situations. In the company of others, be modest and polite as well as patient with those who are not.

Kenaz

The journey for wisdom, knowledge, and awareness is an eternal one. We who will do honor to our faith accept the challenge of this quest sincerely and without expectation.

Gebo

Be kind and compassionate, helpful, and charitable. To your neighbor offer hospitality, generosity, and friendship. Let them return it.

Wunjo

Be happy and free, enjoy life to its fullest and allow others to do the same, but be temperate in pleasing the senses and recognize that certain aspects of human nature must be denied.

Hagalaz

Understand that the powers of fate are innately neutral, and work neither for, nor against us. He who holds what *should*, shall ever regret what *is*.

Naudiz

From necessity we gain strength, courage, and insight. The simple life most often brings forth what a person truly needs—health and happiness. Live for this and scold not those who are lacking in embellishments.

Isa

Only the disciplined can be truly strong, and only the strong can be disciplined. One must *understand* in order to walk upon the paths of power, and one must learn and train to understand.

Jera

Be responsible and industrious. Never shirk from obligations. Life is rewarding for those who will toil for its benefits.

Eihwaz

Give honor to your ancestors and have care and respect in your treatment of the bodies of the dead. Give the praise to them that you hope to have after death.

Perthro

He is wise who will listen to good advice, and noble who will scorn bad. Hear the counsels of the gods and Norns and learn. Those who hear them clearly must not take lightly their duty in sharing providence.

Elhaz

The strong must protect the weak, most especially by never becoming the cold-hearted coward who would oppress or harm them.

Sowilo

Be always a peacemaker, willing to help others settle their disputes and acceptant of the aid to resolve your own. We fight only when all else fails.

Tiwaz

Be honest and true, except when to punish a lie for a lie, and keep all promises, oaths and vows at any cost.

Berkano

Keep strong to your marriage obligations and be wise in the upbringing of children.

Ehwaz

Be sincere and faithful to those who are your true friends. Know who are your friends and who are your enemies: give gifts and protection to the former and cunning to the latter.

Mannaz

The bonds of blood are sacred and unwavering loyalty to family and folk is demanded. Family devotion is manifested by helping them in any circumstance and avenging them in death.

Laguz

Flow around obstacles and blockages, parting and rejoining, but always flowing with the gravity of one's own *örlög*. Water is incremental and tireless, likewise Heimdall's children.

Ingwaz

Find happiness in the arms of another; seek joy in the adventures of sexual pleasure. However, you must not defile yourself with the ignoble behaviors of perversion, sexual violence, or promiscuity.

Dagaz

Exist in harmony with the divine order by living in accordance with the law as set by the gods and Norns. Strive for nobility and live so that you have an honored name and a judgment of approval over your death.

Othala

The best thing we can do for our children is work for a greater tomorrow and hand them down a legacy of wisdom and nobility. Teach your children what is right and watch the seed become a mighty tree!

As you can see, these laws aren't so much "commandments" as they are maxims for living a decent life as a decent person. In most cases, they simply represent the common sense needed to deal with others in any situation, or to simply be noble yourself. If you follow this guide you are sure to be recognized as an honorable person both here and beyond, which is beneficial in so many ways.

Nine Virtues and Nine Vices

An even simpler set of edicts than the Runelaw is that of the Nine Virtues and Nine Vices, which further express many of the laws given above. The use of these eighteen principles is based upon our eschatology and the sacredness of multiples of three in Ásatrú, with nine and twelve being the most holy numbers. Where the Runelaw presents in detail the morals of our religion, the Nine Virtues and Nine Vices act as a standardized credo in which our folk can maintain the values of our faith easily. Some may notice that several of these virtues differ from those used by others, which is perfectly fine and in accordance with our regards for freedom of thought and expression and our lack of a strict dogma. These particular virtues come from a long period of research into the ethics of our ancestors as handed down to us in our sources.

The Virtues

Honesty: The ancients considered honesty to be one of the hallmarks of noble men and women, since liars were often viewed as lowly and vile. Loki himself is the great liar, as well as the great enemy of the gods and humanity. Still, a man must be able to defend himself from the cunning wiles of those with deceptive hearts, which is why men can exchange "a lie for a lie" as part of the *örlög* concept. To be honest, both to others and to yourself is to accept things as they are, which is one of the true inner-strengths. It weakens us to lie; it weakens our integrity and stems from a fear to face reality, to face the truth. In essence, most lies are either told out of fear or malevolence, protecting us from whatever it is we feel we cannot deal with. The bigger the lie, the more we have allowed our power to be taken from us through our deception. Say, for example, you are faced with legal trouble and decide to lie your way out of it. Why? Because you are *afraid* of the repercussions that may be involved with people knowing the truth. Often times, authority figures are much more lenient towards those they know are being truthful. In the long run, being honest usually pays off, especially when you consider the ideals of *örlög*.

Honor: All of us have a sense of honor within us, for this is our innate tendency towards right and good. Combined with the virtue of wisdom, this is where we will make conscious decisions based on the strength of our moral fortitude to determine which actions to admire and which to condemn. There may not be any direct rules against molesting children in our ancient faith (though to rape a virgin was considered worse than any other form of rape, and of course children would be placed in this category), *but does there really need to be for anyone to know that this is morally wrong?* We do not need some dusty old book to tell us that such acts are bad; these are beliefs that are ingrained within us when we are born! Truly, honor encompasses all of our morals, for it is the voice inside of us leading towards the "high road" in all matters. Just as with honesty, there is strength in honor, a strength depicted in the archetypes of our gods and goddesses. Imagine the profound sense of integrity it took for Týr to sacrifice his hand so the Fenris wolf could be bound, or when Ódin fathered Váli to slay his son Hödur for killing his other son Baldur, just to stay true to the law of blood-revenge. We must be honorable and noble no matter what we face, for struggles and obstacles are the ultimate tests of how virtuous a man or woman really is.

Generosity: The ancients had strict rules governing hospitality and generosity, especially within one's land or home. Failure to give heed to this would result in the gods' anger, which could bring about all sorts of calamity. A quick note about this: our ancestors never viewed 'divine wrath' as a direct attack upon an individual. There was no belief that Thór or Ódin would strike you down if you violated divine law. To understand what could happen we must consider the purpose of the gods and goddesses, particularly the Aesir, in the first place. They are the representatives of order constantly battling with the forces of chaos to protect us from the harm that the latter can bring. When the gods or our *hamingja* are angry with us they cease to defend us from these forces, making us susceptible to them, often times leading to an immediate death or otherwise grave misfortune.

Even an enemy must be shown the rites of hospitality, as the gods showed us when the Jötun Hrungnir rode into Ásgard uninvited and was welcomed into Valhalla. However, because our faith is built upon an understanding of human nature, certain limits were placed upon this to keep people from being taken advantage of. An individual could be welcomed into your home for a maximum of three nights, with at least one meal given each night. At any other time, a man could ask of another's food as much as would suffice to supply one meal.

The hero is generous. The degenerate is greedy. The ancient tales paint the lower Jötuns as having avaricious natures, to the point where they would allow their guests to starve to death. The more generous a person was, the more his community respected him, as it should be today. The above should only serve as a guide rather than an order, letting us see the basic concept as it was known. A person might not want to stay at your house for three nights, or you might wish for them to visit for a longer period, and you will most likely want to offer them more food than just one meal a night. The point is to use your best judgment in such circumstances, and decide what's best for you and your situation, while living up to this charitable standard and not allowing yourself to be taken advantage of.

Piety: This virtue may seem to contradict much of what has been stated about the independent nature of Ásatrú, and indeed, some Ásatrúar may contest its placement here. When we think of being pious, as we may consider almost everything religious, one might automatically look at this through the perspective of Eastern religions, for this is what most of us were raised to know. Kneeling, silent, servile, these are the images that come to mind when we hear this word.

It has always been my contention that Ásatrúar must revive this ancient religion by seeking an objective understanding of its living culture. We cannot allow social biases formed from any sort of negative opinions toward Christianity dictate how we practice our faith. There is no doubt that our ancestors had great respect for their gods and goddesses, that they revered them wholeheartedly, or that they placed great value on devotion to them. This is piety! As I have stated, honoring the gods and goddesses, to us, does not put us in a subservient position, it places us in good faith with our beloved deities as the friends and ancestors of our folk. To be pious is to maintain this relationship as we would any other, respecting their names, the rites surrounding them, and the areas dedicated to them. I cannot think of any reason why, in any religion, it would not be important to have such an idea stand out as one of its highest tenets. After all, the divine is the central focus of the belief system!

Courage: Our gods and goddesses teach us to be strong, heroic and brave. These are all qualities that can help anyone to have a successful life, to make something of themselves in a sometimes frightening world. One must not confuse courage with bravado, or think that this virtue should only apply to men or women who face danger on a constant basis. Although such lifestyles are very respected and make for great stories in books and in movies, it is within all of us to be courageous. We all deal with hardship in one way or another; we all reach a point where we come across a circumstance that terrifies us. Courage is not immunity to this fear, for everyone is afraid of something (no matter what some may tell you!); it is simply the ability to do what you have to do to face your fear and overcome it. The coward allows it to consume him and will refuse to move forward, whereas the warrior will rise up and take a stand. Man, woman and child can condition themselves to be warriors by refusing to accept defeat and by embracing hardship. With the strength of the gods blazing within your heart, anything is possible. Nothing is insurmountable.

Loyalty: Together, loyalty and honesty determine a person's trustworthiness. One of the best signs of an individual's worth is whether or not people can rely on them. It takes strength and integrity to be loyal, for sometimes you might be called upon to make unpopular decisions that happen to be the right ones. If your peers unjustly chastised a friend, would you abandon him? When a person goes through tough times they often find out who their true friends are, who are capable of being faithful and who will quickly betray or turn their back on them. Right now, look into your heart and ask yourself if you think you are a trustworthy person. Have you ever stood by someone even though it was uncomfortable or painful to do so? Do you have anyone in your life that you would stand by no matter what, even if it meant your loss of life, limb, or freedom? These are important questions to ask yourself, to contemplate in a way of self-reflection, not blaming others for not being worthy of such devotion, but considering whether or not you could be capable of this. It is a great character builder, something you can work on immediately to improve yourself on the path of honor. To find someone to care about can help us to change any aspect of ourselves we feel needs improvement, for this gives us the incentive to strive for a higher self, for them and for us. Through loyalty we learn to respect others, to defend honor, and to value the bonds we share with friends and kinsmen.

Kindness: This virtue has been discussed at length under the description of its patron, Baldur, who, as the most beloved god, represents the belief in kindness as one of the highest ideals. An inherent relationship with nobility mandates us to never confuse kindness with weakness. Our ethics of chivalry demand that, no matter what our inclination is, we should always try to be kind and compassionate. There is, in fact, power in such expressions, for when we are gracious to others their positive reactions strengthen us, as well as subject us to the forces of *örlög* in returning such favor. When one has gained a true understanding of Ásatrú philosophy, it is easy to see that, in spite of all that is said, our ancestors were still people—with all of the hopes, desires, and aspirations that come with our humanity. They viewed the world around them, and their evolving communities, as part of a synergetic union of natural forces. Although they recognized good and evil, there was no belief in anything absolute, for even the Jötuns could show mercy or honor. It is not individuals, but *actions* that can be disreputable, actions that dishonor those who commit them, like Loki, once in the favor of the gods brought one disgrace after another upon himself, leading to his exile from Ásgard. But is Loki pure evil? Not likely, since he is known in the stories to be benevolent on occasion, and was once so well liked by Óðin that he made him his blood-brother.

Some people have lived such hard lives it is difficult for them to be kind to others, to open their hearts; for they are afraid that to do so will only hurt them. This is why overcoming adversity is so important to us—a man or woman must be able to rise above the pain and suffering they have endured so they may continue to live on joyously and with a loving heart. When you have to deal with hardship you are presented with a choice: you can either allow frustration, anger, or hatred to consume you, like it did Loki and Völund in our lore, allowing it to effectively weaken you to the point where you become jaded and bitter, or you can stand up and refuse to let yourself be overtaken by such negative emotions. As with fear, face your anger boldly, consciously choosing to be empowered by kindness rather than debilitated by hate.

Independence: The prominence of this ideal has been well attested to. That we place high regard on our personal freedoms and self-reliance, which we fully accept are privileges we earn through vigilant defense against tyranny in any of its forms. However, it is important for us to differentiate here between independence and individualism. To be independent is to be able and willing to do things you need and want to do without any interference or reliance upon others. This isn't to say that we will not ask for or accept outside help. It simply means that, in general, we can take care of ourselves, can think for ourselves, and that we choose to do so.

Individualism is the ideal that the interests of the individual should take precedence over the interests of the social group, be it friends, family, or folk. To many, very many, this is an extremely alluring concept. Why shouldn't I be considered more important than my community, my kindred or my people? You see, when individualism runs rampant, without any restraint in its promotion, all collective efforts take second place to the needs of the self. The communal bonds and cultural identities that define our most important aspects of human nature lose their value in the eyes of the individualist. Those countries that further such views, and then try to continue to push "family values" are kidding themselves. What is the point? Why should we care about such things? We care about them because they are what make us metaphysically significant, significant beyond our personal being. They give us all of the things many individualists will admit are missing from their lives: purpose, identity, fellowship, and even love. In embracing a larger whole as part of your meaning in life you connect to something deeper and more profound, something organic, flowing through the lifeblood of your very existence.

Again, there is a difference between these two ideas, though one cannot be seen as canceling out the other. You should not think that our extolment of social groups against individualism represents some sort of fetter with which we would imprison ourselves. Above all else, our freedom as well as our support for others' freedoms must be maintained, no matter what the cost. For the most part, we will promote values of family and folk, but we understand that all circumstances are different. For some "family" may come with horrid memories of abuse and dysfunction, while others may not have one at all! But any of us, yes, any of us can learn to support these principles, where "community" or "family" means mutual respect, reciprocal relationships, synergetic bonds and the fierce defense of each person's rights and independence. To be connected to something greater than ourselves is one of life's highest achievements.

Wisdom: You might think that wisdom cannot be a virtue, since many believe that this is innate, it is something we either have or do not have, whereas the actions involved in being virtuous require a moral choice. However, anyone can be wise, and more so, anyone can choose to use wisdom in any circumstance. If I choose not to get drunk in public places because I want to keep my faculties around strangers, I am using wisdom based on experience. If I choose to immediately tell my wife that whatever dress she is wearing makes her look astonishing, again, that's a wise choice! To use wisdom really acts as the means for which all other virtues can be applied, which is probably why our highest god, Ódin, is its representative. It takes sagacity to know when to use which virtue and how to apply each to the circumstances we face. Wisdom is the ability to assess a situation, and then make an informed decision on what's the best action to take. It involves impulse control and objectivity, two things any of us can learn. You can get into all sorts of trouble if you always act before you think, a lesson that even gods have learned the hard way.

The Vices

Every religion in the world has certain restrictions that generally serve in curbing wanton desires or malevolent tendencies. These taboos represent time-tested principles based upon human experience expressed through the folk-will. Ásatrú, our Teutonic heritage, developed this using common sense and practical thinking. There are no bizarre limitations dictating how we eat, how we talk, how we express ourselves, etc. In fact, these restrictions, as you will see, embody vices that anyone would easily recognize as undesirable. As stated, our eschatology—our beliefs in the afterlife—is retributive, with the powers of *örlög* reaching beyond the borders of life and death. This belief in punishing the damned was formed as a reflection of earthly ideals of justice. If the *Thing* of humans punishes *nidings*, naturally that of the gods would do the same. But, because the dead are immortal their suffering in payment of their crimes is greatly exaggerated and administered in accordance with each specific type of transgression.

There are nine realms below Niflhel, in the land known as Náströnds, each containing places of punishment for certain sins. Below are the Nine Vices and tortures of the damned that accompany them, with references to the sources where these are mentioned.

Murder: Serpents spew venom onto those who dishonorably kill another. Murder, to our ancestors, was defined as secret killing, assassination, which was different from that which occurred through blood-revenge, self-defense, or honorable combat. This pretty much still holds true today, even with blood-revenge, where we have given this power over to the hands of the state. (Sources: *Völuspá* 40, *Sölarljód* 64, *Vafthrúdnismál* 43).

Perjury: Serpents spew venom onto those who violate their oaths. The serpent motif is common in punishments in our lore. When Loki is bound by the gods, Skadi hangs a snake over his face to drop poison down on him, just like the other nidings. Archaeologists have found rings made in the images of serpents, which many believed were used as oath-rings, rings on which sacred oaths were made. The circular design probably represents the eternal bond one has to their promises, but the snakes obviously remind us of those in Niflhel who torment oath-breakers, making them symbols of justice. (Sources: *Völuspá* 40, *Völundárkvida* 6-8, *Skáldskaparmál* 4, *Vafthrúdnismál* 43, *Sigrdrífumál* 23).

Adultery: The waste venom spewed onto murderers and perjurers flows through troughs onto those who violate the sanctity of marriage vows. They are imprisoned within crates made of lead, forcing them to drown in the caustic fluid continuously. Our faith places much importance on vows, especially those between husband and wife. A goddess, Vár, is said specifically to listen to people's oaths and the agreements between men and women, and sees to it that those who break them are punished. In this capacity, she probably has some connection to the

Helthing near Urd's well. In ancient Germania, adulterers, both seducers and the seduced, were severely disgraced. Women would have their hair cut off and would be beaten, naked, through the streets by their husbands. They were marked forever, never again to enjoy the company of men, for no man would have them. Men were worse off—they were buried alive! In comparing our sources, it is possible that this vice was originally more generalized as "debauchery", encompassing the degenerate sex acts that brought shame to those who committed them or brought harm to others. (Sources: *Völuspá* 40, *Germania* Ch. 12, *Vafthrúdnismál* 43, *Hávamál* 115, 131).

Sacrilege: Burning stones are fastened to the hands of those who blaspheme the gods, mock religious rites, or profane sacred grounds. In maintaining our relationship with our deities, we must not insult them or show them a lack of respect, as we would demand from them. Consider this—if our religion supports any belief in the sacredness of any being, place, or object, obviously the profaning of these would be prohibited. When the gods violated the sanctity of Valhalla with the slaying of a witch, Gullveig, a war between the two divine clans broke out with a demand that this act, committed by one of the Aesir, namely Thór, be avenged and recompensed. The demand came from the Vanir. Loki's *nids* include his disgraceful acts towards the gods and their sacred realm, leading him to his punishments in Niflhel. The idea of burning stones, in some sources sacred objects, fastened to the hands of the sacrilegious, probably has some relation to punishing grave-robbers, who desecrate these holy burial sites with their sacrilege and thievery. (Sources: *Sólarljód* 65, *Historia Danica* Book 8, *Vafthrúdnismál* 43, *Lokasenna* 63, *Skírnismál* 35).

Greed: The greedy have their hands fastened to burning objects of their desire, similar to blasphemers. This vice is the predominant trait of Jötuns, and is particularly loathed by the gods and goddesses. Ódin is known to have personally brought dishonor and shame upon those with an avaricious disposition, with his wife Frigga inciting him. One who cannot be generous or hospitable will have few friends, few who will aid them in any way, for, as has been stated repeatedly, relationships must be reciprocal. (Sources: *Sólarljód* 63 & 64, *Historia Danica* Book 8, *Vafthrúdnismál* 43).

Thievery: Bloody runes are risted on the breasts of thieves who carry heavy burdens of lead. The addition of this vice within our morality fully contradicts the idea that our ancestors were nothing more than marauding pirates out to take whatever they could get their hands on. In fact, some of the old stories portray an early "golden age" where treasures could be left out in the open without any threat of them being stolen. For the protection of any group of people, there has to be laws in place that will keep property in the hands of its owners, for without them nothing sacred may be held safely and securely. With their admiration for precious objects, valuable metals and holy artifacts, it should come as no surprise that the Teutons would view those who would steal them with disdain. (Sources: *Sólarljód* 61 & 63, *Historia Danica* Book 5 & 6, *Skáldskaparmál* 43, *Vafthrúd-nismál* 43).

Treason: This could also be called treachery, and those who betray their kin or nation are hung up and constantly torn apart by wolves. You have to understand the importance of this on a national scale, even though it is rarely brought to our attention today. When an individual sells their people out to a foreign, hostile enemy they have practically committed a thousand murders. Their underhanded antics threaten the lives of everyone in their land—people who trusted them, who loved them, who raised them, who helped them. In some ancestral lands, traitors were burned to ash and their names purposely forgotten. In the same sense, to turn against one's friends or family is a shameful act, one that would lead many to distrust the one who betrayed them. We have a union with those in our lives, a union that should be respected and held sacred. (Sources: *Historia Danica* Book 8, *Germania* Ch. 12, *Völuspá* 29, *Vafthrúdnismál* 43).

Slander: Liars and those who utter falsehoods about others, in line with perjurers, wade through the river Vadgelmir in horrible pain. This river is made from the venom of the serpents, whose wattled backs form the hall in Náströnds. As they wade, "Hel's (Urd's) ravens" repeatedly pluck their eyes out of their heads, which we can presume grow back so they can continue this. In an honor-based society such as the one in early Northern Europe lying about someone was serious business. Known as "honor-robbers", they could bring about much harm to those they disgraced. As bad as it is to commit a crime, it is much worse to be accused of one you are innocent of by a garrulous tongue. The role of slanderer is one in which Loki is particularly vested in, possibly furthering the conclusion that Vadgelmir is the stream of venom, since he is punished by the poison of the serpent. The plucking of their eyes might simply be a practical idea—one cannot speak of that which they do not see. (Sources: *Reginsmál* 4, *Sólarljó*d 67 [cp. *Fjöls-vinnsmál* 46], *Vafthrúdnismál* 43).

Cruelty: Those who fail to show mercy are continuously feasted upon by the demons of Niflhel, and they are regenerated after every devouring. They are also said to suffer terribly on the paths to Urd's *Thingstead* even before they are even judged. The marks of torment upon them serve as evidence before the tribunal that they were especially vicious towards others, as does their lack of a *hamingja* to defend them, since she abandons such criminals. The ability to show mercy is the hallmark of nobility in the Teutonic paradigm, for it represents the characteristics inherent within the chivalrous nature of the Nordic warrior. (Sources: *Völuspá* 29, *Hávamál* 150, *Visio Godeschalci* [cp. *Sölarljód* 42], *Historia Danica* Book 8, *Vafthrúdnismál* 43, *Gunnars Slag*r 20, *Sigrdrífumál* 22).

One can easily see how closely related the above Nine Virtues are to the Nine Vices. Most of them have their exact opposites within each list—loyalty opposes treason or treachery and adultery, generosity opposes greed and thievery, kindness opposes murder and cruelty, piety opposes sacrilege, honesty opposes slander, and honor opposes perjury. As long as one follows these guidelines and laws, they will be guaranteed respectability among their people, as well as praise from our gods. Then the lot of the blessed will certainly honor their afterlife. But those who continue to disgrace themselves, who commit vile acts without remorse and without compensating those they have wronged will be stained with infamy, will lose the protection of the gods, and can look forward to the suffering of Náströnds.

To have such a simple, straightforward morality allows each person to be their own authority on how they should live their lives. These laws, the virtues and vices, form the core foundation of our ethical beliefs, so there is no need to strain over obscure textual passages to find rule after rule with which to condemn your fellow Ásatrúar. There is no doubt that these tenets are the basis of an ancient code of honor that forged the principles our ancestors lived by. Respect them, teach them and honor them, then no one will be able to discredit you without first discrediting themselves.

4

Pleasure

"Shun not the mead,
Yet drink moderately,
Speak sensibly or be silent,
None will hold you
To be uncivil
If you retire early to bed.

—Óðin, *Hávamál* 19.

It is important for us, as an extension of our views on Óðinic morality, to look at how we consider indulgences into the various forms of gratification, since these play a major role in how any religious path affects us. Much of my purpose here in this book is to eliminate misconceptions surrounding the Ásatrú faith, and hopefully this examination of our beliefs concerning pleasure will dispel the common myths about the licentious nature of our "pagan" way of life. Simply because we do not favor Puritanism or forced suppression of natural tendencies does not mean that we will act without nobility or even chastity, or that we have some sort of philosophy of "anything goes", ignoring any sense of personal restraint when it comes to pleasing the Self. Our morality may differ somewhat from mainstream religions', but that does not mean it is without validity. One does not need to be a follower of the monotheist faiths, or any religion for that matter, to have integrity and standards. We would consider our ethics valuable and honorable, always reflecting our pious devotion to the gods and goddesses and our people.

To begin, we should consider the boundaries originally set for us when we were children, for these are integral to our understanding of right and wrong later in life. A good example of this is a scenario most parents will likely have to deal with: that of a curious child playing with, or wanting to play with fire. The desire to create fire is one of our most primal urges, which may be a factor in why children are so commonly attracted to the means of producing it. In fact, it is so common that the question is not whether or not a parent will have to face this situation, but how to respond to it when it occurs. A popular method is to take away the source of the fire, then scold or spank the child to remain vigilant so it doesn't happen again. And, in some ways this can be effective. However, imagine how profound it would be for you to actually teach your inquisitive little one how to build a real fire, how to control it, and how dangerous it really can be. Such an experience could teach the child how to respect its power, so any further boundaries set could better be understood. "Because I said so" is an answer given to children to instill fear and a sense of subjugation before a domineering elder, which teaches them nothing positive or constructive.

I discussed this idea with a good friend of mine. He remembered from childhood when his father taught him how to shoot a gun at targets or wild game, to understand the risks involved and handle firearms safely. Not only was this a valuable lesson, it was also a bonding experience between father and son. We cannot shelter our children from the dangers of the world, but we can prepare them to face them bravely and intelligently.

At its core, the above probably best represents the difference between Ásatrú morality and that of the monotheist religions. The latter is absolute, black and white. You will either obey, simply to obey (never mind understanding why), you will follow the very specific rules laid down in their holy books, or you will face eternal damnation. When 'sin' is committed you will either beg for forgiveness or suffer forever. It is a system based on fear and the hope of reward.

Rather than trying to dictate all personal actions, Ódinic morality seeks to educate and protect the folk. Telling your child not to play with matches would most likely pique his or her curiosity. The next thing you know they've set the backyard on fire! As we have seen, Ásatrú sources give us broad guidelines, such as always keeping our word, being honorable and trustworthy in our dealings, being generous and kind; it leaves the details to a person's judgment. Such a doctrine relies on the faithfulness of its followers, granting them the responsibility to make their own choices, hoping for the best. If I impose a thousand rules on someone, for any reason, it shows that I do not trust them or their wisdom in handling situations. The same goes for religious creeds.

For our purposes here, the modes of pleasure can be divided into five categories: sexual pleasure, consumptive pleasures, pleasures of nature, pleasures of the mind, and pleasures in relationships.

Sexual Pleasure

First, sexual pleasure has its limitations and allowances in all social systems, cultures, and religions. All of us have certain points where we will "draw the line", so to speak, in the performance of sexual acts. When restrictions are not placed on such acts any morality will instantly be weakened by the wanton nature of its adherents, for those who cannot restrain such impulses will easily fall into the traps of perversion or sexual addiction. It should be clearly understood that Ásatrú only limits conduct that directly harms the folk physically, emotionally, or psychologically. We are not going to condemn anyone outside our faith for not accepting our morals, and we will not try to contrive odd taboos that unnecessarily suppress our people.

Above all else it should be noted that there are not any limits on the ways a husband and wife can pleasure each other. In fact, the more ways you can come up with, the better, for few things please the gods more than a happy, healthy and long lasting marriage. It is our devotion to family values that leads us in our limitations of certain sexual deeds, but we also focus on the disgrace that comes with harming another for one's personal gratification.

Since our moral principles are based on the needs of practical society, and are not the fear-driven precepts of some Middle Eastern volcano god, the sexual restrictions enforced by our faith act to preserve and safeguard our people, our families, and our nobility. For this reason, there are four primary prohibitions found in our ancient sources, those against homosexuality, promiscuity, miscegenation, and adultery. Of course, sexual crimes, such as rape or child molestation are such obvious *nids* that there is no need for them to be included here. To rape, especially a virgin (which would certainly include children!) was a capital crime in many, if not all Northern European lands.

Sexuality in respect to natural law serves two evolutionary functions. Firstly, it assures propagation or maintenance of one's people, who need to replace their dead for continued survival. This requires at least two children per family for stability, and at least three children per family for growth. When two parents die they need two children to replace them, whereas a third or fourth, etc. will guarantee an increase in the family line; if enough do this it will increase the folk population as a whole. This, more than anything represents the synergetic bond we have with our folk. Secondly, monogamous sexuality assures pair-bondings so that two parents are available to turn their attentions to raising healthy, productive offspring. As individualism replaces cultural identity, family bonds lose their value, along with the connection to one's folk, so that a dysfunctional home life has become the norm. With each generation, the family unit becomes less important, secondary to pleasing the Self in any way imaginable. As this happens, degradation, crime, alienation and addiction will continue to rise as individualists seek to fill the spiritual hole in their lives. Pair-bonded families, where healthy, natural relationships are supported, where kinship and folk are emphasized, will develop as functional entities. In societies where these are promoted, such as in traditional Japanese culture, literacy is extremely high and the rate of sexually transmitted diseases is very low. These facts supersede any claims by those promoting political agendas.

For the ancient Teutons being married by the age of 25 was required of everyone, with a risk of banishment for those who violated this. Such a measure might seem extreme to us today, with our emphasis on the Self, on wanting more money and having more fun. Our modern world today has created the first ever social paradigm where men and women get married solely because they love one another, but in ancient times this could have been done to benefit one's clan, to end wars or form alliances, with love or affection being secondary to these. I am not advocating or condemning either model; I am only making a comparison between then and now. Because of the immense freedom we now have in choosing our spouse, we also have a greater responsibility in maintaining the life of our people. Those who do not replace themselves through responsible reproduction will soon find their folk facing imminent extinction and displacement among others in their own lands. The bottom line is that Northern Europeans are dying out because we are not having enough children, to the point where this has become a crisis of epic proportions. If we cease to exist, the hypocrisies of interracist dogma will have successfully enacted what the worst, most murderous tyrants in history could only dream of: absolute genocide of an entire race.

There is power in promotion, which in many ways is why we have reached the point we have. What we advertise as people and as a people has a significant impact on social trends, especially today in our world of advanced technology. If we turn our back on who we are, if we forget our heritage and ancestry, we will have effectively contributed to the death of our folk. This should be known as the great suicide-genocide! We cannot blame others for this, we can't point fingers or make up hateful, ridiculous propaganda against this race or that, for the fault will be our own. Only we can turn this around and save Northern kind through positive, loving campaigns towards the appreciation of our genetic legacy, which in turn should act as part of an ideal of mutual respect towards all peoples. We will not re-invigorate the Nordic spirit with bigoted philosophies or dead, totalitarian creeds. Race wars, violent coups, belligerent upheavals, all these are the fantasies of ignorant sociopaths who in the end do more harm than good. The spirit of the North merely lies dormant after facing years of adversity on all fronts. To revive it will take compassion, love and understanding, towards our own kind and towards others. We will educate, we will promote, we will help; we will *not* hate, attack, or affront.

The ancient Teutons considered homosexuality a degenerate practice, mainly because it compromises masculinity when a man must put himself in the place of a woman. Also, it is simply an activity that fails to create children for the maintenance of the folk. Not that *all* sex must be procreational, for we will not deny or suppress the fact that sex is indeed pleasurable or that we shouldn't have fun with it! We only need to consider our responsibilities and obligations to our family and folk, and to ourselves, in anything we do. It seems that so many people are desperately seeking *something* to identify with, something to connect to, so often times they will embrace homosexual or promiscuous lifestyles to compensate for the elements that are missing from their lives.

But do not think that, because our faith rejects such practices that we feel it is our duty to attack those who indulge in them, for each individual's life is their own. We are not your parents, nor will we try to be. We Ásatrúar have made the choice to live by these principles and that choice is our own, whereas beyond our nation we can only hope to educate or lead by example. Homosexuality or promiscuity is not "against god", or anything like that, it is something that we choose not to accept because of the harm it brings to our people. Loki is the Jötun of unbridled lust and bisexuality, whose antics are shown in our lore to consume him within his own morass of degrading behavior. But the gods tolerated him as much as they could, until he *had* to be exiled from Ásgard for the crimes he had committed.

Miscegenation *has* to be prohibited, for it can be destructive in so many ways to both individuals involved. If one has a child through interracial sex, which can happen in just one coupling, then an entire genetic line has been broken, one that has developed through thousands of years of evolution. Collectively, when miscegenation occurs on a large scale, the result is genocide. To admit this has nothing to do with hate, it is by all means based on a love and admiration for all races, since it is for their preservation that we speak of such things. If one is to support "diversity" they cannot also present ideals and beliefs that, in the long-term, would eliminate this once and for all. We learn in modern ecological science to value diversity of sub-species and we are told that one of the threats to the red wolf is miscegenation with coyotes. Since coyotes have a high birth rate and can scavenge in a variety of climates, they can "export" genes and still remain a viable sub-species. The red wolf, whose environment is more selective, loses some of its viability as a species every time one carries a litter of half-coyote pups. When scholars use pseudo-science to promote personal agendas regarding the "illusion" of ethnic and genetic differences, they irresponsibly support the extinction of a people, where others would afford such a luxury of survival for animals.

In a sacred analogy, it would only be logical for the gods and goddesses of a folk to desire the continuance of the folk they created, taught, and protected for millennia. Today we speak of "civil rights" as though they are actual weapons against oppression, which I guess in some ways they are. These rights are an extension of natural law, the first of which is the right to survive. Should Nordics be condemned for wanting to protect their heritage? Should we be labeled "racists" or "bigots" simply because we do not want to watch our people and our culture die? The threat to our nations is real, as real as that of the Tibetan monks, the indigenous tribes of Australia and elsewhere, as real as past genocidal threats we read about in history books. It has been projected that within 50 years Europeans will be a minority in their own lands, and without a homeland, something all other races take for granted, all hope for our survival is lost. Can anyone give any reasons why this would be a *good* thing? What's worse, Industrialists, more infatuated with greed than sovereignty or cultural legacies, hope to keep the European workforce maintained by introducing *more* immigrants into Europe, effectively *trying* to replace us! With such attitudes, such apathy towards our genetic inheritance we will cease to exist as a people before the end of this century.

Some may try to convince us that the death of cultural values, which can go hand in hand with family values, would be to the benefit of all. They consider race to be the great world divider, the reason behind wars and hate and violence of all sorts. There is no doubt that race does play a part, and has played a part in some of the atrocities committed in the past, no one can deny this. But then, so has religion, so has political ideology, so has economic status and a plethora of other concepts. Utopian visions should not motivate us towards genocide, for those are the exact reasons attempts have been made towards this in the past. We must truly do some soul searching, looking deep into our hearts and decide what is important to us. As individualism replaces cultural identity crime, addiction, murder, tyranny, etc. will continue to grow as the world's leaders, along with their people, become more and more disconnected to the greater whole and focus only on their self-interests.

Consumptive Pleasures

The next category of pleasure concerns those that are consumptive, i.e. the ingestion of alcohol, food or drugs. Our literature is full of passages that warn us against the dangers of alcohol abuse, though these warnings do not imply any sort of "commandments" for abstention. Ódin himself teaches us, through his own experience, about the perils of excessive drinking. Although imbibing liquor is tolerated, even considered sacred, we are admonished against too much, for the gods know, as do we, that the more intoxicated one gets, the less control they have of themselves. A lot can happen to indignify a person who has become belligerently drunk, who has lost the awareness of their actions.

Liquor, more particularly mead, is the holiest substance known in our lore. It is the great drink of the gods, similar to the Soma of the Hindus and Nectar of the Greeks. So you will not find any teetotaler preachers in the Ásatrú nation. One may choose to not drink alcoholic beverages for personal reasons, but this is not mandated within our faith. Ódin warns us to exercise caution and to be moderate in our dealings with intoxicants. Thus moderation, not abstinence, is encouraged.

In the same sense, we are warned against too much consumption of food. Obviously the gods and goddesses are aware of the dangers of overeating, which can cause obesity, then lead to diabetes, heart disease, and stroke. In many ways food can be addictive, as it fills a void or comforts those who indulge in excess. Often times one simply needs to experience a paradigm shift in order to overcome this, or any other eating disorder. When food becomes a weakness, it is necessary to reconsider how one views it so that it may return to its natural role of being a strengthening agent. Food is energy, nothing more. It may take an invocation of the divine power from our gods and goddesses to help those who are fettered by compulsive overeating (in accordance with proper mental and physical support programs), for their might and inspiration can help us face any problems and win any battle.

Of course, some people can eat all they want and never have to deal with any health risks such as weight gain. Ódin may continually fast, living off of mead alone, whereas Thór's ravenous appetite is legendary! Such edicts against alcoholism and gluttony serve, as with other things, as warnings to us, but are not "deadly sins". Because our deities care for us and love us, they teach us to be healthy and happy, while living life to it's fullest. To be physically fit through proper diet and exercise is probably one of the greatest gifts you can give to yourself, for nothing is more uplifting than maintaining a healthy lifestyle, especially if you have had to overcome adversity to get there.

Drug use is a highly controversial issue in the Ódinic movement. Although there aren't any specific religious guidelines for this most Ásatrúar want little to do with "the drug culture" for we often equate it with weakness, cowardice and degeneracy. As those who strive towards divine and heroic archetypes anything that would sap our strength, our intelligence, or our dignity is repulsive to us.

It is certain that our ancestors employed some form of *sacred* drug use, where hallucinogens were taken as part of religious and spiritual observances, in accordance with ancient herbalist traditions. The suppression of these traditions, which are gaining in popularity today, did not necessarily derive from disdain towards altered states of consciousness, but instead were based on the motivations to systematically destroy all aspects of Europe's "heathen" past. That all attempts to eliminate *any* form of non-medicinal drug intake in many countries have their source and support in Christian fundamentalist circles is no coincidence. As in the past, secular authorities are used to force Biblical morality on us all.

Shamanist beliefs *were* held in the ancient North, and there is no reason why we should deny our faith the resurrection of this ideal. In order for us to do this we must differentiate between sacred drug use and recreational drug use. The former is designed to be a part of a ceremonial atmosphere, under the care of an experienced herbalist, using only natural substances. Sometimes one may choose to engage in these practices without any help, which is fine, so long as you understand the risks involved. Generally, such rituals also involve fasting, sleep deprivation, and/or meditation.

Of course, even recreational drug use isn't something that we condemn. As with most of our ethics we simply try to give aid and warn people against those things that could bring them harm. In our modern world, in several countries, using drugs can put you in prison, get you fired from your job, expelled from schools, etc. Also, it is our responsibility to promote a healthy lifestyle free from addictions of any sort, including alcoholism. When one is imprisoned by chemical dependency they have essentially lost their freedom to an intoxicant, they have become its slave and will often betray all else for the feelings it gives them. All across the world people are trying to restore themselves to sanity, to create some sense of euphoria to drown out the hopelessness that comes with a lack of family and folk values in their lands. As stated, when one can connect to something larger than themselves this can bring a profound sense of meaning to their lives. But, when we feel disconnected, alone, or out for "number one", the world can seem like a cold, cruel place. To make it better, we fill the void with whatever we can. For many, spiritual systems cannot bring them back from the brink because what is offered comes across as stale, callous and mind-washing, redundant even, where one 'crutch' replaces another. When a faith is to heal the scars and wounds of an individual's past, there should be an emphasis on re-invigorating the soul, both personally and as part of a collective unconscious, with strength and power, where one can rise up out of the darkness and find the fires within them to climb their mountains.

Because of the addictive nature of so-called "hard-drugs", we would have to emphatically insist that Ásatrúar stay away from them, for nothing good could come from this. We would not rebuke or "excommunicate" anyone using cocaine, heroin, etc. but we should continuously speak out against this as potentially injurious or even lethal! Anyone who became addicted, to anything, should be helped and treated compassionately, doing whatever it takes to assist them in breaking the chains that hold them to their dependency. Although one could consider such reliance on a drug to be a violation of our Independence virtue, we should not react with indifference, apathy or disdain towards those inflicted with this sickness. Addiction, to anything, is not a character flaw, it is an illness which progresses and develops in the minds of its victims. Some have a genetic intolerance towards addicting substances. We feel that by giving meaning to people's lives through their culture and heritage, through community and family, we can help keep them from falling into this pit of despair.

Pleasures of Nature

Taking pleasure in nature is the spirit of our relationship with our Mother Earth, Frigga. It is the satisfaction in observing, and being completely absorbed in the natural world, where the mind is silenced and all the senses are in tune with your surrounding environment. Beyond meditation, it is the ability to appreciate all of the miracles, the *true* miracles of the universe. Many of us live so isolated and alienated from nature it is hard to place value upon this experience. Connection to the land is a vital part of our existence, even if this is not readily apparent. Anyone can take time to be moved by the dawn, or to enjoy the cool breeze of a field, to listen to the sounds of a flowing stream, and the mating calls of local wildlife. The bond that we have with the world around us is sacred, and it is our duty to honor it, and all life, from different peoples to different species, to the plants and rocks; the sky above and the ground below are invariably connected. This union, or universal synergy, is represented by our most holy symbol, the World-Tree, Yggdrasil. There is no denying the sanctity of this ideal, for to our ancestors it was one of the highest philosophical concepts. Throughout our sources, we read of a people's immersion in the beauty, awe, and immensity of nature.

Pleasures of the Mind

It is the same with pleasures of the mind. The Sagas, Eddas, and Histories are replete with mentions of skalds, visionaries and sages, who were the equivalent of our modern scholars and scientists. Archaeological digs have found Bronze Age remains of board games, which were the forerunners of chess. There is even the possibility that our ancestors had books, perhaps even large collections of them, long before the Christian invasion, for historical records describe evangelist kings, most notably Charlemagne, burning hundreds of volumes as well as libraries and universities. The point is that the early Northern peoples admired intelligence and wisdom; they were not the ignorant savages some have made them out to be. During their harsh arctic winters they would partake in leisurely activities that stimulated the mind and furthered their personal evolution.

Pleasures in Relationships

There can be the pleasure of friendship, which can be, and usually is one of the most significant aspects of our lives. To offer friendship is to commit yourself to a person in a way that is honorable and noble, where our sacred tradition of "gift for gift" will help to maintain the bonds we have with others. This is *not* a folkish ideal, for there is no need for us to isolate ourselves from the rest of the world. If you were to become friends with someone who is not of your folk, the mutual respect you *should* have for one another should motivate each to honor the other's cultural boundaries. In this sense, our faith *is* ethnic, but is *not* ethnocentric, for we should try to develop friendships with those of other cultures and other religions, in any way that we can. Of course, one must use wisdom in dealing with anyone, and it is always imperative for us to see to it that we are not taken advantage of. I am reminded here of the adventures of Arab explorer Ibn Fadlan, whose dealings with the Rus on the Volga river (in the land named after this tribe—Russia) led to a prolific friendship. At the same time neither tried to impose their beliefs or customs on each other, a great model for us today.

Gratification of the senses must be experienced in a way that does no harm in the deepest and fullest sense. Pleasure must be in moderation and in a healthy context, which helps to preserve a vital, functional society and a mentally and physically wholesome person, living by natural laws as typified and overarched by the divinely manifest tenets of the gods and goddesses. We have, in our body of texts, and the isolated survivals of our faith in practice, the meta-example of a spiritual dynamic, which allows the individual's enjoyment of life and the need to create and maintain a stable and productive civilization.

5

The Warrior

"*A king's children should be*
wise and silent
and daring in war,
everyone should be
joyous and generous
until his hour of death."

—Ódin, Hávamál 15

"*Wherever you know of harm,*
regard that harm as your own;
and give your foes no peace."

—Ódin, Hávamál 127.

Probably the most popular, and yet most misunderstood aspect of Teutonic culture is that of the warrior, as many factors combine to create a false perception concerning its origins. That period in history known as "The Viking Age" has created images of "barbarians" raping and pillaging, murdering with reckless abandon, caring not for the sanctity of life. Although we should not over-romanticize them as innocent victims of libel, there is no doubt that the Vikings' story has been severely distorted by those who eventually conquered them; often to the point where these ecclesiastic chronicles depicting their history cannot be trusted.

We do not deny that our ancestors were fierce combatants, whose martial prowess was even lauded by the Romans; nor do we reject the idea that these men and women were capable of displaying the savagery they are known for. However, there are two primary reasons why this should not reflect negatively upon them or upon our faith. First, it is selfish and pompous for anyone to impose their standards of living upon others, past or present, for this denotes a false sense of superiority and prejudice in considering other cultures. Many people in secular society have tried to condemn the Bible for its portrayals of violence and bigotry, using this very egocentric train of thought. Sacred books, be they Christian, Muslim, Hindu, Ásatrú, etc. were written long ago and represent civilization as it was then. By our standards today, anywhere you look the world was seemingly a much darker place, so attacking the contents of these texts is to try to place our values on those long since dead, when their perceptions clearly would have been different. One would have to be incredibly self-centered and naive to think that humanity has always been, or should have always been like us today.

Viking Raids

Also, in spite of the fact that the early records are greatly exaggerated, there is a perfectly logical explanation for the bloodthirsty dispositions Christians witnessed in Viking raids, one that has nothing to do with their usual mannerisms. It is extremely important in considering this, that we recognize Christianity as an invading force against the indigenous populations of Northern Europe, which was but a continuance of previous incursions initiated by the Roman Empire. To illustrate this point I would like to give a brief history lesson:

After the death of Carloman in 771, his brother Charles, or Charlemagne became king of the Franks. Charlemagne was one of the cruelest tyrants the world has ever known, who forced Christianity upon several nations in a sea of blood. Through his zealotry, he embarked upon a vicious campaign against the Saxon "heathens" in order to bring them into the new religion and make them a part of his empire. His soldiers had no concern for those they killed, be they men, women or children, for as "pagans" their lives had little value. At one point the Franks had told the Saxons at Quierzy (Kiersy, near modern Brussels in Belgium) that those who would not kneel before the alien god would be killed. The natives heartily refused, ignoring their threats, which brought forth an unmerciful slaughter at Verden (near the Weser river in Germany) in 782.

The Scandinavians were well aware of the atrocities their southerly neighbors were facing at the hands of the Carolingian empire, as they had received, and sheltered many refugees and aided the rebellions. It is believed that the leaders in these regions gathered to conceive a plan to deal with this invading menace. They knew that attacking the Franks head-on would have been disastrous, even suicidal. So the idea was to attack "the church" as a whole by selecting isolated areas devoid of Charlemagne's and Rome's awesome military might, then using gue-rilla tactics which had proven efficient to them in the past.

Their first target: the wealthiest monastery in all of Europe, located on Lindis-farne Island just off the coast of Northern England. These churches were financed by local tribes who were heavily taxed as subjects of the new religion, or who were simply repressed by the reigning powers. Viking raiding traditions were more about adventure than piracy, for exploration and daring undertakings were an intrinsic part of their culture. So leaders simply used this adventurous spirit to help fight against the incursion, for they knew that *their* lands would be next. That thievery was their primary motive actually defies what we know of Viking society, especially if these raids were officially sanctioned. The purpose behind stealing from the Christians was to take back what had been stolen, in the form of church taxes and seizures, from their neighbors, whom they had aided. Such lev-ies became ridiculous for "heathens" and were even unreasonable for the newly converted. This was the case in Lindisfarne where a 25% tax was demanded of peasants, along with requirements for labor and buildings whenever possible. No doubt the monks ruled their territories with an iron fist, subjecting their followers to their foul lusts and greedy temperaments.

So it was that on June 11th, 793 C.E., just eleven years after Charlemagne's attack on Verden, three Viking ships landed at Lindisfarne, "The Holy Isle", and the Teutonic folk made their mark against the Christian faith. They had no intentions of killing anyone, for the monks were rounded up and separated from their assailants' activities. But in their fervor these Christian priests began tor-menting and mocking their attackers, which so enraged the Vikings, remember-ing Verden (as some were probably from there), that all were executed. This began a defensive campaign that lasted many years, even when Scandinavia had to deal with its own zealous monster, Olaf Trygvasson.

Now, take a moment to put all this into perspective. Imagine if, say fanatic Muslim regimes managed to push their "jihad" into your land. You've heard of the horrors committed against those in lands very close to you. Perhaps you even have family in the areas taken over. You know they will be in your homeland soon. Like the Christians of that time they would convert or kill, then force survi-vors to live under their extremely oppressive rule. Your family would be mur-dered, your home burnt to ash, your land conquered. What would *you* do?

I would like to point out that certain measures have been made by the Catho-lic church to apologize for the atrocities of its past, and this should be praised and honored. Our purpose here is to relate history as it is, though we hope that we can eventually heal the wounds that separate our faiths in an effort of peace and co-operation. The church needs to be accountable for its history, but it is not our place to condemn them or the path they have chosen because of this. In the same sense, individuals of *any* faith: Muslim, Jew, Buddhist, etc. who will reach out to us as friends should be given the chance to prove themselves. We should not let fear or prejudice dictate how we react to those around us, nor should the past, no matter how recent, be our sole guide in our relationships.

The first thing we can learn from all of this is that we are all just people (as were our ancestors); we are just people making it through each day as best we can. We will meet psychopaths, zealots, fools and liars who will paint all the wrong pictures of those things we hold sacred. This is an inevitable fact. *Any* religion can be shown in a negative light, *any* creed can be described as dysfunctional or barbaric, for all ideals have that one invariable and yet uncontrollable factor: people. We could spend years amassing evidence against Christianity, Islam, Judaism, Marxism, Capitalism or any other ideology we can think of, or we can try to manifest our own beliefs in a noble, respectable manner to serve as a higher example for all.

The treatment of our Viking ancestors in history books has to be taken with a grain of salt, for there is no doubt, as modern science has well attested, that they were an extremely intelligent, civilized people trying their best to exist in one of the harshest periods imaginable. Irresponsible scholars, who ignore Christian conversion tactics and the possible impact of this new, invading religion fully display their bias against these indigenous cultures when supporting the "savage" Viking perception. Some have even tried to claim that Christianity was introduced into Northern Europe peacefully, which really shows that when they read the histories they only see what they want to see.

The Valhalla Imagery

By far the most disastrous misconception surrounding our warrior ethic is in the Valhalla imagery, where it is falsely believed that the only way we can obtain a blessed afterlife is if we die in battle. In order for us to actually accept this ludicrous idea we would have to view our ancestors as wild, belligerent fighters (which, as shown above, seems to be the intention in some aspects) with no belief in defensive battle tactics, since death would be favored over victory, as even walking away victorious from a fight made one susceptible to dying of old age, sickness, or accident. In every single source left for us we do not find any reason to believe that the ancients ever conceived such a notion, nor do we find any record of "suicide squads" rushed at the enemy for any sort of strategic advantage.

If these warriors were truly devoted to the ancestral ways, and we have no reason to doubt they were, then someone would have noticed such a peculiar tradition and written about it somewhere, especially if some of the more passionate adherents were throwing their lives away in deep religious fervor. No such records exist, not even in the foreign annals where we would expect them! The Berserkers themselves, with their wild battle fury, were not thought to be suicidal or to have been more desirous of death in battle over victory and life.

The origin of this false imagery lies in the erroneous interpretation of our eschatology, where Christian views of the afterlife and Christian cosmology have overlapped our own. When the Bible was first translated into Greek it was decided to interpret the Hebrew "Sheol" or "Gehenna", a designation of their Underworld, with "Hades", that of the Greeks. However, unlike the Hebrew conception, Hades is not entirely the realm of punishment for the damned. Controlled by the *god* Hades it is divided into two regions: the Elysian Fields for the blessed dead and Tartarus for the condemned. Hades himself is a benevolent deity who cares for those who lived honorably and piously, and who punishes wrongdoers.

Later, when the Bible was to be translated into German, or more particularly, the Gothic tongue, the same method was used, correlating the Teutonic Underworld, known as Jörmungrund, with the Semitic. Like Hades, the Teutons' world of the dead has its fields of bliss, known as Hel, and its realms of the damned, called Niflhel. In heathen times the goddess Hel was a benevolent deity, identical to Urd, the highest Norn. However, the usage of "Hel" in the Bible, which was termed "hell", became so popular that it superseded all other designations and became the common form still in use today. Because of this popularity Christian scholars needed to coincide the ancient lore, where this originated from, with that of their holy book. In order to correspond with the ideas concerning the land of hell, the goddess needed to be changed into an earlier demon from the lore, working alongside their "devil", Satan or Lucifer. This is what led to the confounding of Loki's daughter, the half-dark, half-white (literally!) patroness of disease, and ruler of Niflhel as Urd's servant, who was confused with our beloved *dís* of fate.

The Teutonic cosmology was then arranged ethically, as in the Hebrew, with heaven as the 'good place', earth as the blend of 'bad' and 'good', and Hel as the 'bad place'. The three worlds of Ásgard, Midgard, and Jörmungrund (the Underworld) parallel this somewhat, but the dualistic moral archetype is completely alien to us. With the loss of our Elysian fields, and consequently the Helthing that judges the dead, only Valhalla remains as a place for a joyous afterlife and, consequently, only heroism remains as the means for the gods to grant us this. Thus, those who die of old age, sickness or accident, no matter how worthy of respect or reward, are doomed to be among the damned. That such a ridiculous idea has survived as long as it has is tragic in its own right, for it devalues decent men and women who have not lived engaged in combat. Even Sigurd, that most famous hero of the Völsung clan, stated that "some are valiant who have red-dened no sword in the blood of a foeman's breast", showing that our ancestors did not see war and fighting as the only means of gaining honor.

It should be further recognized that dying in battle is not the only means of getting into Valhalla, which again would create a bizarre suicidal form of combat strategy. Also, it would have kept some of Germania's most beloved heroes, who may have died outside of battle, from feasting with the gods, while one who never touched a weapon could join the elite after dying in their first confrontation.

The term "*Valr*" is usually taken to mean "one slain in battle" as it serves as a prefix for such words as "Valhalla", "Valkyrie" or "Valfather" (Ódin). It actually means "one selected by an assembly, or chosen for the destiny that awaits them in another world", in other words the "Valr" are the select, the chosen, the elite, those who will ascend to Ásgard and become part of Ódin's and Freyja's warriors, called the Einherjar. As in life, the ultimate purpose of the Einherjar is to protect their families in Hel, during Ragnarök—doing on a cosmic scale what they did in life—sacrificing for the common good. That one has to be *chosen* to become one of these elite warriors certainly implies that one had to *earn* this status. This would explain why *all* of our ancient warriors were obsessed with their reputa-tions. Their status is earned through honorable life and heroic deeds, which defended their people for what is right and good. One cannot stumble across her-oism or 'accidentally' end up in our ancestral "Hall of Fame", for the gods and goddesses decide at the Helthing where each of us will spend our afterlife. Because of this one could not live ignobly or unmercifully and expect to reside with our benevolent forefathers and deities. A hero is, as he or she has always been—the epitome of chivalric and stalwart action, who will put his/her life on the line to help and save others. Their sacrifice is why we have always respected and revered their station, for without them peaceful existence would be impossi-ble.

Admiration for Heroism

The skaldic or bardic traditions were strongly linked to early Northern European society, and had deep Indo-European roots, meaning that our ancestors valued the storytellers among them. Just as it would be incorrect to use today's action films as the basis for believing that all modern people thrive on violence, it is the same when we look at the ancient tales. The fact is, heroes make for good stories and sagas, which is why accounts of their adventures greatly outnumber those of any other class in all cultures in all ages. But this does not mean that we, or those before us, have ever favored war or violence over peace and prosperity. Our sources specifically describe a people who admired and longed for an ancient past where all lived harmoniously and happily. The great Teutonic epic, as it is pieced together, depicts a progression of universal corruption, where the worlds passed from the Golden Age to the ages leading towards a downward spiral of strife, deception, and degradation. It is clear from viewing this in its proper context that the "axe-age and sword-age" was deeply lamented by early Ásatrúar, as it should be today. As stated, they were people, with all the hopes and desires humans hold in their hearts, so naturally they would wish for peace over war. Their admiration for heroes and heroic deeds stemmed from a realistic understanding that freedom, sovereignty, security, and tranquility cannot be maintained without those brave men and women who are willing to fight and die to protect them. Denial of this in religious systems has led to hypocrisy on one side, where non-violence is preached while soldiers are sent off to kill and die, and apathy on the other, where those who fight for freedom are disrespected or taken for granted. Our religion does not establish such psychological conflicts. A warrior is a valued member of any society.

It does not matter if we agree or disagree with the politics involved, or if one is friend or foe; those putting their life on the line should be given their due respect. We may be taught to love our allies and hate our enemies, even if we personally have no conflict with them. "They" are "evil", "we" are "good". But the other side also feels this way, considering all of us as they would those in direct conflict with them. The fact is, none of this is true, which our ancestors recognized when it came time to fight. They saw two sides with a dispute that could not be settled with words, so the time had come to settle it with weapons. When enemies died they were given funerals and paid tribute to as if they were allies, for it was believed that the anger one held towards another in life should not extend beyond death. There are records of confrontations settled in a way that could actually be used as evidence for a more humane standard of combat than that found today. On some occasions, when two leaders came into discord with one another, they would opt to resolve the dispute in single-combat, known as "*Hölmgang*" ("Island Going", for these would be held in isolation on small isles), so that fewer would have to die. It would have been easy for them to rouse their armies against each other, but they chose to spare the lives of their people, bravely handling the situation solely between the two of them. Could you imagine any politician doing this today? They would never even consider putting themselves in harm's way, though in the past leaders stood at the frontline of battle, willing to sacrifice themselves in any way for the good of their nation. My, how times have changed.

The Warrior Ethic

So, exactly what is the Teutonic warrior ethic? Today it could best be expressed as a creed of inner-strength and courage, which does not necessarily have anything to do with violence. The Teutonic warrior faces *any* struggle with a valiant, noble heart, prepared to do whatever it takes in the protection of his family, his people, and what he considers to be right and just. The chivalrous nature of this ideal forms our core principles of decency and fairness, in peace and in conflict.

Because of attempts to pervert this ethos, I would like to explain that we do not, in any way, support terrorism, in any of its forms. We do not enjoy the suffering of any life form and will not harm innocents for the sake of a political agenda. No one can be honorable if they seek to hurt or kill those who will not fight, who have given no reason for the assault against them, who do not deserve to be attacked. And for anyone who would make excuses, allow me to make this perfectly clear: those who have not directly harmed or oppressed you are not your enemies and do <u>not</u> deserve to be attacked! Only cowards will harm innocents, as bullies will not fight those who can actually defend themselves. Our ancestors considered those not in the business of war to be off limits when conflicts arose, and so it should be today that we will not fight unless we absolutely have to against someone who forces our hand. We should want peace, value it and admire it, for those who will seek settlements over war are truly noble.

On the other hand, we will not be weak, nor will we be passive. Every Ásatrúar has a responsibility to themselves and their family to know some means of self-defense. Children should begin learning at an early age, traditionally starting near their twelfth birthday. The discipline and confidence developed from this is priceless and allows us the ability of being prepared for any situation we may face. Like the martial artists of the Orient, we learn to fight so we will not have to, using these skills for protection, while always seeking to be a peacemaker first and foremost.

Being a Hero

Some may be naturally drawn to a life of heroism and action, which is perfectly fine. One must understand that violence is something that happens; no matter how much we wish the world could exist without strife, it does not. When this arises we *need* warriors who will stand up to defend those who cannot defend themselves. It is not that we are giving in to what we accept as an inevitable conclusion of life, that we embrace the condition of the world with all of its harsh realities. We simply do what we can to make sure that we can face these harsh realities and protect our families, our communities, and our folk.

For those who would dedicate themselves to such a life I would recommend considering work as a soldier or police officer, as these can act fully within the bounds of law in protecting the people of their land. Because of legislated morality, where police are forced to arrest and imprison people for so-called "victimless crimes" a wedge has been placed between society and law enforcement. It does not have to be this way: we can make an effort in support of those men and women who will be there when you need help, if you have been assaulted, robbed, raped or have had a loved one murdered. As with soldiers, we cannot let politics keep us from honoring those who are prepared to make the ultimate sacrifice for our safety and security. There are probably plenty of laws police officers disagree with, which they wish they did not have to enforce, but they still have a job to do and should only be respected for the position they are in.

Of course, your choices are not limited to a career in community or national security. We should never have to feel helpless in any situation, and we will not if we are prepared to take the initiative to make our areas safe. Those willing to stand up for their right to a happy, peaceful existence can initiate all sorts of programs and ideas. Neighborhood watch, community meetings, safety seminars, there are *so* many avenues for us to use in protecting all that we hold dear.

Misguided Ideals

Let's face it: the life of a petty thug, a half-wit "revolutionary", or a paranoid "conspiracy theorist" isn't exactly glorious. So far, these are the premier means of "protecting" the folk conceived. It's always interesting to hear one speak highly of their 'righteous' conflict, the 'war to end all wars', where if "we just kill this certain group of people" the world will be all sunshine and rainbows. That *all* warmongers feel this way is just a matter of circumstance. But then, someone else might come along they would disagree with so all they need to do now is eliminate *them*, then another comes along, then another, continuing a cycle that will never end so long as disagreement is understood as only being settled through violence. The belief in "no-compromise" is what starts wars, while it is compromise itself that ends them. We should not place any faith in those who would glorify senseless destruction and/or malevolent slaughter. They are not warriors; they are sociopaths devoid of human compassion and empathy. "Might is right" is wrong, dead wrong, for it completely ignores the fact that we have a choice to be merciful, kind, and helpful towards others; moreover, that we have a duty to do so! By its philosophy rape, murder, child molestation, any disgraceful act is justified simply because one is strong enough to inflict it upon others. That anyone has ever taken this foolish concept seriously is a true testament to the moral degeneracy our ancestors feared would lead to the end of the world!

I will not deny that there are several policies instituted by our governments that I strongly disagree with. In a perfect world we would not be slaves to corporations, would not have our rights continuously threatened by special-interest groups, would not have to worry about our privacy taken or our freedoms whittled away slowly but surely. Unfortunately, we do not live in a perfect world, so we have to accept things as they are, while trying to change them in a positive, uplifting manner. No one has ever witnessed a manmade catastrophe and thought how great it would be to join the individuals involved. No one has ever looked upon the crimes of brainwashed fools and thought of them as admirable or as perfect role models. We will not change the world by trying to blow it up! No matter how valid your ideals may be, no one will be able to appreciate them if they are manifested in a dishonorable way—such as through the harming of innocents or other forms of belligerent behavior.

We also cannot change anything through paranoia, within ourselves or in trying to spread it among others. It is easy to fall into the "conspiracy" trap, if you ever learn of any, which can quickly take over your life. In saying this I am not denying or validating these theories, I am only stating that, unless or until we actually face danger worrying about it is useless. This is part of being a warrior: to never fear the unknown and to face life on life's terms. Is the government keeping tabs on us all? Possibly. Is there anything we can do about it? Probably not. All we can do is help people by educating and empowering them, giving them a sense of worth and meaning, for the only sickness is that which keeps us from saving ourselves. If we can give the gifts of confidence, self-respect, and healthy self-image we will have truly done a service to our fellow humans. With these anyone can deal with any situation they come across, no matter how overwhelming or scary it may seem.

The Power of Choice

Everything we do is a choice. To be a warrior one must *decide* that they will follow this path. When a woman fends off an attacker, she *chooses* to be a warrior, when a man stands up for a cause or ideal, he *chooses* to be a warrior! When we are stricken by trauma, which could paralyze us with fear, but make the conscious decision to not let it break us, we are warriors. To be weak or strong, to do or not to do, to act or be passive, to be bold or oppressed, all that happens to us is based on the choices we make, and our greatest freedom, yet our greatest responsibility is in making them. The warrior knows that with every path taken there must come a consequence, good or bad. The purpose of courage is to accept these consequences in a dignified manner, always living without regret. If one lives honorably, regret is meaningless, for even when we make decisions that have negative results we will know that we did what we thought was right at the time. Some may even try to criticize us for our folly, but nothing can change what has happened, so all we can do is learn from our mistakes. To do so, we must first have the humility to admit it when we are wrong, needing to keep our ego in check. If mistakes we have made involve some sort of infliction against others, we will seek to make amends in the best way we can. This is the way of honor.

The warrior is one who embraces struggle, who sees hardship as a teacher and obstacles as lessons. From very early on suffering and pain are the ultimate guides towards wisdom—if we burn our hand on a stove or in a fire we learn not to touch them; if we get bitten by an animal we know to be wary of it, if we trip on a stairway we learn to be more careful. The same should be applied when we face more complex forms of distress. More than anything, the warrior trains him or herself to endure, to accept what happens as it happens. To do this is merely a matter of choice—*you* decide if you're going to get upset when the toilet clogs, when the bills pile up, or if your children won't stop screaming. You can yell, throw things, fly into a fit of rage, or you can handle the situations in a proper manner, so problems get fixed and things get done. 'Acceptance' is by no means passivity; it is simply deciding that you will not let situations weaken you mentally, spiritually, or emotionally. We cannot control what happens to us, we can only choose to learn from all of our experiences without complaint, without allowing them to sap our strength. No matter what, the warrior perseveres, never quits, never accepts defeat. What needs to be done, will be done, even if plans must be changed, new directions taken or new ideas explored. He or she will always stay the course to obtain his goals.

Most importantly, the heroic ideal teaches us to live life to its fullest, with good humor and a positive outlook. It is important for us all to strive for greatness, setting a higher standard for our descendants and ourselves. To leave a legacy of nobility for future generations is our obligation to them, so they may have ancestors who will serve as proper role models for the continuance of this tradition, passing it on through the ages. All of us are capable of this, all of us can make the decision to be warriors, and all of us should. It is worth it for us to understand and live within the principles of higher evolution, to follow "the paths of power", where we exist in accordance with the ideals of integrity and wholesome values. Furthermore, we are worth the time and effort it takes to embrace this way of life. The Nordic warrior can live on in our hearts, evolving through time, along with civilization—which it parallels—and what we know to be right and true.

6

Marriage and Children

"A son is better
even if born late,
after his father's death.
Memorial stones seldom
stand by the road
unless raised by kinsman to kinsman."

Óðin, Hávamál 72.

When we get married, we make a solemn vow to stand by our spouse no matter what. The restrictions placed upon us by religious law should not have to act as a leash that keeps us loyal, we should <u>want</u> to be true to those we have committed ourselves to. If you are only devoted to your wife or husband because some edict tells you to, yet feel temptation calling you from all around, chances are you will eventually answer that call. Marriage isn't about dedication to a certain path, it is about dedication to each other, to love and honor one another in all the ways we can. When a faith condemns adultery, upholding the sanctity of the wedding vows, this is only the final wall, the last resort in making people keep their oaths, for certainly their violation is dishonorable. But long before this is ever considered it is the *relationship* that must motivate us towards what we have to do to keep our commitment strong.

Before you ever make such a commitment there is one thing that you absolutely *must* do: eliminate any and all high expectations you have towards your significant other. This is very important. I'm not talking about the basics here; obviously we expect our spouse to not cheat, lie to us or about us, or physically harm us in any way. But when we look at the person we love today, expecting them to always be perfect, to always be just the way they are when we paint all of our romantic images in our heads, we are bound for disappointment. People aren't perfect, they won't always live up to your expectations, and there will be times when you will argue to the point where you will not even want to look at each other. Marriages, *all* marriages will hit rough spots, no doubt about it, but these are the times when our relationships gain *real* strength.

Earlier I discussed the ethics of the warrior, which partly embodies the idea of being empowered by hardship. Such a concept represents our personal struggles as we experience them throughout our lives. Once we are married two people become one, so now the ideal expands to meet both of your needs, in strengthening your bond. You must be warriors, together. In early Roman accounts German fighters were greatly feared if their women were beside them, for their union represented a force of power to be reckoned with! The relationship is an entity that must be fed or it will starve and eventually die. We feed it with love, with respect, with fairness, with loyalty, and with reciprocity. When we face difficult circumstances together this entity helps us to endure, as support for each other increases our personal power, which is the same as power for both. We should take our vows with our spouse seriously and support them in all endeavors.

Married in a Community

But relationships are not only strengthened by hardship, they can also develop or grow through a connection to community. As with the warrior, we are personally empowered by our work in the service of those around us and our folk, which now extends to the marriage. Having close ties to the community allows us to feed our relationship-entity with the love and respect we gain from those within it, which in turn allows us to do the same for them. When a couple cuts themselves off from the rest of the world their isolation will take its toll on their marriage, as they lose their sense of union with a greater whole. It would be no different if we shut ourselves off alone. Although this may not seem readily noticeable to some, once you have reached out to the community you will see the difference.

Up until the Christian era our ancestors spent thousands of years living in tight, close-knit tribes where all had to support each other for the sake of survival. Because of this, the need for communal service is ingrained within our DNA. It may not be easily recognizable, it may not even seem relevant, yet it is a part of who we are and will quickly be understood as vital to our happiness once we take the steps in working for it. Today we feel that we can build walls to keep neighbors out; then try to keep ourselves comfortable with our addictions to television and other gadgets, to sex or drugs or alcohol or whatever it is we need to fill the void. The answer to true happiness is right in front of you! The little old lady across the street, the kids who play in your neighborhood, the family next to you: Community is all around you, and all you need to do is reach out to them, help them, be a part of their lives. More than just throwing backyard barbecues we need to be of service, to be the ones everyone can count on, to be proactive, a vital part of the area we live in no matter where that may be! When a married couple becomes part of this greater service, *this* will be the glue that binds them and their family together.

There has to be a greater, spiritual connection for a wife and husband to maintain their bond. A "warrior ethic", community, spirituality; these are the time-honored methods of keeping people united. Modern media can spew out all the techniques in the world about "a better sex life" or "a happier union"; they can scream it out until their faces turn blue, but without the above concepts promoted as significant the divorce rate will continue to be extremely high. Think about it, divorce was once practically unknown to our ancestors (though it did occur on rare occasions) *even though they only knew the person they married just moments before the proposal!* Why? Because they had a strong warrior ethic, strong community support, and strong spiritual systems. All of these are expressions of a higher form of love, inspiring us to commit ourselves to enduring all the pain and suffering with all the joy and success, where we connect our marriages and our families with the world around us, and where we seek to forge a spiritual bond as much as an emotional and physical one.

The spiritual union is developed through both hardship and community, but also in trying to understand and appreciate your spouse on a deeper level. It takes courage to do this, for it involves opening your heart in a way that could be difficult for some to do for themselves, much less for someone else. To do this you have to set your ego aside and tell your wife or husband what you truly feel without concern for judgment or disdain, meaning that you cannot judge or devalue them when *they* do it. You can also connect in this way through joint spiritual practice, meditation, appreciating nature, or getting involved in a project together. All sorts of avenues exist to strengthen the marriage of spirits, which will deepen what you have physically and emotionally.

Raising Children

The highest priority for all of us is in the proper rearing of our children. This should not only apply to Ásatrúar, but to everyone in every land, for the next generation will always reflect the values *we* instill in them. It only takes a small amount of foresight to realize the responsibility we have as parents, as teachers, as mentors or as anyone who may impact a child's life in one way or another. A tree cannot grow if the seed is not planted. We must play our part in securing a brighter future for our descendants. This is not intended towards the accumulation of material wealth either; we have to accept our obligations to them by protecting our environment, our culture and our values so they will have a world of tomorrow that will be safe and promising, validating the very existence of us all. If we do nothing, if we only concern ourselves with ourselves, individualism will replace all that defines what we know as civilization, as our world falls prey to the corruption resulting from this. This is not a hypothesis or a belief based upon moral principles or doomsday prophecies, it is an undeniable fact—as the family unit breaks down, so will society. When appreciation for folk and family lost its value in the Roman and Athenian empires, among others, they quickly began the decline that would lead to their fall. When the Self overrules the many, when all that matters is gratifying the wants and needs of each individual, a nation cannot survive, for its leaders and its people cease to concern themselves with the community at large.

Facing Challenges Together

All families, as all marriages, will face challenges. It doesn't matter what your religion is, what your race is, how wealthy or how poor you are, no one is free of difficulty. Your children must learn the lessons of this from an early age so they can become well rounded, healthy-minded adults. It isn't our job to coddle them or shelter them from the struggles they will encounter, they *must* encounter. I am not saying we shouldn't protect our children from harm or danger, of course we should. But, when they do meet harsh circumstances you can use wisdom to determine when to help them and when it will be helpful to let them work through the problem themselves so they may learn from it. If we do everything *for them*, if we fight off every possible struggle, they will never learn to do it for themselves and will become overly dependent on us. Sooner or later they are going to have to fight their own battles, and the sooner the better. At their earliest ages we will have to do almost everything for them, but with each year, as they grow older we have to gradually introduce these ideals of independence and self-reliance. Our duty as parents is to socialize our children so they will become successful, noble grown-ups. By "successful" I mean that they will be able to achieve their goals and hopes and dreams and that they will never have to settle for second best. These are not expectations *we* should demand of them, but rather ones we should teach them to have of themselves. In teaching this we must also give the tools that will help them overcome disappointment (another form of hardship), to give them wisdom, confidence, strength and validation.

We cannot, must not delude our children with fantasies of "perfection", which usually come with *our* expectations. To do so is to set them up for failure, which can be devastating for a child. We give them guidelines and boundaries, teach them valuable lessons that will mold their characters as they grow up. In essence, we have a person's life in our hands, which is a tremendous responsibility. If you force it into their mind that they must walk a certain path exactly as *you* see it, the moment they fall short they will feel like they are not worthy of you. Their self-esteem will be shot and the further they disappoint the more they will fall into self-destructive patterns. Guide them, yes, but do not create an image they can't live up to. Teach them to imagine, then act.

True Family Values

Everything we do as parents affects our children's behavior. This is why it is important for us to advocate *true* family values, which should not in any way be confused with the political agenda of "fundamentalists" to force their morality on the world. True family values are the antithesis of individualism, which can only harm any and all communal relationships we try to build. When individualism is prevalent selfishness supersedes all else, as ideals surrounding any form of social group begin to decay. The groups themselves may continue to exist, but only as shells of what they are supposed to be. They become dysfunctional collections of *individuals*, rather than synergetic wholes. The group must be an extension of the self, not a contradistinction of it.

Parents today often embrace the egotism of "parental instincts", thinking that everything we need to know about raising a child is ingrained within us. This may work for animals, but they do not have the complex emotions and great amount of needs and desires we humans have. Parenting is a journey of discovery that comes with learning all that we need to know to help raise our children from those who have already experienced this. You only need the humility to admit that you don't know everything and are willing to learn or do whatever it takes to meet your obligations as a parent. At one time, before the invention of mass media, this was one of the purposes of tribes. In a tribe, parents could share the time-tested techniques that would insure their success in raising their sons and daughters. Without that personal connection to community so many are left searching for answers in the dark, hoping they can find the right path for their family. Others simply go through the motions and hope for the best.

Dysfunctional families have become the norm in our society, just over the last twenty years. This is unacceptable. Although we will not judge those who have no choice but to live in such conditions, it is important for us to work towards a higher standard, where families have both a mother and a father figure in a healthy, loving environment. For those who live in broken homes or unhealthy environments, it is *your* job to break the cycle when it comes time to have your own family.

Again, individualism is to blame for the lack of strong, functional family units in our lands, for one cannot create a wholesome social structure if their own interests come first. And herein lies the problem: Mom may scream all the time because *her* emotions and how she expresses them are more important than the impact this may have on her children; Dad may drink a lot because *his* indulgences must come before a secure, harmonious home for the entire family. Some will even keep their children dependent on them because of *their* wants and needs. When we become parents we are no longer "the Self", we have become part of something bigger than this, which should come with the realization that *we* do not come first!

Do not think, either, that is it is too late to deal with any negative circumstances infecting your home life. It is *never* too late to deal with problems, even if they are long-standing, you only need to first recognize if and when there is one, then have the courage to handle it. This can be hard for many; because they feel that if they admit there is a problem they are failures as parents. What's funny is that when you *do* admit this, and work to fix it this is the very thing that highlights your success! You can't sweep negativity under a rug and expect it to go away, your problems can accumulate until they blow up in your face. You have to be proactive in finding appropriate solutions for whatever troubles come at you. *This* is the hallmark of successful familial relationships.

Synergy Of The Family Unit

To have a family is to be a member of something so profound, so fulfilling, so loving. With this experience comes the greatest joys, the greatest sense of accomplishment, and the greatest feelings of affection you will probably ever know. But, at the same time, there comes the greatest responsibilities and obligations to the other members. We become part of a synergetic whole, which must work together in order for it to work at all. "I" am no longer as important as "we".

That means that I have to do what it takes to maintain a stable, functional family unit so my children will know what it is like to live in a happy, loving home. This doesn't mean that I will try to shelter them from the realities of the world, it means that no matter what they will know that I support them and love them and will do what needs to be done for their benefit in any and every circumstance.

As we guide our children into becoming successful adults, one of our main focuses should be to help give them purpose and meaning in their lives. This might be difficult because it is something we have to *make* them do, if not anything else. We have to be the adults and decide what's best, as we lead them down the road *they* will choose. We cannot choose it for them, but we can't allow them to give up at the first sign of difficulty or decide to waste their lives. We have to teach them to search for true inner peace and happiness through their accomplishments, while educating them against the empty, superficial nature of quick-fix joys found in today's pop-culture. All of us need purpose, we need something that gives us a sense of worth, so we may appreciate ourselves and what we have to offer. This will come through noble service for the good of the whole, no matter how big or small. The chemist spending every day in his lab creating a new medicine that will save lives, the engineer making sure our buildings and bridges are safe, or the construction worker putting food on his family's table. We all have a calling, and to answer that call, to face whatever challenges that come with it makes us warriors. Those who make sacrifices for the greater good, no matter what they are doing, are no different than soldiers, police officers, or firemen, or any other form of heroic service. Their sacrifice is made by a choice to endure whatever must be endured; to do what they feel must be done. When this has become our greatest joy, when the *climb* of the mountain is just as important as reaching the top, *then* we will have walked the paths of power. Nothing less than devotion to creating significance will do, if we are to set a higher standard for ourselves, for our people, for our world.

The foundation of a happy home is a happy marriage. Children pick up on your habits very quickly, so if Mom and Dad are always fighting don't be surprised when your kids start to express over-aggressive traits, or experience some other type of behavior change. Parents will fight, this is an inevitable fact of marriage, but it is up to you to be responsible and try to keep the yelling out of the reach of children's ears. If this is unavoidable always reassure your children afterwards, letting them know that you both love and care for them and each other. Also, watch what you say. Don't say things you don't mean in an argument or moment of anger; children will always remember what you said. At the same time it is important for Mom and Dad to do whatever they can to work out their issues. Again, have a little foresight, if you realize that a little problem today could become a big problem in the future, do what you can to resolve it in a calm, appropriate manner. Don't constantly complain or nag over petty disturbances in your life, and *understand* that the world was not designed to make you happy; just try your best to maintain a wholesome, loving bond between you and everyone else in your group. The healthier the relationship between the parents, the healthier the overall environment will be for the entire family.

The Initiations

As children get older their needs and wants change, as do their attitudes. One of the most important things in the life of a teenager is their identity: who they feel they are as a person, their accomplishments, their tastes, their desires, even their standards. With the cultural identity missing, they often seek out substitutes that can be destructive or dangerous. Without the empowerment of the folk-will they are susceptible to the mindless enslavement of consumerism, peer-pressure, drug use, gangs, etc. Some will even feel as if they have no identity at all, nothing connecting them to their world, which can lead them to depression and thoughts of suicide.

No doubt, when a child reaches puberty, new challenges arise that many parents aren't prepared for. However, there is an ancient tool left to us by our ancestors, nearly forgotten today, which can help our youth in the difficult path of their teenage years. In tribal societies certain observances were utilized to mark the time when a boy became a man, or a girl a woman, which still takes place in some cultures today. That this specifically occurred around the age of twelve in almost every civilization is no accident. This is the time when puberty normally begins, when the natural signs of adulthood begin to be seen. The rites of passage were only given to boys, allowing them a sacred initiation into manhood, which began their journey of becoming an adult. Girls are different, for it has always been understood that they begin this journey when they have their first menstrual cycle. For the former, often times painful tests of endurance would be required, symbolically representing the death of the boy to make way for the birth of the man.

It may be shocking for us today to actually consider hurting our sons in the name of some "archaic" tradition. But this can be such a beneficial event in the life of a boy/man, one that has to be manifested in one way or another. That our society lacks a significant initiation is in part due to the influence of the church in its suppression of the cultural expression of indigenous peoples. When these rites are wanting, boys feel a constant need to try to "prove" themselves with dangerous stunts, unnecessary violence, or excessive alcoholism or drug abuse. Deep inside most boys want to be men, but there is no event that naturally signifies this transition, so if an external source does not mark a point for manhood to be achieved, boyhood may continue even into old age. Think about all of the modern images of grown men who never "grow up", who want to play and have fun and live life for the self until the day they die. No responsibility, no maturity, just "boys will be boys" forever, which for them is indeed true in its most literal sense. It sounds tempting doesn't it? Maybe I'm just being an old fuddy-duddy and should lighten up, eh? But what happens if you need to rely on one of these people? What happens if you find yourself in a position where you need their help or you might lose life, limb or freedom? What if we *all* thought this way? The truth is that our world and the foundations we have built our ideals of social relations are based on the spirit of service, to be able to trust and help our fellow man. Without this, when Self is the highest concern, true men need to stand up who will gladly place others *before* themselves.

A grown boy is ill-equipped to handle any serious problems, too concerned with his next good time to show any real loyalty. When it's time to party he's great to have around: a good laugh, sociable, yet unable to create significant relationships and unable to appreciate anything other than superficial ideas. The same goes for girls afraid to become women. Then they reach old age and realize they have nothing to show for their lives, no legacy to pass on to future generations. In the end the world is not better or worse for their existence.

The initiation ceremony for Northern Europeans has ancient origins, where many symbolic factors come into play. The boy should be separated from his parents by a male elder of the family or tribe, taken to a secluded area for a number of days, and then made to withstand some sort of ordeal. It is believed by some that when Ódin hung himself on the World-Tree for nine nights, fasting and wounded by his spear, this was *his* rite of passage. From this he gained wisdom from his uncle, Mímir, "Bölthorn's famous son". We would not want to literally re-enact every aspect of this event, for certain passages lead us to believe that this resulted in Ódin's actual death and rebirth, but it can be used as a guide in creating our own rites using symbolism. The most important aspects would be the separation from the group by a male elder, the symbolic death and rebirth representing the transition from boy to man, and the teaching of wisdom, passed down from generation to generation. Please be careful in doing this, do your homework, talk to individuals from groups with a long history of established traditions in such observances, such as the Native Americans, for pointers on how it can be done effectively without endangering your son's life.

Once the initiation was complete and the boy had become a man, with the elder's wisdom imparted on him, it was customary for him to take his first voyage of exploration. This was considered important, for the man must learn the ways of the world beyond, as the boy had at home. For the Teutons, adventure was a part of a religious need to enrich one's reputation, so he might become selected for Valhalla after he died. It was also necessary for when he would later court a maiden he wanted as his wife. When a man asked a woman for her hand in marriage it was her, or her guardian's, obligation to ask him questions regarding his knowledge of the world and all the lands he had visited.

Just as much emphasis should be placed upon the first time a girl experiences menstruation. This exclusive trait of women is what gave rise to the rite of passage given exclusively to boys, and, in part, probably had something to do with why women were considered sacred in ancient Northern European societies. *Nature* tells girls when they have become women, when they have become fertile and begin to release eggs. When this happens the women of the family and clan should gather in celebration to welcome the girl into womanhood, letting her know that she has come of age. Acknowledgement of these stages is not only significant, it can be vital in helping a child to learn to accept the ups and downs of being an adult. An added bonus for girls is that it allows them to know that they don't have to be ashamed or embarrassed by a perfectly natural process.

There is a reason these observances take place at such an early age. They do *not* represent the immediate jump from youth to grown-up, but rather mark the beginning of a gradual progression. A boy is not a full-grown man at the age of twelve, nor is a girl ready to have children simply because she has become fecund. They have to finish the process of fully developing before they are ready to live on their own. But now comes the time when he or she should be given more responsibility and more independence, both of which should go hand in hand, balancing each other out. As they get older their duties will increase with their freedoms and privileges until they are ready to begin their lives outside of their parents' home. Although hidden for some time, the ancient tradition of the journey into adulthood, which has thousands of years of experience behind it, could serve us well if we re-introduced it today.

The Happy Home

The gods and goddesses favor happy homes and healthy children, which is why several deities are devoted to their protection. Frigga, Freyja, Urd and her Norns, Hoenir, Mímir, Thór, Heimdall, all play their part in helping us and inspiring us to do what's best for our families. Every step is covered by our ancient traditions, from courtship and engagement to marriage, then pregnancy, naming the child, and so on.

There is a delicate balance to keeping your home peaceful. One of the things that we all wish to avoid is pushing our children away as we try to instill morals and standards in them. We do not need to try to be their friend. That is not our job. Our job is to guide them and socialize them. However, if we try to force a way of life upon them, especially a *religious* way of life, we can easily lead them down a self-destructive path. One of the biggest conflicts children meet in mainstream, monotheist religions is the idea that there is "only one way". This is the same as demanding a perfection that cannot be achieved, for when they fall short they feel worthless. When you tell someone that they will either be "a good Christian" or "a bad person", whenever they cannot stand strong in that faith they lose their self-esteem, then embrace their new life as "bad". This is why so many prostitutes, porn stars, and strippers come from so-called "strict religious backgrounds". We cannot express our religious beliefs in a negative way and expect positive results. When we use a faith to treat our children like garbage they will grow up to resent you and everything you hold dear. So not only will you have turned them away from an entire religion, you will have turned them against your family! Faith and spirituality should be something that is uplifting, empowering, something that creates positive experiences within its practice. The last thing it should do is *cause* misery and suffering, for anyone. We shouldn't consider religion to be a magic formula for a happy "perfect" life, but when it is the source of dysfunction or pain it has really ceased to have any worth to us.

To be a spouse, to be a parent, these are difficult, yet extremely rewarding jobs. It is our duty to our families to put *them* first, as they will put *us* first. The give and take, reciprocal communion between husband and wife and parents and children is as ancient and sacred as the very existence of humanity. It represents a higher, spiritual bond where all are important, where all are valid. If one becomes invalidated, or, on the other hand, self-centered, the balance of these interpersonal relationships will be broken, which can lead to dire circumstances if it is not repaired. If we accept these challenges with open arms, we will be rewarded with so much love, and with a legacy that will live on after we have moved on to the next world. We are called to do this by the gods and goddesses of our people; we *must* do it for the sake of all civilization.

7

The Land

"Four things are given for your profit, with the names air, water, land and fire. But Ódin will alone be the possessor thereof. Therefore, I advise you, you shall choose yourselves just men who deal out fairly the toil and the fruits so that none be free from work nor from the duty to defend."

—*Freyja, The Oera Linda Book.*

With all the philosophy, with all the ideology presented in this book it must not be forgotten that Ásatrú is first and foremost a nature religion. All of our gods and goddesses have a relationship, in one way or another, with the natural forces prevalent in the universal order. Ódin is the god of wind, Thór lord over thunder and lightning, Frey is the patron of harvests, and so on. This divine link to these phenomena represents, to us, the connection of all life in every corner of existence, as they reach out across the worlds to affect our planet.

As civilizations seek progress through technological advancement above all else, human beings continue to be further separated from our environment as time passes. In looking at the powers of the gods and goddesses through their archetypes we can see that the balance between naturalism and human development can and should be maintained. Our world is sacred; it is our Mother Erde, Mother Earth, a name for our highest goddess, Frigga. Our *universe* is sacred, it is Yggdrasil, that holiest of symbols representing the synergy of all things. Once we begin to recognize and place importance upon our relationship with our world habitat, we will then be able to grasp the need to protect it at all costs. More than just wanting to secure the planet for future generations, we should want to defend it because it is the holiest of all objects to us!

Ásatrúar feel the power of earth all around us. We do not need to experience miracles through extravagant magical displays, we do not need artifacts or buildings to feel connected to divinity. It is all around us, in the forests, oceans, mountains, plains, and valleys; it is everywhere we look, for our Mother Earth sanctifies all living things. Our miracles are in the sunrise, in the birth of a child, in the flight of an eagle, for we live in awe of all the natural wonders of the cosmos. Although we may have temples, our "churches" are mainly the sacred groves (called "holts" or "lunds"), where we may fully appreciate the gifts we are given in nature, for as organic beings our awareness of the flora and fauna surrounding us is viewed as truly spiritual.

Since the introduction of the Roman paradigm our connection to the land has been suppressed. For centuries, European people have been disconnected from their bond with the earth and the life on it, replacing it with a desire to conquer everything in their path. It is only recently that valiant efforts to save the environment have begun to be effective in the face of rampant industrialism. Until then, we moved from nation to nation, dominating peoples, threatening cultures, destroying landscapes, wiping out entire species of animals. When indigenous, nature based religions are exchanged for belief systems that view the world as a toy for mankind to exploit, our sacred planet will be the first to suffer. From such irresponsible considerations, we have seen whole ecosystems annihilated, and we continue to deal with the consequences of actions made generations past.

The earth is not ours to exploit, conquer, destroy, or harm in any such way; it is our home, it is the land of our birth, the place we grew up, the soil that rests beneath our feet at this very moment. It is responsible for us as much as we are responsible for it. Scientists today have begun to understand that underlying the incredible balance of natural habitats across the world there *must* be some sort of intelligence, a consciousness that understands how to maintain this balance as it constantly compensates and adapts in response to change. This is known as "The Gaia Theory", Gaia being the earth goddess of the Greeks, the equivalent of our Erde-Frigga. More often than not science comes full circle in recognizing what was once well established among the ancients.

From this we can see that our planet is a living entity working as hard as she can to be a home for us. When we poison her with pollution or lack of population control, we weaken her, allowing the forces of chaos to be unleashed. Hurricanes, blizzards, tornadoes, tidal waves, all destructive forces were believed by our ancestors to be products of the powers of the Jötuns, which the gods and goddesses can only defend against if we help them to do so. We help them by honoring them and offering to them, by living decent lives, and most of all by playing our part in protecting the environment.

But how do we do this? First, it is important for us to understand and seek to defeat the Roman model of thinking, within ourselves and others, through education and community values. As long as this infects our people, the sacred world revered by our ancestors will continue to be a plaything for multinational corporations and the common man. If we return to our native cultures, we can begin to rebuild the *spiritual* relationship we once had with the earth. Even if one chooses some other path, the very least any of us can do is eliminate the god-complex that has clouded our thinking for so long.

If we can once again see the world as an intelligent entity we might consider the *örlög* factor in our dealings with her. As with any relationship, we should strive for reciprocity, so that every time we take something from her we should give something back. Cut down a tree, plant a tree; if you hunt or fish, take part in efforts to insure the growth of the species you kill; if you own or work for a company that consumes natural resources, see to it that these resources are renewed, if possible, and see to it that responsible, eco-friendly policies are implemented throughout every facet of your industry. We cannot allow greed, laziness, or selfishness to stand in the way of our obligations to the planet we live on.

In ancient times, the connection to the earth was truly synergetic, for people could not have survived without the gifts of Mother Erde. The celebration of annual festivals revolved around agricultural cycles that were necessary for their very existence. Medicines, food, tools, homes, all things we take for granted, were once taken directly from nature, so they would have to be renewed for future use, maintaining the life of everything and everyone involved. In our modern world, because so much of what we use is manmade, we have to choose to reconnect with the sacred world around us, and realize that even the things we make ultimately originated from the natural elements. No matter how advanced we become, how well we will be able to manipulate these elements, this will always be an undeniable truth.

We will accept our place as natural beings, we will embrace the use of natural remedies for our health, we will again rejoice in the cycle of the seasons, we will recycle, use sparingly and do what we can to protect our planet's resources. These are the ways for us to re-institute our spiritual bond with the environment. It is a responsibility all of us must take seriously, or we will face dire consequences. Each year natural disasters become more frequent as global warming takes its toll, showing us exactly why we have to respect the earth, or *we* will be the ones to perish.

Environmental Behaviors

In realizing the interdependence of the universe, it should also be understood that behavior affects the world around us as well. This may be why our ancestors viewed natural disasters as forces of chaos, striking down "sinful" populations unprotected by the gods and goddesses. We affect our environment with everything we do. Someone working on an experiment in a lab is going to create direct and indirect stimuli upon their work, as molecules interact with one another on a sub-atomic level. Such effects permeate the atmosphere with all sorts of bio-radioactive energies manifesting mental, emotional, and physical actions. Just as we may influence an entire room of people without ever saying a word, just by *being* we can contribute to the overall state of the global bio-field which affects our atmosphere.

Expand the personal principle to a worldwide scale. If individuals can influence their immediate surroundings, imagine the power of the alliance of all collective unconsciouses: the massive energy field created by the general well being of humanity. If we are consumed with hate, anger, malevolence, or selfishness our planet will react to this. As manmade calamity continues to get worse, natural destruction will rise as well, for we are one with the land. It affects us and we affect it. Consider our emotional reactions to weather, how when it rains we can feel sad or drained, or happy when it is sunny and warm. On all levels we are connected to the earth, even in ways not readily understood. Thus we have to be bold enough to make the decision to live for all life, to live for Yggdrasil, meaning that we will cherish humankind, animal-kind, rock-kind, whatever kind we meet both here and beyond.

I am sure someone right now may be reading this debating its validity in his or her mind. They might be correlating it to things they do not like or do not approve of; they might not agree that there is any evidence at all for any "connection" to the universe. But does any of that really matter? We can argue logistics all we want, but does it change the need for being a good person, for respecting your fellow man and the planet you live on? Whatever your motivation may be we all know deep inside of us that this is right and true, but we have to decide that we will accept it as valid for our lives. No one can force you to live honorably, this can only come from within, and it must be a product of *service* and *action* much more than words and thought.

The Way is Lost

When a certain way of life or ideal becomes disdained by a significant population of the people, everything remotely linked to that ideal may become subject to censure even if it is not among the reasons the main creed is disliked. For example, the rise and fall of Nazism brought about a long period of infamy for all things connected to Germanic culture, even if they had nothing to do with the Third Reich and its constituents. During the American Civil War, the freedom of black slaves was a byproduct of Northerners' ill will towards the South, which had seceded from the union. They wanted nothing to do with Southern culture or Southern lifestyles, so they sought to do away with anything resembling this. Since slavery was such a major facet of the Southern plantation economy, the logical conclusion was to abolish it. This development of social biases expanding beyond the originally discredited ideal is actually what began our separation from nature, and our adoption of the Roman paradigm.

As Rome invaded Northern Europe a wedge began to be formed between the nobility and the lower classes, as Roman leaders sought to indoctrinate them into their way of thought. This especially became true after the Empire was converted to Christianity. Those who remained united with the land, who revered the old ways were called "pagans" or "heathens", both terms designating those living in the forests, in the "heaths", not a part of so-called "high civilization". These became derogatory labels similar to our modern "hillbillies" or "bumpkins". Soon these "heathens" would become the objects of scorn, as would all they represented. Heathen gods became Christian devils. Of course, the church certainly played its part in all this, but the general feeling was that reverence of nature was "bad" or "evil", while exploiting it was our "god-given" right!

Later, when science began to rebel against Christianity the same thing happened again. Rejecting all that is considered "religious" early scientists painted a cosmological view that was very cold and mechanical. With the church dictating anything considered sacred, there arose a battle between science and faith, which was extremely polarized, with no chance of compromise on either side. Had the ancient religions been allowed to continue to thrive without interruption such a conflict would never have been conceived, for they were the inspiration and origin of all the sciences known today. It is said that the Dark Ages set us all back 2000 years in our technological advancement.

Local Action

Another way we can reconnect with the land is by supporting or taking part in local agricultural services. Farming or gardening, once so integral to survival, is a powerful way to understand and appreciate the earth's cycles. Rather than remaining dependent on the processed foods of large corporate entities, buy from your farmer's market or directly from the farmers, beekeepers, or ranchers themselves. This will not only aid in local economic growth, it can also be a healthier choice for your family, since much of this food will be free of pesticides, steroids, and other harmful chemicals. Of course, when you grow your own food, *you* have total control over what goes into it and what does not, plus you gain the added benefit of your personal accomplishment. Catching, hunting, or growing the things you feed your family is an extremely empowering way to live, for it insures independence from any entity, while instilling pride in exercising such freedom.

When members of communities come together to support each other, to give aid to one another, to help keep their local area strongly united, and to keep the land clean, this can only result in uplifting the spirits of everyone involved. *Many* outlets exist for you to do this, and community action is the first step you can take in performing beneficial services for those outside your family. Charity, generosity, social awareness, none of these should be disconnected from our surroundings, focused only on people we will never see or lands we will never visit. They begin right here, in our own backyard, then continue to extend out to the global community. We take action by being kind and compassionate to those around us, by cleaning up our homes, our neighborhoods, our streets. We take action by becoming aware of the fact that we live in communities and are therefore a part of them, no matter where they are. Shutting ourselves off from our neighbors only ignores the ties we have with one another, and serves to alienate us from the world in which we live.

The Law of the Circle

Every living thing is subject to the natural law which dictates that all life is born, lives, dies, and is reborn. This is a fundamental concept within the world's nature religions, including Ásatrú. The highest example of this is in the cycle of the year, where the land re-awakens in the spring, with its thriving support of life, then dies every winter, only to revive again. This too is the foundation of our belief that we will be reborn after we die, that, in fact all creatures, mortal or divine, are subject to this.

Odal

In ancient Europe, there existed a tradition that played a part in our ancestors' appreciation of the land. It was called the "*odal*" and was so sacred that one of our runes was named after it (also called "*Othala*"). The *odal* was an inherited property or estate, passed on from generation to generation. It was an institution built upon the obligations felt towards descendants and the demand for personal independence expressed in our heritage. The idea of land ownership, when not based on greed, can be the perfect means of protecting the environment. Before the size of one's personal property, on average, shrank to less than an acre, communities spread across vast territories, which were protected *because* they were owned. No need for preservations or parks, since the care taking of the earth was vital to the sustenance of one's own home. Plus, with so much of their beliefs focused on the sacredness of the world, the respect given to these surroundings was a religious experience. Even if you only own a small piece of land in a residential neighborhood you can still work to make it a valuable inheritance for your children. We need ancestral lands, given to descendants with each passing, so that the connection to the earth and to the community can be truly valued and honored. Even if none of this is possible for you, you can still make the choice to respect local ecosystems as literally part of your home.

This concept may be hard for some to conceive, since for many, property ownership represents walls built to keep others out. "This is *my* land, you stay out! Private property!" To the ancients, living in a certain area did not give you the right to keep people off of it. In fact, it was your duty to extend hospitable welcomes to anyone who came on it, unless their intentions were malevolent. If they came to steal or destroy or hurt your family, by all means one would defend their home. However, if their intentions were peaceful you were obligated to show them hospitality, even if they were enemies. So, in essence, owning the land only gave you the right to live on it and defend it, nothing more. This could be a valuable lesson for us.

The Gard

An enclosure which we would have dedicated to the gods and goddesses is called a Gard. These could have our sacred groves ("holts" or "lunds"), or temples ("hofs"), or both established within them. The Gard is considered to be a large tract of land (cf. Ásgard, Midgard, etc.), usually with some sort of interesting geological feature or some legend attached to it. The actual area where rites and festivals are held is called a Vé.

It is important for Ásatrúar to establish their own Gards as we reconnect to the ancient ways. In our modern era, we will need to do our best to make sure that these areas are safe and secure. However, we are still bound by the Gebo Runelaw in extending hands of friendship to whomever comes with peaceful intentions. These holy grounds are supposed to be peace-steads, no different than those in Ásgard itself, so violence and strife are strictly prohibited within them. Those who come into conflict with each other will have to take their affairs elsewhere. It is also important that the area is kept clean and that all treat it as if it were their own land. It should be given a name, for in our religion naming something is a means of sanctifying it, giving it a true place in the society of our people. It should be respected as a sacred place, with ceremony added in whatever way deemed appropriate to get this point across.

Aurvangaland

The first of all *odal* lands, or ancestral lands should be considered by Ásatrúar to be the holiest, most celebrated territory on earth, but recognition of this has been all but lost. For some, Ásatrú makes them think of Norway or Iceland as the premier Scandinavian countries of our lore. Others may think that this is all a matter of fancy, that local tribes revered local lands and each would try to place mythical events within their region. Saxony would be held sacred to the Saxons, Denmark to the Danes, Frisia to the Frisians, etc. There is no doubt that, to an extent this is true. However, there is evidence that there was a land most honored among the Teutonic tribes. The histories of the East Goths, the West Goths, the Longobardians, the Swiss, the Gepidae, the Burgundians, the Herulians, the Franks, the Saxons and the Alamannians are all united in their expressions of the belief that the Teutonic homeland, the greatest of *odals*, was called Scania, Skandia, or modern Skåne, the southernmost tip of Sweden. In the ancient lore it was called the Aurvangaland.

Some sources point to the probability that our ancestors believed that this is where the first Teutonic pair, Ask and Embla, were created by the gods Ódin, Hoenir, and Lódur. They walked along the coast on the northern edge of Skåne until they found a tree growing, which they used as the substance to make the two people. It may not be a coincidence that an ancient city lies along this coast by the name of Lund, which means "The Grove". It is also interesting to note that the most ancient Scandinavian settlement, some 12,000 years old, was found at Mölleröd by Finja Lake in Skåne.

Later, the god Heimdall came to Midgard to bring culture. The story, as it is pieced together, tells us that he came as a child in a self-propelled boat filled with implements and a sheaf of grain, which he would use in his teachings. The land he visited was called Svithjód, which is still the name used for Sweden by Icelanders today (Icelandic is the closest remnant of the Old Norse tongue). In some sources it is stated that Svithjód was named after Ódin himself, who is also called Svidur. Certainly there is a connection here between the area where Ask and Embla were created and where Heimdall landed, since this would have to be the place the Aesir had left the humans to develop. This is even more likely when we consider that all of the earliest sources outside of Scandinavia point to genealogical origins in Skåne for every Teutonic tribe. Heimdall here founds the first royal dynasty, known as the Skjöldungs or Scyldings, through his descendants of human birth, Skjöld-Jarl (also called Borgar) and Halfdan-Kon. Interestingly enough, this was the first noble line of Denmark, and the city of Lund is especially known to have been a capital of the kings of Denmark in the early Middle Ages. In fact, Skåne was originally a Danish territory and remained so until the 17th century when it came under Swedish rule, though the entire realm was still known as Svithjód in the most ancient times. Related to this is the idea that the name "Danes", as Sophus Bugge suggested, comes from *Khthôn*, "earth", and means autochtone—"indigenous people". This would explain why *Danskr tönga*—"Danish Tongue" is synonymous with *Norroen*, the native language of ancient Scandinavia.

Svithjód was thought to encompass several lands beyond Sweden itself, though this was its central and primary territory from which it received its name (meaning "Land of the Svi or Sviones", cp. *Germania* by Tacitus). Even Finland was once considered to be a part of this nation. The myths placed Svithjód in direct connection to the gods or legendary heroes, such as Ívaldi-Svigdir who was considered to be one of its most ancient kings. Baldur himself, under the name Fjalerus (Falr), is said in Saxo's *Historia Danica*, to have been governor of "Scania". In Ynglingasaga, both Njörd and Ódin are made into Swedish rulers. The Christian euhemerists, dismissing our gods as mortal kings, placed Valhalla in Sweden (*Gylfaginning*).

"Skåne", said to be named after the goddess Skadi, whom ancient kings proudly claimed their descent from, is the original territory from which Scandinavia got its name, which we can see from its alternate designations: Scania, Skandia, Skandza, etc. All points thus lead to the likelihood that this was the most holy land to our ancestors, mentioned in the lore more than any other as the scene for various mythical and heroic exploits. Sweden itself, Svithjod, contains more runestones, and has been the site where more artifacts of our faith have been unearthed than any other nation. That Uppsala, where the most famous temple in all of our religious history once stood, is in Sweden should make us aware of its relevance. The temple was said to have been built by our god of agriculture, Frey.

We should not take the existence of a sacred *odal* land lightly, for as higher mortals and deities serve as archetypes for us to live by, our holy primordial home can act as the model for which we can honor *all* lands. This could be the first place we direct our children when they begin their journey into adulthood, since nothing could be more significant than a pilgrimage to the most honored area known in our stories. It is said that for this very reason, that Skåne is our ancient home, we should always pray facing North. To visit the land we have prayed towards can be a very spiritual experience. To hear the tales of the old gods and ancient heroes can captivate the imagination, while actually looking at the scene where their adventures were thought to have taken place can indeed be a powerful event.

Of course, every Germanic tribe is important, and all have their part to play in the rich cultural history of our heritage. Any nation in Northern Europe can be validated as significant to our religion in one way or another, and many have sacred sites we can go see. Unfortunately, much of the information regarding local legends, holy steads, or pre-Christian religious geography has been lost. There are place-names which correspond to names of gods, goddesses, heroes or other beings or things in our lore. Westphalia (now the western realm of Germany) was named after Phol, Falr, identical to Baldur, Frisia was named after Freyja, Odense in Denmark was named after Ódin, etc.

We don't *need* some foreign territory to convince us that the earth is something we should respect. We know that no matter where we live all around us is sacred life. The reverence toward the ancient odal land provides us with a real, physical connection with our ancestral culture; it is a place where we can go to walk in the footsteps of the gods, where we can see the actual sites of ancient battles, where we can visit the graves of our earliest forefathers. Even if science places our point of origin elsewhere, this should not take away the spiritual significance of appreciating what was once believed by all Teutons to be the cradle of our folk. We should also keep in mind that scientists can and have been wrong, but that is not really the point. The point is that Skåne is sacred to us, sacred to our lore and sacred to our ancestors. This should be enough for any of us.

Nature's Defense

As followers of a nature religion it is our duty to promote the sanctity of our Mother Earth. We can teach people the importance of her cycles of life, death and rebirth, honoring all of these stages as vital parts of the natural order. Our beliefs on the "sanctity of life" do not extend towards a fear of death, which we understand as just as necessary a part of life as birth. Living is indeed important to us, but we are not going to reject death from our doctrine or label it as "evil", or something to be afraid of. In nature we see birth and death as part of a continuous balance, part of every ecosystem that we are included in. We are not supernatural beings, no matter how much we would like to be, and eventually all of us will die. Trying to escape or deny this is pointless and serves nothing, for it is an inevitable reality.

We will educate people on all factors that threaten our environment, so they can take the proper actions against them. It is not healthy for us to sit back and feel helpless about what is happening in our world, nor is it necessary. There are so many things you can do, in your home, in your community, in your country. All you need to do is make the decision to stand up and do it! Take action. Become involved. Forget about social biases regarding groups you may not approve of or do not wish to be associated with. We're talking about doing the right thing, what's right for you, for your family, for your planet. If you do not want to be associated with someone, *don't* associate with them, but don't let this be an excuse for not taking an active role in service of your land and community.

8

Folk

"For the eighth I know,
What to all is
useful to learn;
where hatred grows
among the sons of men—
I can soon set it right."

—Ódin, Hávamál 154.

No doubt, this is *the* most controversial aspect of our religion. In today's society we are led to believe that there are only two sides of the fence regarding matters of race: you are either a racist or you are anti-racist, with nothing in between. No compromise, no shades of gray, it's very black and white: "you are either for us, or against us", say both sides. But how has that worked for us? The world continues to become more and more violent with each passing year, with no hope for relief. Hate groups spout their propaganda, which is really nothing more than a list of complaints, and never even come close to getting their point across. When an idea about a certain group becomes a mainstream bias, it is very difficult to overcome that; it is *impossible* to overcome it while feeding the stereotypes used against you. Anti-hate groups are anything but; most have personal agendas they end up carrying out in hateful, often brutal ways. Whether you hate someone because of the color of their skin or their beliefs, you are a bigot all the same. You would think that an "anti-hate" group would try to combat any and all forms of hatred by teaching love and compassion, not attacking others because of the way they think.

There is an alternative to this ongoing battle, one which should stand out as the most natural, balanced way to consider racial issues: that being mutual respect. I'm going to tell you right now that it is our obligation to life, to the universal order, to denounce prejudice, to denounce oppression, to denounce tyranny in favor of a creed that will allow us to appreciate everything that exists. We are all a part of Yggdrasil, each of us products of divine power and evolution, with a bond connecting us to all things, including all races, all religions, and all ideals. To deny this is to deny who we are as part of the great scheme of existence.

Our connection to this all-pervading creative force begins with ourselves, and then spreads outwards to the rest of humanity in a specific order. I am first a member of a family, then an extended family, then a folk, then humankind, etc. I refuse to believe that anything is an accident, that things do not happen for a reason. I am the person I am because of two things made up of thousands, hundreds of thousands of smaller factors: genetics and experience. Without a grateful recognition for both of these, when one's experience becomes their sole motivator they either become self-centered or self-depreciating. This is the core problem with the race debate: one side sees no value in others, the other sees no value in themselves. We cannot accept the validity of any form of higher power, or in evolution for that matter, if we cannot find worth in the heritage, both genetic and cultural, of all peoples, including our own.

The Inferiority Complex

Before we go any further with this there is something that must be mentioned for the sake of the argument. Those who claim racial superiority over others are missing the point entirely. Any race on earth can collect all sorts of information on the history of their people, their contributions to science, to civilization or whatever and use this to justify ideals of supremacy. The reason this turns many off is because it can be the first tool used in the oppression of others. There is simply no other reason why anyone would need to make this claim. Generally, those who feel it necessary to state that they are better than others actually feel inferior in some way; much like a coward who is always beating his chest, trying to act tough, it's overcompensation. Superiority should not be anyone's concern, since it can in no way be truly beneficial to anyone involved, even those who would claim it. When we separate ourselves as better than others, as better than *nature*, our isolation keeps us from truly valuing the diversity of our world. Since no civilization could thrive in such circumstances, no one gains from such beliefs.

Many use the feats and contributions of heroes past as "proof" of the superiority of their race. One should not hold their own greatness in the accomplishments of another, for this is without merit and can keep us from making our own mark. Although we should honor others, of all peoples, for their wonderful contributions to civilization, our ultimate query should be 'what will I do? What sort of action can I take to make our planet a better place to live in?' The improvement of the self should, in the end, be a tool with which we may help others do the same.

But there is a logical explanation for the reasons why so many feel frustrated and angry, why matters of race continue to create conflicts in our world. When people are not respected, when they are not treated with dignity, when they are not made to feel like they have worth, they will try to find someone to blame for this, and will then plant seeds of hatred in their hearts for those they view as the source of their problems. This goes for anyone. This is why our connection to life must begin with ourselves, for we have to learn self-respect before we can extend this to our fellow man. Let's consider how "self-respect" is applied here: the dictionary defines "respect" as "willingness to show consideration or appreciation for", which is exactly what we need to learn on so many levels. We must learn to love ourselves as children of the gods and of nature and as members of humanity, which is a much different form of self-love than that which arises from individualism. To love oneself is important, but it is only the beginning, as we will seek to become manifestations of higher love that extends to all living beings.

For the same reason, it is important to love one's self-kind, one's folk, which begins with one's family. We can no longer accept the "black-white" paradigm where we either hate races or beliefs. This is not helping anyone, it is only causing more strife than ever before. Just as any race can build up information to claim superiority, it's easy to demonize any people, any culture on the planet. It is the same as with religions—races are made up of people, and people make mistakes, do bad things, even *evil* things, but that should never be an excuse to condemn or invalidate entire groups.

The Ideal of Mutual Respect

Imagine how effective this idea of mutual respect could be, if we all were to use it. So many people of European descent are ashamed of their heritage, afraid to be linked with this movement or that belief system. Even spirituality isn't sacred here, for so many look to the East for what could be found in their own backyard. Some impose upon other cultures, such as Native American, Hindu or Buddhist, rather than connect with their own ancestry, which they seem to be embarrassed by. It's sad that we have allowed ourselves to fall into such a state, where all that we have become through thousands of years of evolution and cultural development is now the source of shame. The fact that only whites turn to other cultures for an identity, where all others proudly embrace who they are, is proof of this. No one is to blame for it other than us, since *we* are the ones who hold the folk-will within our hearts; *we* are the ones who can accept or reject our past for what it is, not what we would hope it to be.

When two sides of an argument are all that's permitted within the social strata there is no way anyone can make an objective decision, since the arguments of the two accepted sides will fall into direct opposition, usually because of factors other than what is being discussed, keeping them from reaching any sort of resolution. Such is the way with the topic at hand. The leftists and rightists will occasionally come out of the woodwork to fight it out and remind everyone that they despise each other; then, as always, each retreats to their corners without any solution, any means of establishing peace. Furthermore, the ideals themselves can then overshadow what is right and wrong, as members of each side first consider what is in accordance with the side they are on. This is why there *cannot* be a compromise with the current model, for this would compromise what it means to be active on either side of the political coin. Forget whether or not an idea is "good" or "right", the concern becomes "does it conflict with my or my group's views?"

We should always think of what is good and right first, over all other things, and if our beliefs conflict with this then perhaps we should reconsider our priorities. It is not right to invalidate an entire race of people, no matter what that race may be. That is it; it's that simple. No excuses, no justifications, no historical analysis. It is time for us all to make the conscious decision to put an end to the hypocrisy involved with this issue. When one race is put on a pedestal to the detriment of another, nothing good can come of it. This is why we need *mutual* respect. Today's media continues to express the double-standard regarding appreciation of all peoples and all cultures, except those with Nordic blood. They can't even speak of it! Any race in the world can shout out from the rooftops how much they love their genetic inheritance, but whites must always show respect for others, never for their own. If they *do* express admiration of their self-kind they could lose their job, be ostracized in their community, or in some countries even be arrested, even when their actions have nothing to do with "hate". To even try to make any statement promoting a love of our people is an act of "racism", even though it is *this standard* that is more bigoted than any ever known before.

Mutual respect—I can revere my ancestry, my folk and still have room to honor others at the same time! Such is the truest form of celebrating diversity (that popular, yet often misused "buzzword"), I can think of. No group of people should be oppressed, no one should have to be singled out and spit on because of the color of their skin or what they believe in. Some seem to forget this when dealing with those they disagree with.

To Be Appreciated Again

As stated, Ásatrú is an ethnic religion. It is the faith of our ancestors that developed as part of our cultural expressions, meaning that it is one with who we are, genetically and spiritually. There are literally hundreds of religions all over the world, and yet only a handful are "universalist", meaning they seek to encompass all of humanity into one doctrine. All others are cultural; they not only designate a specific pantheon, a specific morality, specific traditions, they also represent a specific race and nationality. Australian Aborigines, Native Americans, Japanese Shintos, Hindus, all these faiths focus on the cultures they manifest, for they are expressions of the folk-will. The only group, as I have said above, that has sought to "cross-over", or infiltrate them is whites, who feel lost without a native spirituality they can be proud to call their own. Because we are used to the Christian Universalist creed we feel we should be allowed to adopt these foreign beliefs, even if their natural adherents disagree.

Even worse, some groups have opted to eliminate the folkish foundation of Ásatrú by making *it* Universalist! I will not make accusations or conjectures on why they do this, I can only say that we should not be ashamed of who we are, nor should we let fear drive us away from our ancestry. The only thing we can do here is take action for the benefit of all. We have to rethink our positions, reconsider our choice of banner, to objectively stand up for what we *know* is right. Through education and spiritual awakening we can teach the world to love and value Northern Europeans again! We can begin a cultural revival that will at least disassociate racial love from racial hate, which can act as the catalyst for true harmony amongst us all. As long as any folk is devalued in the search for this, it will never be achieved.

For anyone who may doubt that any of this is an integral part of Ásatrú faith I only need to point out the Vikings as the highest example. During "The Viking Age", and probably before, the men and women of Northern Europe held a strong passion for learning of and appreciating other cultures, while still identifying with their own. They traveled all over the world as part of an established tradition beginning when a youth came of age. When women were courted their first questions to their would-be husbands were "Where have you been? What can you teach me and our children of foreign lands and foreign peoples?" Such a custom could only have developed through a deep-seated admiration for all races. But not once do we ever see in our records any sign of the lack of respect for whom our forefathers were as a folk, which has become so prevalent today.

You can't say, with any shred of validity, that an entire race is either "good" or "bad", it just is. It is what it is. You see, as much as we may try to deny it, even with biased pseudo-science, there is a reason why we look the way we do, act the way we do, think the way we do; our genes give us our identity as much as culture, upbringing, or experience. This genetic inheritance has worth. It should not be mistreated as an excuse to oppress or harm others, or as a means to promote a false sense of superiority, but it has worth as a natural part of our existence, our connection to who we are, which we call "the cultural identity". In fact, all else pales in comparison, for every other identification we can conceive would be man-made. One's country is nothing more than lines on a map, a flag, and some traditions and laws. We share our gender with every other living creature, yet many would use this as others would race in separating themselves from the opposite sex. Beliefs come and go, but nature has given us the only signs of our specialty. In the same way a tree is a tree, or an oak or birch; or a flower a flower, or rose or lily, we are products of creation or evolution, and we come in a special package of our very own! It doesn't matter how this came to be, how many genes produce it or how many we share with all other life forms, there is a reason why we are who we are and what we are.

The Strength of a People

The degradation, then eventual destruction of society always begins with the rejection of folk values. Why? Because they empower the people, allowing them to stand up against institutions that would enslave them. When we reach a point where aspects of our heritage are outlawed in our own lands, where our people turn away from who they are, where we have allowed ourselves to be the only race that can be ostracized in the mainstream, this represents a broken spirit, one which had kept us strong in the face of centuries of adversity. So, some lash out with hate while others regress with self-loathing, almost like the dual reactions of abused children. On both sides we can see a sickness, one that only *we* can cure ourselves. We will not re-awaken our Nordic spirit until we realize that it is a re-awakening that we *need* for our continued survival. Until then, so many will continue beating their heads against the wall in futile causes. Our weakening has allowed individualism to replace our cultural identity. In other words, appreciation for the larger community has become an obsession with the Self. "Me, myself and mine" has taken the place of "we, us and ours".

The first lessons we learn about our relationships with others begin with our family, so this is the foundation for which we build our ideas of community. From the start our communal bonds are forged through blood, which extends further to the folk, to our genetic community. When the folk community is invalidated, the global community becomes invalidated in the hearts of those who do not feel valued. It may seem romantic, even beautiful when we discuss racial harmony as something that should just happen, since it seems so right, so noble. I don't think any of us would deny the great benefit the world would receive if we could all just stop fighting over our differences and learn to strive for peace. But we can't work for this by ignoring these differences and then, at the same time, using them against one group for another. The result is oppression, which leads to frustration, then conflict. How can we Northerners become viable members of the global community if we cannot even accept our place within the folk community? While our heritage and the sovereignty of our homeland are stepped all over we sit back and shrug our shoulders without any consideration of what we are giving up. Global community is an ideal of validation for all cultures; we cannot be by-standers—we have to be active, we have to be ethnic!

The Right to Survive

Say for a second that you want nothing to do with any of this, that you don't agree with anything I've written. Fair enough. But can you, in good conscience say that your heart has turned so far away from Northern kind that you actually wish it no longer existed? With the waning Nordic spirit our folk have ceased to grow by not replacing our dead with sufficient births. It is apathy that is killing us, and those who do not care will be remembered as just as involved in our extinction as any who might physically try to do us in.

It is not our place to condemn personal decisions to engage in interracial relationships, which is in part to blame for our low birth-rate. Anyone who does this certainly has the right to do so and should not be put in any sort of negative light for their choice. Those who would attack them are missing the point. An idea is not a weapon with which we can hold all others to our will, where we can tell them how to live their lives. Although we cherish our folk, we also believe strongly in freedom, and would not violate this by dictating our beliefs to others.

However, per the first natural law, we have a *right* to survive, meaning that we should be allowed to promote positive folk values to our nations. We would practice mutual respect even with those who have sexual unions with those outside their race, no matter how much we may disagree with this. It is their choice to live how they wish, not ours. We will teach those we can about the importance of the cultural identity, doing all that we can to present a loving, positive doctrine aimed at the benefit of all. Those who will not listen to us are certainly free to do so. But those who will not give us a voice, who willingly, maliciously go out of their way to hold us down are no different than the Nazis in their oppressions and attempted extermination of Jews, or the communist Chinese in their assault of Tibet, or any other tyrants craving genocide.

That's right, genocide, the killing of a race. Whether this is done quickly with guns or poisonous gas, or over many years with hateful propaganda, with the assault on a people's spirit, dead is dead. There cannot be any finger-pointing here, though, because it all begins within ourselves. Each individual has to make the choice to overcome our current status and reach for something higher, personally and as a member of a folk community. *You* have to make the choice, right here and now, to begin using mutual respect in your daily life. If you are a racist, start trying to find a way to redirect your thinking towards an admiration for other cultures and races, eventually working to apply this in dealing with them. If you have lost touch with your heritage begin studying this, your genealogy, the history of your family, wherever you may hail from. If you are anti-racist perhaps you could begin trying to understand and differentiate actual racism from positive, folkish values, then teach this to others so we can all join together in eliminating the menace of bigotry. Do you think racism hasn't harmed Northernkind? It's undermining of all our cultural precepts has threatened our very existence, so that in the end white bigots have done more harm to their own folk than anyone else!

The Rise of Bigotry

Make no mistake; the idea of racial superiority among whites began as part of the Roman paradigm. The Nazi vision of an "Aryan Germany" was based upon the movement of German crusaders in "The Holy Roman Empire" centuries earlier, where Rome's institution of conquering replaced the Teutonic paradigm of co-operation. The reason this took place was because Rome became a centralized, single power built upon a single claim of Roman superiority, whereas the Teutons were made up of a collaboration of tribes living independently of one another. For the latter, co-operation, while not always successful, was necessary for survival. As Rome grew in power all those outside her borders became increasingly reviled, classed as "barbarians" (a Latin word meaning "foreigners") who came second in place to the so-called "civilized" Roman inhabitants. When the Romans conquered other nations they indoctrinated them into the beliefs of their homeland, extending this concept of "superiority" to their allies. Eventually all of Europe would embrace this, which would become the prime motivator for later imperialist campaigns against non-Europeans. Not that racism did not exist before Rome, certainly this has always been in every land in one way or another; however the overall mentality of a people can be deeply affected when their country has been invaded and taken over. When we adopted the Roman paradigm our folk-will rejected our natural ideal of mutual respect.

It may seem hypocritical of me to write about appreciating all peoples while condemning Romans. Certainly I think that Italy has one of the most beautiful, vibrant cultures in the world, with a rich past full of noble warriors, brilliant thinkers, and masterful artisans. Although the Roman Empire bears the name of its greatest city, this became as much of a detriment to its own people as it did the lands it conquered. In its later era Roman government ceased to care at all about the citizens of any of its provinces, so it isn't and shouldn't be any sort of a negative reflection on the natives of Rome, who happened to be the first to fall prey to the empire's power.

Pro-Self-Kind Ethics

It is only through the positive promotion of pro-self-kind ethics that we will be able to awaken the Nordic spirit, and effectively save our folk from extinction. It is only through promotion of mutual respect that we will be able to take our rightful place as members of a valid culture. The first step towards this is looking in our hearts to see what worth we can find in who we are, in everything that we are.

You might think that I'm proposing an abstract philosophy here, without any experience in what I am expressing. Words are useless if not put into action, which is why I try to live with the values of mutual respect on a daily basis. I have to say that the only difficulty I have faced is with whites of either side of the fence, who have either lost touch with their cultural identity, or exploit it to meet a hateful political agenda. I have yet to come across any member of any other race who can find fault in this. After all, *they* have never stopped enjoying their ethnicity, *they* have always reveled in pride for who they are and where they come from, so such an ideal just comes naturally to them. I talk with people of all races and all walks of life to try to understand what I can do to work towards this concept.

For me, it has become a very profound way of looking at the world and those within it. It has been a way for me to connect with others while the admiration for my own heritage swells in my heart. I have learned that I can love who I am; I can *love* that I am a white man and not be afraid of admitting that, without hating others in the process. Anyone can attack me for this if they wish, but I *know*, deep within my soul, that I am doing what is right and honorable, even if it is unpopular.

Hating others reflects upon no one other than yourself. Think about it—you can utterly loathe a person next to you while they go about the business of their day; you might attack them or hurt them, but this is only a temporary solution to your feelings of rage, feelings they could completely ignore. At the worst, they would have to deal with a brief negative impact from your hate, based on your actions against them, while you may be consumed with this, letting it take over your entire life. So you hate, and they are really unaffected. In the end only *you* are the one harmed as your hatred consumes you, then keeps you from functioning as a decent human being. All the justifications in the world can't make up for the fact that only you are the victim of these negative emotions. To overcome them, to work towards a healthy world-perspective, is the hallmark of courage and the sign of a true Nordic warrior. While we should defend ourselves from attacks or affronts, even in defending the honor of our family and our people, such would not be an act of hate, but rather a rightful response in the name of natural, higher love. The tribal bond we share with those of our folk mimics that of many animals and every race on earth, who would do the same in the protection of their own, as they should.

It is my sincerest hope that anyone reading this who has filled their minds with self-loathing against their own folk will find it in their hearts to accept us for who we are. It would be easy to claim that we Ásatrúar have a hidden agenda, that we are trying to pave the way for hate, or that the words we speak are just lies. If we can learn to be compassionate towards one another, even if it is simply to agree to disagree, we might be able to actually shed some light on those who do *real* harm to all peoples through hateful propaganda and social agendas. I don't want to be the enemy of people I do not know, whom I have never wronged, have never harmed. All I want is to keep our folk and our heritage alive so that future generations may enjoy it and appreciate it. All I can do is what I feel is right in my heart, which I am sure most would agree with: all we can do is what we feel is right. If people wish to hate us for this, at least we will have known that we did our best in working for our beliefs in truth and honor. Perhaps, in adopting what I have said here we may begin moving towards an ideal of true racial harmony, for a celebration of true diversity through mutual respect.

Reverse Discrimination?

It's disheartening when we see the discrimination our folk now meet on almost a daily basis. Children are expelled from school, fights break out, arrests are made. And what for? For attacks against members of other races? For violent protests against government policies? For terrorism? No, for simply having the courage to stand up and say that they are proud of who they are. Nothing more. In several European countries and elsewhere there are "race laws" banning symbols and actions, which often effect innocent people who are not affiliated with hate groups. Have we come so far that we will suppress even benevolent ideas, such as pro-self-kind ethics or mutual respect, out of fear that they may perpetuate that which is most despised by society? And when will it end? Are we actually headed for extinction without anyone caring or lamenting our demise?

We all know what's right and what's wrong, what's fair and unfair. All the indoctrination in the world cannot take that away from us. You know what is inside your heart, what you are capable of and what you are incapable of. Perhaps, if I am effective, my words have touched you in some way and we, and by "we" I mean every person on this planet, can move forward for a brighter day for us all. No doubt this will take courage, it will take determination, but when men and women have truth behind them no force can stand in their way. Only together will Europeans be able to fully revive the Nordic spirit in all of us. Even if Ásatrú isn't your choice of path to do this, any positive way that you deem appropriate for yourself and for your family can only be honorable and righteous.

Why do I feel so strongly about re-awakening the Nordic spirit? Because, not only am I of Nordic descent, I am passionately devoted to the idea that this can be a powerful beginning to a new era of mutual respect among all races. Once the world had a dream that forced integration was going to fix all racial problems in existence, yet all this has done is create yet more problems. Affirmative Action has taught us to not judge a person based on the content of their character or abilities, but solely upon the color of their skin. Media outlets believe if they constantly bombard whites with messages that they must always care about others and never about their own, that they will eliminate racism once and for all. You simply cannot devalue one group to uplift another then expect positive results. Now, we have a choice: we can either continue to express apathy or even disgust towards our ancestry and laugh away while we become extinct, or begin finding joy, profound joy in who we are as a folk. Like I've said, it will take courage. You will have to be brave enough to not be embarrassed by your past, while recognizing that certainly, as among all races, religions, and creeds, some have done bad things. But that is no excuse to ignore or demonize the rich culture and beautiful history of our people. Be positive and focus on positive things, neither point fingers at others nor allow them to guilt-trip you into rejecting your blood. Do this and together we will start to re-institute our folk as a viable, significant entity within the global community. Alone we are but one, united we are the strength of a nation!

Ásatrú is a name we have given to the sacred cultural expressions of our people, which existed for thousands of years before the coming of Christianity. Whether you like it or not, the blood of our ancestors flows through the veins of every person of Northern European descent. It is a natural part of who we are as people, and as a people. It can become the bridge upon which we walk to join the rest of the world in celebrating diversity among all nations. It can become the means for us to tear down the walls that divide us on issues concerning the very existence of our genetic identity. If we give up, if we let our folk die, I at least hope that we can preserve the remnants of our past so future generations may remember us as a noble people, with a heritage worthy of appreciation.

All over the world cultures have held family and folk values in high esteem. Our religions teach us that these are sacred; that they are, in effect, the very backbone of our civilizations. If we ignore them, the downfall of society will be the result, as we have failed our future generations. This is emphasized in the ancient texts:

"Brother may become his brother's bane, and blood is spilled between siblings' sons; hardship is in the world, much whoredom, axe-age, knife-age, shields are cloven, wind-age, wolf-age, ere the world succumbs, no man dare spare each other".

—Völuspá 46 on Ragnarök.

"And the brother shall deliver up the brother to death, and the father the child: and the children shall rise up against *their* parents, and cause them to be put to death."

—Matthew 10:21-22 on The End Times.

"Though they, blinded by greed, do not see evil in the destruction of the family, or sin in being treacherous to friends, why should not we, who clearly see evil in the destruction of the family, think about turning away from this sin (of inter-clan war) O'Krishna? Eternal family traditions and codes of conduct are destroyed with the destruction of the family. Immorality prevails in the family due to the destruction of family traditions."

—Bhagavad Gita 1. 38-40.

"Then, is it to be expected of you, if you were put in authority, that you will do mischief in the land, and break your ties of kith and kin? Such are the men whom Allah has cursed for He has made them deaf and blinded their sight."

—The Qur'an, Sura 47:22-23.

9

Today's Religion

"No man lacks everything,
although this health is bad:
one is happy in his sons,
one in his kin,
one in abundant wealth,
one in his good works."

—Óðin, Hávamál 69.

Ásatrú has existed for thousands of years, with relics dated as far back as before history began to be recorded. It is a religion that has stood the test of time: it has been attacked, suppressed, misrepresented, demonized, falsely accused, and denounced, yet it still lives on in the hearts of its adherents, even though much of the above still occurs. We simply cannot let it die, for to do so would be to kill a part of ourselves, since the ancient beliefs and customs it represents live strong in the souls of every person of Northern European blood. Love it or hate it, it is still very much a part of who we are.

It took Christianity over 800 years to officially convert every European nation, which tells us a bit about how important these indigenous faiths were to our ancestors. With constant campaigning, proselytizing, and military force the Christians did everything they could to break the Nordic spirit. Some say the old ways never actually died out, they just went underground for the safety of the fol-lowers. That these religions have re-emerged in the last century lets us all know that we will never be completely broken down, so long as there are those of us who will do what we can to keep our heritage alive and thriving. Even if we reach a point where to do so will threaten our lives, if society gets to the point where we will be purposely suppressed, as it has before, we will continue to work for the salvation of our people and our cultures.

A Living Nation

The Ásatrú community, which we call "The Ásatrú Nation", "The Odinist Nation", or "The Nation of Ódin", was established in Australia by Alexander Rud Mills around the turn of the 20th century. Else Christensen would later spread it in the Americas beginning in the late 1960s, and so would begin its expansion around the world. Today, almost every, if not every country with a European population has some group of noble individuals struggling to bring the Old Faith back to its previous glory. Our nation is vibrant, diverse and filled with intelligent people, most with fiercely independent natures. It is said that no two Ásatrúar will think alike or see our faith in the same way, which is exactly how we would have it. Dogma has no place in our sacred path; neither does priestly hierarchy or formalized "sects". The ideals of self-reliance, which permeate our belief system, are so important to all of us that such things could not exist within our community without compromising this in some way. Even sects cannot logically remain, for there is no dogma, no *set* standard where we *have* to think or act according to one single interpretation of our sources. Because of this such divisions are unnecessary.

There have been attempts made in the past to create sects among our adherents, but these usually do not come to fruition. The first of these was based on a misunderstanding of the difference between the terms "Ásatrú" and "Odinism", with many thinking of them as designating two specific and separate "groups" within our community. For anyone who *still* thinks this is true it is time to debunk this falsehood once and for all. When the neo-Odinist group in Australia was founded they used the term "Odinism" to establish the rebuilt religion, since this had already been used among the scholarly community as a label for these beliefs for some time. Later, the word "Ásatrú" would be utilized by Scandinavian organizations, namely the "Ásatrúarfelag" in Iceland. Icelanders have an interesting tradition in use today, where modern words such as "telephone", "computer", "internet", etc. are brought before a special committee which then comes up with a suitable word for their native tongue. No doubt this is how "Ásatrú" became standard in every Scandinavian language, changing only in dialect for each one.

One of the men who helped get Ásatrú established as a recognized religion in Iceland over twenty years ago was Thorsteinn Gudjonsson, whom I had the privilege of corresponding with for several years before his death. In all the information we shared, all the letters we exchanged, I never found any indication that the Ásatrúar there considered themselves to be any different from those calling themselves "Odinists". In fact, every division ever formulated between the two, Ásatrú and Odinism, seemed irrelevant by his explanations of the views he and his constituents held and hold to this day.

Some have said that Ásatrú focuses only on Scandinavian culture, but this is not true, several Ásatrú groups recognize and institute contributions from Saxon, German, Frisian, and other groups. Others say that we only celebrate the Aesir and ignore the other divine clans, but this has no foundation in reality. The word "Aesir" is used in a general sense on many occasions in the ancient texts, representing all the gods and goddesses. That the word "*Ás*", though technically designating a God of the Aesir clan, is used often to mean "a god", is proof of this.

The fact remains that there is no difference between Ásatrú and Odinism; they are two words denoting the same religion. Choosing one term or another is merely a matter of preference. Arguments can and have been made for why one should be used more than the other, but such debates are pointless. Both are modern terms, both have their advantages and disadvantages. Our ancestors, when forced to make a distinction between their religion and Christianity called their sacred path "Forn Sed", meaning "The Ancient Customs", so this too could be used.

I chose to use Ásatrú myself years ago because of my friendship with Thorsteinn and because it has been officially sanctioned in the lands our forefathers believed the European folk originated from (see Chapter 7). To me, it seems to reflect the polytheistic nature of the faith, more so than Odinism, but this is just my opinion. I really don't take this too seriously and will often times use the words interchangeably, which I would recommend others to do. It just isn't that big of a deal. Know that there is not, nor has there even been, an "official" distinction.

Probably arising from the belief that "Ásatrú" signifies primarily Scandinavian traditions, new groups have popped up using localized interpretations of the "Ancient Customs". The Theodish folk focus primarily on Saxon ancestry, while the Irminists base their ancestral path on German heritage. Let me first say that I have a tremendous respect for these groups and think that the efforts they have made in the renewal of these beliefs is truly commendable. As long as we continue to respect the bond that we have in celebrating these traditions it does not matter what our particular interpretation is. We are all pretty much on the same path, whether we use Icelandic or Old Norse or Old English or German words and concepts makes no difference at all, we are all members of Ódin's Holy Nation.

Ancestral Distinctions

Our ancestors had a natural, long-lived means of establishing folk distinctions, which represented a larger relationship between all peoples. Individuals were members of families, from the immediate family to the larger, extended "kindred". Kindreds grouped together into clans, clans into tribes, and tribes into nations. With each link in this chain a set of traditions would be celebrated, which would eventually form the diverse cultures spread out all over native Europe. Families would have a special set of customs they would follow, which may or may not include the kindred; clans would follow their customs, tribes would follow theirs, nations theirs. In the end, all still worshipped the same gods and goddesses, but in their own way, which celebrated the independence of the folk and the shared bloodline of all. Such a model could be valuable in reforming our cultural identity, for it gives us particular steps in doing so, while honoring the actual method used in Northern Europe centuries ago.

Allow me to put this into perspective. My family is generally considered to be my parents, my siblings, my grandparents, and now my wife and children. The extended family: aunts, uncles, cousins, second cousins, great-uncles, etc. are all part of my kindred. When a group of families come together under one banner this alliance, which can be solidified by intermarriage, is called a clan. Many Ásatrú or Odinist fellowships today would fall into this category. When many clans came together this is a tribe, which could be considered the larger Ásatrú/Odinist groups today. More appropriately, tribes would be the conglomeration of various clans within one's state, province, county, or country. In the past, tribes were bound by location and an ancestral name of a tribal founder, such as the Istaevones or the Hermiones, or some other signification, such as the Longobards ("Long-Beards", a name believed to have been given to them by Ódin himself). However, modern technology allows us to maintain close ties from long distances, so geographical location might not be as important as it once was. Finally, as stated, the nation itself is the collaboration of all of us, a great union of our people working in steadfast devotion for our faith, our folk, and our families.

Land *was* integral to tribal relationships, for each division came with a territory of its own, spreading from small homesteads to entire countries. Nations were established as the realms of tribes or alliances with others, with all the culture and heritage that came with each group. Perhaps we could one day make this valid once again, while never forgetting the union of the overall "Ásatrú Nation" that we have created in our re-awakening. Families can become part of communities, building clans to form tribes, which will then recognize their place within the country they inhabit as a part of the folk identity, possibly becoming viable entities within their lands.

Clans may become tribes through blood relations as well. For instance, if the father of several sons is a clan founder, then each of these sons in turn establish their own clans, then the overall group would be a tribe, named after the father's original clan. Such was the case with Ívaldi and his three sons: Völund, Slagfin, and Egil. All of these divisions then have their particular divine protectors, Norns who represent the luck of the people, who watch over us and aid us when possible. For the individual is the *Mannsfylgja*—"Man's Fylgja", identical to the *hamingja*. The *Kynsfylgja* looks out for the family and the *Aettarsfylgja* protect the clan or tribe. Such a divine correlation to these divisions shows how sacred they were to our ancestors.

Building a Community

We have talked about developing large, folk-based communities in our nation for years, yet few, if any have been truly successful at this. A lot of it has to do with how many perceive such a way of life, which in many ways has been influenced by isolated cults or bizarre organizations, which shut themselves off from the world. Some believe that a "community" must be built on some compound, or on private land where we won't have to deal with others, where we might stock up guns for protection, or "train" for any conflict that may or may not arise. For one thing, it costs a *lot* of money to set up something like this, money most people do not have, money best spent elsewhere. Also, in such a situation you are *going* to instill fear in those around you towards you and your group, which can lead to all sorts of trouble. Is this what we want? Do we want other people, especially those of our own folk, to actually be afraid of us? I think not.

Integrated communities are the best means of creating strong, locally respected groups that can thrive within each area. When those around you fear you it will be next to impossible to be taken seriously. Consider the old hermit in your town, which almost all have, and think about the rumors and innuendos told about him. Some say such people are devil worshippers, others may say they kidnap children and lock them in the basement, all kinds of stuff. Usually this is just amusing banter or trivial gossip, but when several people gather and have such things said about them it can escalate into more strife than it's worth. However, when you act honorably and nobly you will find you have more advocates than if you try to hide from everyone. This could also help you if you were to ever face any difficulty in dealing with law enforcement, which can sometimes be just as reactionary as rumor-spreading locals.

Not that you should spend every waking hour trying to impress or kowtow to the whims of area residents. It is very likely that you may have problems with some who just do not appreciate any beliefs being practiced near them, if they are not those they grew up with. No matter what you do in life there will always be someone who doesn't like it, so all you can do is what you know to be right. As long as you handle yourself in a respectful, dignified manner, remembering that you are a representative of your family, clan, tribe, etc. what anyone says behind your back is irrelevant. When one starts telling lies about you and your friends, including the media, it is your duty to address these nobly, but with a stern determination against them.

All you need to do to start building an integrated, folk-based community is pick an area, probably the one you live in right now, and start a group, starting uniting families into clans. Offer information on our faith, emphasizing *teaching* rather than proselytizing as you let more and more people know about our ancient ways. Once a few have come together you might consider "importing" others by helping Ásatrúar find deals on real estate near you. As your community grows so should programs offered in service to it, such as faith-based daycare, schooling, tribal economy, and so on. So much more goes into this than just meeting for ceremonies or discussing traditions. In fact, these are but a small part of the larger cultural picture that defines our religion. It takes some work, but developing and establishing a community can be immensely rewarding, leading you all into so many areas of effective, pro-active living I could not begin to list them here. Be creative! Be supportive! Look at your group not as a stale manifestation of a cultural *aspect*, but as the vigorous, flourishing embodiment of an entire society!

First and foremost, when you are a part of something larger than yourself, you have to accept this and embrace it, for you can no longer consider yourself alone. That means that what you do reflects upon the others in your group, even if this is just your family. If you, as their representative (which all the members are), make yourself look bad, you make everyone connected to you look bad, and vice versa. This is a responsibility that you have to them, which you must not take lightly.

Interpreting the Ancients

In this book you may have noticed some traditions that may seem archaic or superstitious in our day and age. As with all religions we view the ancient customs as containing deeper spiritual wisdom that has taken the form of the stories and ideals handed down to us. This wisdom can speak to us in any number of ways, which is why it is important for our religious scholars to consider this in the writing of texts. Every word, every ceremony, every song, every cultural expression of the ancients is in one way or another connected to the divine, which should be our goal in creating such things today. In recording these traditions we should seek to keep them as is for the sake of allowing people to find their own interpretation. The tendency is to give the author's own opinions regarding the symbols and concepts, rather than leaving this up to the folk. We may work to bring the ancient ways back to their former glory, before the coming of Christianity corrupted them, but it is up to each individual to determine how they want to look at this information.

Certainly, no Ásatrúar believes that there is a great big tree in outer space connecting all the worlds together, or that several deities in Viking garb fly across the sky bringing the sun, the rain, the wind, etc. Typically, we try to view our beliefs in a logical context, which often coincides with modern science. I would like to give here a review of the major interpretations utilized by our people. These should give anyone a foundation to build their own personal beliefs, no matter which path they choose.

Nýall—Founded in Iceland in the early 20th century by physicist and dream analyst Helgi Pjeturss, this scientific philosophy seeks to make sense of all things considered "supernatural" (which to us is a misnomer). It has several aspects, including the idea that our dreams are *actual* events viewed from afar, ideals on the origin of life, the afterlife, and so on. For our purposes here I will only briefly explain the theory concerning the existence of the gods and goddesses in accordance with this doctrine. Since Nýall philosophy is founded on scientific principles, the basic concept is that deities are higher life forms living on advanced planets elsewhere in the universe, whose powerful life-force, called "bioradiation", played a role in our creation from DNA, RNA and proteins. These deities are living, breathing, biological entities and, in the same sense, are our most ancient ancestors, though their place in the evolutionary scale is much, much higher than ours. Our relationship with them is realized through dreams and telepathy, which are energy transfers that empower them as well as us. Whenever we pray or observe the rites, or have any sort of so-called "religious experience" we are energized by them and they by us through actual, physical, and energetic processes.

All of this is based on sound theories well established in the scientific community, and much of the concepts within Nyáll are gaining ground as time passes. All one needs to accept it is to believe in evolution, to believe that mankind is not the pinnacle of evolution, to believe that there is life elsewhere in the universe (which most people do), and to believe in telepathy. The latter has practically become a scientific fact as several experiments have proven that thoughts can be projected from one mind to another. Trying to make logical sense of the universe was the very reason religion developed in the first place!

Spiritualism—Some see the gods and goddesses as ethereal spirits living on some other plane of existence, possibly another dimension of reality. This is a well-known concept common to most belief systems. What's interesting is that some physicists and mathematicians have recently discovered amazing theories that may well prove that these other "planes" or "dimensions" are real. If these theories pan out they could very well change how we perceive metaphysics. Some factions in the academic community have always been behind the spiritualist movement, which began in the 1800s in Europe, with the many secret societies that were formed at the time. In fact, it was this movement that began the "German Renaissance" which *could* have been the starting point for the Odinic revival, if it had not been tainted by political regimes, or damned by the onslaught of two world wars. Spiritualists started asking questions that others were afraid to know the answers to, questions that would later become a part of valid scientific queries.

Vis Numinis—A term coined by the Roman historian Cornelius Tacitus, Vis Numinis signifies the positions of the gods and goddesses as symbols of nature, or their relations to the community affairs and culture of the folk. We would usually recognize this in their duties or descriptions, such as Ódin being the god of the wind, of wisdom, the runes, language, spirit, breath, etc. Mainly we would use this in describing the meteorological school of thought, where our deities and stories are viewed solely as representatives of natural phenomena. There is no doubt that this is a valid explanation, even if one follows any of the other paths listed, since our lore does provide us with clues regarding each deity's place in the universal order. This has probably been the longest standing viewpoint in the academic community, although some have used it as an attempt to invalidate the ancient ways as simple-minded superstitions. There cannot be a more logical means of worship, when one reveres the sun and sky, the oceans and earth, the world around them, which they can see and touch, hear and smell. For many who do not focus specifically on this belief, reverence of nature still plays a vital role in their spiritual lives, for as we know, Ásatrú is a nature religion.

Archetypes—The famous Swiss psychiatrist, Carl Gustav Jung, began developing his theories on archetypes around the year 1913, which stemmed from his lifelong interest in mythology and ancient religions. Jung believed that every race on earth has its own deeper unconsciousness, which he called the "collective unconscious", and we call the folk-will. The archetypes are part of this concept; they are patterns of thought or models of behavior, which have developed through the centuries. These archetypes allow people to react to situations in ways similar to their ancestors, as these are deeply rooted in the collective unconscious. Ancient gods and heroes, according to Jung, are therefore expressions of the folk-will, as well as guidelines leading us to greater wisdom.

As with Vis Numinis, it is easy for us to recognize these archetypes in the lore no matter which interpretation we lean towards. In fact, the models of behavior and ethical lessons taught to us by the model of each character in the sources are part of our deeper spiritual understanding of the ancient tales (see Chapter 1). We look up to the gods and goddesses as higher examples of the virtues we humans aspire to, for inspiration in our daily living.

No matter how we look at our inherited faith it is important for each of us, in a personal sense, to find practical applications for what it has to offer. Long ago religion and science were united as one, without any conflict between the two. Ásatrúar do not wish to conform science to a strict dogma, or create lavish theories to force the academic community to accept our religious beliefs on anthropology, cosmology, etc. We tend to do the opposite—find already existing theories and see how they might fit with the ancient design. So far this has been tremendously successful, on all fronts. What's more, by the standards taught to us by our All-Father, Ódin, we must always seek out, promote, and support new forms of wisdom and learning. For far too long, under Christian rule, we have had to live by the idea that faith *has* to defy logic and logic *has* to defy faith. With our religious renewal we wish to bring back the way of the ancients, where higher understanding of the forces of the universe was not only permissible, it was their passion! Science, to us, is a religious experience, as we reach out to all its avenues to gain wisdom and intelligence and reconnect with nature by striving, first and foremost, to understand it. We will be its students and its teachers, not its opponents or detractors.

Everyone who reads the ancient lore must first understand that our ancestors were extremely poetic; so much of what has been passed down comes to us in allegory and metaphor, which certainly overlies the deeper truths hidden within. What is amazing is how even back then technologies such as computer games (the "tables" game, a forerunner of chess, of the gods which will play an opponent by itself) and flying machines (symbolized as animals, animal drawn chariots, or animal guises) were thought of. Some believe that visions of such devices came through dreams of actual more advanced worlds elsewhere in the universe, where others may see them as prophecies. It is up to each individual to make sense of these poetic images as an integral part of their spiritual enlightenment. Some will write books on their interpretations, which can then help others in their search for a better understanding of our sacred wisdom. And we do need to understand this, for to do so is to gain an insight into our own being, as individuals and as a folk. We work hard to put the ancient epic back together because it is a part of our heritage and as such calls to us as sons and daughters of our deities to know of them, learn of them and the secrets they hold. The myths are important in this awareness of the divine, and therefore are so much more than just symbols or literary fancy.

The Paths of Power

Previously I have mentioned "The Paths of Power" without describing exactly what they are. We use the word "paths" in its plural sense because there are many ways one can journey for personal empowerment. They do not lead to a destination; they *are* a destination, a goal in and of themselves, since we see the struggle for attainment as more valid than that which can actually be attained. Basically, to walk the Paths of Power is to reach for higher evolution, to seek to constantly improve yourself mentally, physically, emotionally, and spiritually. This is not for the weak of heart, for it requires discipline and an ability to look past the ego for something better, something stronger. Moreover, these paths are the means for one to become a vessel of pure action in the service of their people. After all, talk is cheap and men and women are most noted for what they *do* rather than what they say. You can read this book, find some things in it you like, then set it down and probably forget about everything in it in about a week or so, or you can make the commitment, right now, to begin striving towards enlightenment and empowerment. If you have to, make a vow that you will begin living with honor and integrity, that you will stand up for who you are and where you came from, and that you will live according to principles you know and feel in your heart are right and true. Then decide what types of actions you will make in your daily life towards that end; you could start teaching positive folk-values in your community, meditate by yourself or with family and friends, find ways to protect your environment and support your local agriculture. There is an infinite amount of things you can do for your faith, folk, and family; you are only limited by your imagination and your willingness to act.

Interfaith Outreach

You may have noticed that a few times in this book I have described Christianity in a somewhat negative light. It is important for us to recognize the mistakes of the past (and of the present) so we will not make them again. Christianity has a very dark role in the history of European religions, which we cannot deny or ignore as we try to piece together the remaining shards of our shattered faith. However, we should not condemn Christians, or members of any other religion for that matter, simply because of the path they follow. We will also not turn our eyes away from ignoble acts performed in the name of any religion, including our own. It is necessary for us to play our role in the global community, which we can do if we follow the ideas of mutual respect. Part of this will entail outreach programs so that we can work to maintain peaceful relationships between us and those of other faiths. Remember that honor is a reflection of the Self, so our actions towards others should not have anything to do with personal biases or prejudices, but rather should serve as a higher example of kindness and compassion. We are honorable because it is right to be this way, even if we come across a vicious criminal our actions should be just as dignified towards them as they would be towards someone we highly respect. I have heard people say that they would "get" so-and-so because they don't like them, or would attack them without provocation, not realizing that this makes them no different than the person they are after. Their actions show what kind of person *they* are, not the one they have wronged.

We can reach out to other religions—Christianity, Islam, Judaism, Hinduism, Buddhism, etc. with a spirit of friendship that can only be deserving of respect. As we learn of their traditions we can teach them of ours. Whatever the results, we tried to do what was right, and will continue to do so whenever we have the chance.

If we are successful in our attempts to revive the ancient concept of mutual respect towards all, and I am optimistic that we will be, we might begin to find validation for Ásatrú in the hearts of our own people, who may realize the virtuous nature of our path. We have to try everything we can to re-awaken the Nordic spirit in all members of our folk, no matter what it takes. If one thing fails, try another, then another, then another, remembering to be patient and compassionate, without trying to force our beliefs on others. Never give in and we *will* be heard, we will realize the rebirth of our once great race!

Conclusion

Why Ásatrú? The technologies of the modern world have brought all nations closer than ever, allowing any of us to learn of and choose from hundreds of paths in our search for spiritual meaning. Some are ancient, some are not, but all have something to offer. Many people may even fall into the pattern of donning a new religious cloak with their changing moods, while others might combine several different faiths into their own hodgepodge of traditional wisdom. However, there is one thing no other creed can give you, no matter what is said: a connection to your heritage. Whatever your race or nationality may be the ancestral ways of our forefathers call out to us all. Your genetic inheritance links you to them in the same way it does your family line, so whether you would connect to Teutonic Ásatrú, Chinese Taoism, African Yoruba, or Caribbean Santeria, *all* of us have an ancient path to return to. Revered, honored since the dawn of humanity, the voices of our ancestors will not be silenced by a few hundred years of theocratic dictatorship. Like the boys of indigenous tribes, upon their initiation into manhood, we must be brave, we must be bold, and we must accept our places as members of a folk, all of us. Enslavements to superficial, fashionable lifestyles have replaced the deeper living once held sacred all over the world. We have an uphill battle in trying to reach into the hearts of those indoctrinated by self-loathing, or other-loathing ideologies, but our struggle will be rewarded with the continuance and fair treatment of the legacy of our forebears.

I cannot speak for others, all I can tell you is that my personal experience has been incredibly enriching as I have grown in this way of life. Deep inside all of us, we have the mettle to forge that special bond with our gods and goddesses, those of *our* people, for they are out there, they are a part of us, in blood and in bone. Ásatrú can be the light that shines within us, the very soul of our being which can lead us toward our higher selves. The beacon is lit; we only need to walk towards it!

Practical and to the point, Ásatrú philosophy teaches us to not get too caught up in the complexities of existence. There is no need for the divine to be an abstract conception of omnipotence; we can appreciate the power of the gods as beings that are real, in the sense that they are not perfect. Our stories tell of mistakes they have made, and bad circumstances they have met with. This, to me, is the most profound ideal found in our sources—that we cannot expect all to go well for us just because we worship the Aesir and Vanir. Because there is no single deity controlling all of reality in our belief system, there is no consideration that divinities have the blame for the wrongs that befall us, as part of some "plan". *Wyrd* is *Wyrd*, not even the gods have power over it. They can influence it, just as we can, but they can never control it. Their imperfections do not make them inferior as higher powers, in comparison with monotheist gods, but are in fact testaments to their beauty, to their wondrous beings, which we can relate to and ally with. What the holy powers do give us is the strength and inspiration to face life's challenges with a brave spirit and a noble heart. This is their greatest gift to us.

I can honestly say that by following the ethics and ideals handed down to us through the centuries your life can certainly be changed for the better, something I know from experience. Once you accept an honorable path, where morality is imposed for the improvement of mankind, there is no way this cannot have a strong impact on who you are. We can begin listening to our conscience again, for these are the words of our *hamingja* leading us on our way in the struggle for true integrity. Simply by realizing that we are recompensed with what we have given, that a gift will be met with a gift and a lie for a lie, we can understand our place in the world, the connection we have with others.

If we reject this, thinking that the Self should be placed above all, our decadence will be the death of us. We have to have a reason, a real reason to want to live to help others, rather than help ourselves. By becoming active in our community and with our folk we will find meaning for this so that others may follow our example. Actions always speak louder than words, which is why we should use the information in books, such as this one, to motivate us to do something positive in the furtherance of these higher values. Don't just sit around thinking about how much you liked or disliked what has been said here...Get up! Get moving! Make the choice *now* to take part in our cultural revival. We all have to employ high-minded, proactive principles in our daily living. This requires careful consideration and discipline in determining what should be done and how one should go about doing it. First, one needs to consider their skills, talents, and interests, then use these to their maximum benefit for everyone around you.

What so many are in need of today is direction, a purpose for their lives, to give them meaning and worth. As long as we reject our past and fail to meet our obligations for the future our folk, every folk, will continue to fall into the downward spiral that has trapped millions across the world. One may feel isolated and alone because that is exactly what they are. Until you find significance in your blood you are but an individual, a creature cut off from the powerful bond of family and folk. We humans can concoct all the excuses, all the complex theories we want, but nothing will change the fact that we are who we are, we are what we are, so all we can do is celebrate this in every possible way.

To be free, to be independent, to be valued and respected—these are the most basic desires of all people. But to get we have to give, such is the way of *örlög*; we have to plant the seed to reap the harvest. To be free we have to work diligently against those forces that would oppress anyone. To be independent we must break the chains of dependency that fetter us all, no matter what form these chains come in. To be valued and respected we have to value and respect others, both on a personal and cultural level. The only thing that stands in our way as we walk the Paths of Power, the only obstacle blocking us from recognizing our true selves, the only ones keeping us from something greater is us. We have become our own worst enemies, but if we choose, we can overcome the Self to reach for our destiny, what the gods and goddesses had intended for us all along.

APPENDIX A

The Role of Women in Ásatrú

by Katia Puryear

Few could argue with the fact that over the past few hundred years, there has been much confusion concerning the self-identity of the women of our folk. Our women generally just don't seem to know what roles they should play within the family, as well as in society in general. Even our perceptions on how to act, or feel, or look have been clouded in our modern world. For men, this has always been fairly obvious, but for women recently it hasn't, and this is due to many reasons I will briefly discuss in this article.

Women find themselves pondering where they fit in best—as career-driven individuals, mothers, single & "independent", or as wives. They also wonder what personalities suit them best with these decisions—Authoritarian? Caregiver? If a woman is kind and giving, is this natural, or does it equal some sort of weakness? Should we follow the trends and advice that modern day society has set for us? It's almost as if we have lost all female instincts on how to be and feel like a woman. It's enough to make your head spin! With all this confusion, it truly isn't abnormal to hear that Teutonic races are the least likely to reproduce at this point in time, with an average of 1.4 children being born to every Northern European woman, as compared to an average of 3+ in other races.

The roles that the women held in our ancestors' days were defined and stable, vastly different from the uncertainties we face today. Let's start with taking a look at our Goddesses. One only has to consider our lore to see the respect and reverence paid to female divinities in their roles of mother, wife and warrior. They loved all and were loved by all. Our ancestors worshipped the Goddesses as fervently as they did the gods. They did not view one gender as inferior to the other in the least. Each had their own realms of expertise, but they were all equally important to the every day lives of our ancestors. Our earliest parents viewed women in high esteem when it came to their knowledge. Ódin is documented over and over going to the Norns and Goddesses for enlightenment, as well as consulting the Valkyries for assistance in times of war. And of course, there is his wife Frigga, his companion and constant consult, who was even shown to have out-witted Ódin in one instance as displayed in the Longobard's Saga. Frigga herself is mother to the most major gods and is highly revered by gods and men alike. Our All-father never ended his quest for knowledge, and more often times than not this quest would bring him before a female entity. Not to mention that the Norns, composed solely of women, hold the responsibly of weaving the fate of all…even that of the Gods! This type of power would certainly not be held by a gender that was generally understood as unintelligent and/or incapable of making wise decisions.

Now let's focus on the Northern European human standpoint. Men held their roles of providers and husbands and fathers, they handled those roles well, and that must be respected. The family certainly couldn't survive without the provisions their men supplied. But women were always the vital drive of the community, the positive energy that kept families going and tribes thriving.

Sexism was not even a concept in the time of our ancestors; they simply did what they had to do to survive. The fact that women stayed at home with the children wasn't an option—they had to do it for the family's survival. A man certainly couldn't bring a young infant with him hunting. This would be absolutely impossible. Additionally, it was imperative for the woman to be around the young children so she could nurse them. Their arrangement was simply a matter of practicality and common sense. Another important fact that many overlook is that when the men were not out hunting or fishing, they stayed at home and helped raise the children as well. Spouses were equal partners with a shared goal: to ensure their family's survival. The home was the center of their lives and all they did revolved around that.

This doesn't mean that the wife's role during that time was less important. Quite the contrary. While men were out hunting, or in war, or out discovering foreign lands, the wife had to make sure the family was taken care of and had to assume practically every role the husband usually maintained during his absence. This included caring for the children, cooking, cleaning, carpentry, harvesting, plumbing, farming, sewing, healing, educating, and also important—she had to know how to defend her family in case of invasion at any time—just to name a few. The woman in charge of the home during that time was viewed with much respect, and had many responsibilities in the community as well. For example, our female ancestors were held responsible for organizing the religious social events of the community. Carrying keys on her belt, which unlocked all of the doors in the home and symbolized her power over the household, identified her as mistress of the home. Even when a woman aged and her daughters had children, they were greatly respected amongst the community and were consulted for advice on many occasions. What incredible responsibilities our ancient mothers held! The testament we have to their success in these roles is the fact that we are here, existing now. They kept their families safe and cared for, and to call them simple housewives is disrespectful to their accomplishments, which ultimately are every one of us. We should all be proud to have had such strong matriarchs, who have kept the blood of our ancestors running through thousands of generations.

I remember reading a theory once which claimed that the proof that our ancestors did not value women was that when under attack the enemy would often seek the death of the women and children first, the idea being because they were the "weakest" and easiest to kill. This is a complete misinterpretation of historical facts. The reason that the enemy would seek the death of the women and children first and foremost is because, if they were capable of killing them all, this would guarantee the end of posterity for the clan and would result in its extinction. It is mentioned in Tacitus' *Germania* that just the thought of their women and children being captured made the warriors fight even harder. Women represented the future of the clan and needed to be safeguarded at all costs.

Since the beginning of our folk, our women have been associated with the power of life and it's endless circle of creation. This most obviously being due to the fact that women carry children, but there were many other reasons as well. The driving force of the universe has been nicknamed Mother Nature (often compared with Frigga), as she is the All-Mother, who brings forth life to us all. Women have a natural tendency to turn all that we deal with into something positive and good. We generally have a kind disposition and want to see people cared for and happy more than anything else. Our benevolence is not a fault, though in ancient times this was reserved for her family and tribe, and it has been greatly manipulated during the conversion from a Tribal society to a Universalist one.

I believe one of the major factors in how the woman's role was blurred through our folk's historical line is through the sudden lack of community support. The tribes that our ancestors formed were vital keys to either their survival or demise. Teutonic families were usually composed of two generations living in a home, and everyone pulled their share of the burden, including children. This was beneficial for many reasons—the more hands in the household the more help there was, so the family in general would be better off. This is why in our ancestors' time having many children was not considered a burden at all; it was considered a blessing from the Gods! The older children, grandmothers, and the community in general helped raise the smaller children at the time; the community was not just the neighbor you waved to on occasion, it was a team of individuals that cared for each other and worked as a tribe, with each other and for each other. This was also smart because ensuring that your neighbor would survive would ultimately lead to a better chance for your family's survival. This is how our ancestors managed to thrive, with extremely large families, for thousands of years.

The major setback for our women was during the conversion of Europe by the Roman Empire to Christianity. Suddenly our strong, independent, intelligent women were ordered to sit back, be quiet, be submissive to their husbands and accept any lifestyle he deemed fit for her. There was a dramatic shift in the roles one held in the bond of marriage, where once husband and wife were equal partners, now the woman was deemed less worthy than the man. This arrangement is not uncommon in Middle Eastern culture, where one does not need to look far to see how women are treated in these societies even today.

Christianity's holy book, the Bible, is a prime example of how women are generally depicted in this faith. The only woman with a role in the New Testament was Mary Magdalene, who was a prostitute! Even worse, the Old Testament is filled with stories that depict women as temptresses and traitors. According to the Bible, the root of all human evil began with Eve, who not only damned humanity to pain and suffering but then tricked her husband into doing the same. Then, a few chapters later we learn about Job's wife who ridiculed him in his time of need; then Jezebel, the evil ruler who tried to kill prophets; and Delilah, who cut off Samson's hair during his slumber and rid him of his strength…these are only a few examples; the list goes on and on!

What a difference these stories are from our lore, which depicts the Goddesses as beautiful, kind, loyal deities who were good natured and granted gifts of wealth and love to all. A story of Freyja comes to mind, who lost her beloved husband Svipdag-Óð and circled the universe in a desperate attempt to find him, and cried tears of gold out of heartache. While our lore states that the first humans, Ask and Embla, were equally created from trees and given equal gifts by the gods, the Christian doctrine implied that man was created in God's image, then a small part of him was taken later on to form his wife. Such drastic ideological differences are so prevalent, it truly is no wonder that it took the Roman Empire hundreds of years of tyranny and suffering to convert Northern Europeans into their doctrine. Our women went from strong community leaders to sullen, un-empowered objects that didn't have a choice in how they ran their families, or how they were treated by their spouses.

In the middle of the 20th century, women finally had enough and decided they were long due some of their rights back. It isn't surprising that this caused extreme hostility within the home and led to a major deterioration of the family structure. Though the revolutionary women's movement has done some great things to re-establish our valued status, we still have a long ways to go before regaining the stature we held in the prime of our folk history.

As for additional roles that Teutonic women played in the community that should be resurfaced today, history shows that before the mass conversion women were the ones responsible for healing and medicine/potions in the community and served in the role as doctors and midwives. Later, the church placed men into the positions they believed deserved social status, such as priests and doctors—women were forbidden to practice these roles and those who continued acting as midwives were the first to be labeled as "witches" and would usually be put to death. But for millennia before that, women held the roles of healers in the community. It is assumed that they handed down books of recipes of personal herbal remedies throughout generations, so mothers could aid their families in the healing process, and some of these remedies are still utilized today (this is without a doubt linked to the "witch's book of evil spells" we read about). There is also supporting evidence which shows that the more experienced women in the community helped the younger mothers with child care issues, household advice, and even showed some of them how to use the rhythm method for birth control. This is obviously a part of our female instinct and there is no reason why women shouldn't do our best to revive those traditions today.

The history of our women across the ages also acknowledges our special connection with nature. I'm sure that any woman reading this can remember some kind of technique a motherly figure in their life used to help their body heal faster. Your mother usually knew just what to do to cure your cold, or sore throat, or upset stomach. For example, I remember when I was a child my grandmother told me that if I were to ever get stung by a bee, the best thing to do would be to put a little honey on it. This alleviates the swelling and helps with the pain, and is a down to earth, simple solution for a common event. So this female instinct truly has never died, it was only suppressed for a long while. Nothing will make a mother feel more content than watching their child slowly gain their strength back after being weakened physically by a virus or injury. Northern European women everywhere need to work towards re-discovering this calling and acting independently of the medical corporations whose focus is solely on making a profit. If I were to bring my child to a modern-day physician after being stung by a bee, most likely the doctor would prescribe some kind of chemical, which they might only recommend because they own stock in the manufacturer. The media has played such a fine tune in making our mothers doubt their own instincts, and corporations have teams of individuals dedicated to convincing us that we need to believe their hype and purchase their products if we really do care about our children. A wise woman always needs to remember that our capitalist society isn't based on ANY kind of community; it is centered around businesses, whose sole intent is to make us distrust our ancestral instincts, all just so they can make money.

Now of course in some cases medications are necessary due to the deadly illnesses and ailments that have developed from simple bugs to mega-viruses (since they have become resistant to the antibodies). If you think about it, an antibacterial soap kills 99% of germs generally. But the 1% that is left behind is usually a super germ that is too strong to be eliminated. These super bugs left behind on surfaces multiply, and what you end up with is an army of germs that are impossible to destroy using solvents. The truth is that germs in small doses have never hurt us; in most cases our bodies will fight them off and our immune system will become stronger to fight the bigger ones because of it. Our female ancestors knew that, but of course they didn't have the media preying on their insecurities the way we do now. The commercials that exploit women's fears of their children becoming sick will try to convince us that this is because we didn't use a certain type of product. This is just corporate manipulation. Keeping a tidy home is definitely important, but making our own natural solvents the way our ancestors did is truly the best way to upkeep a home. This is the least harmful to our family and won't have any adverse effects on nature. My personal rule is, if I can't pronounce an ingredient or I don't know what it is, I won't spray it on a surface my children could eat off of and ingest it. If you have become spoiled and enjoy the particular smell of say, lemons in a cleaner, then it is simple to make a base solvent and add some lemon juice to it. Somewhere along the lines we obviously have lost touch with nature, as she has provided all kinds of solutions for our ailments and for the upkeep of our homes in every respect, and it is our duty to her to look at natural alternatives before resorting to chemically infused, pre-packaged products. We need to always remember that we are not above nature; we are a part of it. Nature has always cared for us in the past and will continue to do so.

The issue of childbirth is one of the major events that I believe has been corrupted the most in our recent history. In our pre-Christian society, a pregnant woman was viewed as being the closest to our Mother Earth as humanly possible, and she was considered in complete harmony with nature and was thus at the peak of her female intuition. When a woman went into labor, the community of women came together and assisted her by massaging her, chanting and even dancing around her. This was considered a celebration of life and everyone's aim was to make the mother as comfortable as possible. What a contrast from when the male-dominated authorities took over, and women began giving birth in hospitals surrounded by surgical tools and a sterile, cold environment. Delivery was never treated as an illness in the time of our ancestors, but rather a joyous, natural event. Our ancestral spirit still resides in us today, as we are still the same folk. As long as we give nature a chance, the gentle hands of our female soul will guide us along. We don't need to always believe a doctor in a white coat simply because society tells us to. Our instincts kept our folk living on for thousands of years; we need to learn how to trust them again.

The drastic change in views on childbirth are not surprising really, as our Christian counterparts view this as a punishment from their male god, which all females must suffer from due to the lack of self control of the woman who had 'sex' to give us life! We must also consider the notion that the virgin Mary was to be revered because she was capable of giving birth without having sex, which is completely unnatural. It's no wonder that recent generations have no idea how to give birth anymore; we have suppressed almost all of our natural instincts on this for hundreds of years. During that time we have been made frightened by childbirth, informed it is dangerous, and needed to be under the strict supervision of a team of medical experts. Thankfully, some progress has been made in recent decades, as birthing centers and the aid of midwives are on the rise again. Though delivering at home was the only option for our mothers, we can certainly use medical advancements to our benefit by using a birth center or having the proper emergency resources available to us in order to make the delivery as safe for the baby and mother as possible.

There are many options for Teutonic women who want to aid their natural childbirth. Meditation is an amazing tool to help deal with pain, which should be exercised all during the pregnancy. A pregnant woman should take the time to honor Frigga, our patron mother who aids women in childbirth. It would also be respectful to hold a ceremony for the Norns and ask for their blessings in delivering a healthy child. Most importantly, one must remember that our faith focuses on personal evolution and wisdom, so it is imperative to read as much as you can about childbirth and aid yourself in being the most resourceful mom that you possibly can be for one of the most important days of your life!

It is also important to make the baby as comfortable as possible during his/her stay inside your body. Your child is bonded with you, so every emotion that you feel, he/she feels as well. Any expectant mother will tell you that when a sudden, loud noise occurs, you can feel the baby jump in surprise. The best way to keep your baby relaxed is to stay calm and relaxed yourself. Experiment with aromatherapy, listen to soothing music, and try not to get upset to the point of yelling, ever. The last thing you want your baby to feel is sad or frightened; avoiding such is a primal instinct for a woman. The same goes for when the infant is born. Many women today are having water births, as in times past, and most will say that they find the experience to be extremely relaxing for themselves and for the little one. Our ancestors did this all the time and well attested its effectiveness. Try to put yourself in the place of your child—in complete darkness, swimming in fluid, and muffled noises all around since you came to be. As traumatic as the birthing experience is for the mother, it is even worse for the baby, for at least the mother is aware of what is going on! By putting yourself in the place of the baby, would you really want to bring them into the world in a room with bright lights, loud noises, and a man in a big green outfit, sporting a surgical mask, as the first thing you see? That sounds quite traumatic doesn't it? The first thing that a new person should feel is the warmth of the mother's body, the first smell he/she should experience should be that of his/her mother's skin. This will do both the baby and the mother good, and they can recuperate from this traumatic experience together. Of course, in some instance medical intervention is necessary, and since these options are available to us now we should never jeopardize the life of the mother or child. However, I believe too much emphasis is put on assuming that you have no other option but to head to the emergency room simply because you are contracting, when there is no real signal for distress and this is simply nature running its course.

A woman should always consider breastfeeding as well, simply for no other reason than this is obviously how our Mother Nature is providing food for your baby. Breast milk is filled with vitamins, minerals, and important antibodies your baby is unable to receive from manufactured formula. There is nothing shameful about breastfeeding, it is a natural provision for the baby, and if anyone around you is uncomfortable with this act it is solely their problem and nothing for us to concern ourselves with. Look at the animal kingdom, all mammals breastfeed their offspring! We are objects of nature, and even though we live in a technologically advanced world, that fact remains the same and always will. Breast milk is the healthiest thing for your child to receive nutrition from, and it is also the easiest for them to digest. Recent studies have even linked formula use to the epidemic of childhood obesity. The only thing that is important is the best nutrition for your baby. Does anything else matter more than that?

Another important aspect of the Teutonic woman was that of the warrior. In this day and age it may feel like women have nothing at all to do with war, but this certainly is not always the case. History shows that Germanic women used to fight alongside their husbands in battle, and our sources often depict women having important roles when it came to times of war. The most obvious are the Valkyries, females entities of war, trained and ready to assist in battle at any time. There is even proof that women fought along with their husbands in the ranks of war, such as is seen in Saxo's *Historia Danica* Book 5, where Gunvara (who is Freyja) stands by Erik's (Svipdag-Ód's) side and fights with him in battle. There are also many other female warriors found in this text, such as Alvild, a maiden who ravages the seas as a pirate, and led a band of women in her campaigns (*Saxo* Book 7) and Ladgerda, who was "a skilled female fighter, who bore a man's temper in a girl's body, with locks flowing loose over her shoulders she would do battle in the forefront of the most valiant warriors." (*Saxo* Book 9). It has also been documented that, if women were not in combat themselves, they would often sit on the sidelines of war to cheer their husbands and fathers on, and the cheering was such a driving force for the men that they would usually virtually annihilate their opponents. This is where the modern concept of cheerleading originates from, as organized sport is actually mock warfare. Besides these facts, Germanic women were also said to have helped their sons learn the laws of battle when the fathers were away, and the mother would give her son his first shield and sword when they celebrated the beginning of the boy's journey into manhood.

Now of course, this was a different era and these types of scenarios wouldn't be applicable in our day and age, but the fact that women are strong entities more than capable of defending themselves and their families rings true even today. In order for men to be productive providers for their families, they need support and praise from their spouses, in the same ways that men need to support women in their choices for the family. Relationships worked because they were reciprocal and each had a need the other filled. Besides the power of the female persuasion, women have also been noted for their physical capabilities as well. There is the story of the woman who's child was under a car, her adrenaline took over and she was able to lift the car which was dozens of times her own weight, and saved her young child's life. Women are also protectors of their family, and this is one example of the strength within us and what lengths we will go to protect them. This protectiveness and might is a trait of a warrior in itself. However, it is our duty to take this a step further. If an intruder broke into your home in the middle of the night, would you have the wits and the physical strength to protect yourself and your family? If a man assaulted you while you were walking to your car, would you be capable of fighting him off? The ancient day perils of warfare don't exist for us any more, but these every day threats certainly do and we need to be realistic about them, as well as ready for them at any time. While we cannot stop bad things from happening to us, we certainly can do our best to be prepared for them, mentally and physically. There are various tools available for us in this regard, such as self-defense classes for women organized through Martial Arts schools and through local police departments. Some women enjoy sports such as boxing or even wrestling. Also, by continuing our quest in the Odinist lifestyle, by constantly evolving and working towards self-enlightenment, our wits will always be about us, and we will be more adept at handling situations. We are important enough, our families are important enough for us to commit ourselves to this. We owe this to both ourselves and to them.

It truly hurts me when I see mothers that are at their wits end because no matter how hard they try, they cannot seem to do it all for their families. As we covered earlier, in ancient times the entire family and community helped raise children, and nowadays it isn't even clear how a woman is supposed to act or what roles she should hold. We have burst through the chains that held us down for so long, so it is only natural that now we are at a stage where we ask ourselves: 'Where do I fit in now?' Women naturally have a generous disposition, so we can often find ourselves trying to do it all in a society where the role of the housewife is generally viewed without any kind of social status (when it is indeed the most important job there is!). This is understandably frustrating and disheartening. It is our duty, as women, to assist our fellow kinswomen in any way that we can, and try to re-establish the concept of community that our predecessors held so dear. We should find strength from our mothers and try to learn from the roles they held, before they were brutally distorted by the authorities of an alien faith. Since we are returning to our native roots, the conversion back to our natural ways is an easy one that just requires an open mind and determination. The goddesses and Norns are always there for us, we are their daughters and they will respond if we are sincere in our requests for assistance. We naturally want to be good wives and mothers. Men and women are very different, but these differences are what bring us together. One balances the other out, and this creates true role models for the children. The fact that our ancestral religion is coming back to light again shows us that the spirit of our folk never died, it was merely hidden for a while. The tribal aspect is returning to us in many ways, such as with the women's movement, with alternative medicines making a rise again, with tattoos, artistic expressions, etc. We need to embrace this calling from our ancestral spirit.

We are returning to our natural, vital ways and this is a wonderful experience we must welcome with open arms.

Special thanks to Kathy Metzger.

APPENDIX B

The Hávamál

The following poem is *the* most sacred writing known in the Ásatrú faith, which serves as the core foundation for much of the philosophy in this book. These are the words of Óðin, giving us wisdom and practical advice as a father to his children. Often times you can read a verse several times and get a new understanding each time. There are verses that contain words particular to our religion which new readers might not be familiar with. In such cases I would refer to the catalog of terms or glossary in the back of this book. The translation is based upon those of several interpreters, including Viktor Rydberg, Benjamin Thorpe, Henry Adams Bellows, and Lee M. Hollander, set in an easy to read format.

1. All doorways
Should be looked into
Before going forward;
For it is difficult to know
Where foes may sit
Within a dwelling.

2. Hail the generous ones!
A guest has come in:
Where shall he sit?
He is in much haste,
Who has to prove
himself by the fire.

3. Warmth is needed
For he who has come in,
And whose knees are frozen;

Food and clothing
A man requires
Who fares over mountains.

4. Water is needed
For him who comes to feast,
A towel and hospitable invitation,
A kindly reception,
If he can get it,
Discourse and answer.

5. He needs his wits,
The wanderer who travels far:
At home all is easy.
He is a laughing-stock
Who lacks words to speak
When he sits among the learned.

6. No one should be proud
Of their understanding,
But rather be cautious in conduct.
When the wise and silent
Come to a dwelling,
Harm seldom befalls the cautious;
For no man will ever have
A firmer friend
Than great sagacity.

7. The wary guest
Who comes to the feast
Keeps a cautious silence;
He listens with his ears,
Seeks with his eyes,
So the wise man observes.

8. Happy is the man
Who obtains for himself
Honor and good reputation:
Less sure is that
Which a man must have
In another's breast.

9. Happy is the man
Who holds in himself
Honor and wisdom in living;
For bad counsels
Have often been received
From another's breast.

10. A better burden
No man bears on the way
Than good sense and manners;
That is thought better than riches
In a strange place,
And it gives a refuge in grief.

11. A better burden
No man bears on the way
Than good sense and manners;
A worse provision
He cannot carry on the way
Than too much beer-bibbing.

12. For beer is not,
As it is said,
Good for the sons of men;
For the more he drinks
The less control he has
Of his own mind.

13. The heron of oblivion,
Which steals one's wit
Hovers over the *sumble*.
I was fettered
With this bird's fetters
In Gunnlöd's dwelling.

14. I was drunk,
Very drunk
At cunning Fjálar's;
It's the best *sumble*
When each gets home
Retaining sense and reason.

15. Wise and silent,
And daring in war,
Should a king's children be;
Everyone should be
Joyous and generous
Until his hour of death.

16. A cowardly man
Thinks he will live forever
If he avoids the fight;
But old age will
Give him no peace,
Though spears may spare him.

17. A fool gapes
When he comes to a house,
He mutters to himself or is silent;
But all at once,
If he takes a drink,
Then is a man's mind displayed.

18. Only he is aware,
Who wanders wide
And has experienced much;
By what disposition
Each man is ruled,
Who possesses common sense.

19. Do not shun the mead,
Yet drink moderately,
Speak sensibly or be silent.
None will hold you
To be uncivil
If you retire to bed early.

20. A greedy man,
If he is not moderate,
Eats to his mortal sorrow.
Oftentimes his belly
Makes a joke of a silly man,
Who sits among the wise.

21. Cattle know
When to go home
And then cease from grazing;
But a foolish man
Never knows
His stomach's measure.

22. A miserable man
With ill-conditioning
Sneers at everything:
One thing he does not know,
Which he should know,
Is that he is not free of faults.

23. A foolish man
Is awake all night,
Pondering everything;
He is tired
When morning breaks
And nothing has changed.

24. A foolish man
Thinks all who smile at him
Are his friends;
He does not realize it,
Though they speak ill of him,
When he sits among the clever.

25. A foolish man
Thinks all who smile at him
Are his friends;
But he will find,
When he comes to the *Thing*,
That he has few advocates.

26. A foolish man
Thinks himself all-wise
If placed in unexpected difficulty,
But he does not know what to answer
If he is put to the test.

27. A foolish man
Who comes among people
Had best be silent;
For no one knows
That he knows nothing
Unless he talks too much.
He who previously knew nothing,

Will still know nothing,
If he talks ever so much.

28. He thinks himself wise,
Who can ask questions
And converse as well;
No one can
Conceal his ignorance,
Because it circulates among men.

29. He who is never silent
Utters too many
Futile words;
A babbling tongue,
If it is not checked,
Often sings to its own harm.

30. Do not mock another
Who comes among your kin,
Although he is a stranger in your home.
Many a one thinks himself wise,
If he is not questioned,
And can sit in a dry habit.

31. He thinks himself clever,
The guest who insults guest,
If he takes to flight.
Certainly he does not know,
He who chatters at the feast,
Whether he babbles among foes.

32. Many men are mutually
well-disposed,
Yet will torment each other
At the table.

That strife will ever be,
Guest will irritate guest.

33. A man should often
take early meals,
Unless he goes to a friend's house;
Else he will sit and mope,
Will seem half-famished,
And can inquire on few things.

34. The way to a bad friend's
Is crooked and far,
Though he lives by the road;
But the paths lie direct
To a good friend's,
Though he is far away.

35. A guest should depart,
Not always stay
In one place:
The welcome becomes unwelcome
If he continues too long
In another's house.

36. One's own house is best,
Though it is small;
Everyone is his own master at home.
Though he has but two-goats
And a straw-thatched cot,
Even that is better than begging.

37. One's own house is best,
Though it is small;
Everyone is his own master at home.
He is bleeding at heart

Who has to ask
For food at every meal-tide.

38. Leaving his arms in the field,
Let no man go
A foot's length forward;
For it is hard to know,
When on his way,
A man may need his weapon.

39. I have never found a man
So bountiful or so hospitable
That he refused a present;
Or of his property
So generous
That he scorned a recompense.

40. Of the property
Which he has gained
No man should suffer need;
For often what was intended for the dear
Is spared for the hated;
Much goes worse than is expected.

41. Friends should gladden each other
With arms and vestments,
As each can see for himself.
Givers and requiters
Are friends longest,
If all else goes well.

42. To his friend
A man should be a friend,
And requite gifts with gifts;
Men should receive

Laughter with laughter,
But leasing with lying.

43. To his friend
A man should be a friend,
To him and to his friend;
But of his foe
No man shall be
His friend's friend.

44. Know if you have a friend
Whom you fully trust,
And would get good from him,
You should blend your mind with his,
And exchange gifts,
And go to see him often.

45. If there is another
Whom you trust little,
Yet could get good from him,
You should speak fairly of him,
But think falsely,
And pay a lie for a lie.

46. But yet further of him
Whom you trust little,
And you suspect his affection,
You should laugh before him,
And speak contrary to your thoughts;
The gifts should resemble requital.

47. I was once young,
I was traveling alone
And lost my way;
I thought myself rich

When I met another:
Man is the joy of man.

48. Generous and brave
Men live best,
They seldom cherish sorrow;
But a cowardly man
Dreads everything;
The miser is uneasy even at gifts.

49. In the field I gave
My garments to
The two tree-people (Ask & Embla):
Heroes they seemed to themselves
When they got clothes.
The naked man is embarrassed.

50. A tree standing
On a hill-top withers;
Neither bark nor leaves protect it:
Such is the man
Whom no one favors;
Why should he live long?

51. Hotter than fire
Does friendship burn for five days
Between false friends;
When the sixth day comes
The fire cools
And all the love is ended.

52. Something great
Is not always to be given,
Often little will purchase praise;
With half a loaf

And a half-drained cup
I got myself a comrade.

53. Little are the sand grains,
Little the wits,
Little the minds of men;
For all men
Are not wise alike:
Men are everywhere by halves.

54. Each one should be
Moderately wise,
But never over-wise;
Fairest are the lives
Of those men
Who know much well.

55. Each one should be
Moderately wise,
But never over-wise;
For a wise-man's heart
Is seldom glad,
If he is all-wise who owns it.

56. Each one should be
Moderately wise,
But not over-wise:
Let no man know
His *örlög* beforehand;
His mind will be freest from care.

57. Brand burns from brand
Until it is burnt out,
Fire is quickened from fire:
Man to man

Becomes known by speech,
But a fool by his bashful silence.

58. He should rise early
Who desires to have
Another's life or property:
A sluggish wolf
Seldom gets prey,
Or a sleeping man victory.

59. He should rise early,
Who has few workers,
And go to see to his work;
Much remains undone
For the morning-sleeper:
Wealth half depends on energy.

60. A man knows the measure
Of dry planks
And roof shingles;
Of the firewood
That may suffice
Both measure and time.

61. Let a man ride to the *Thing*
Washed and fed,
Although his garments are not too good;
Let no one be ashamed
Of his shoes and pants,
Nor of his horse,
Although he have not a good one.

62. All who will be known as sage
Must be ready
To question and answer.
Let only one know,

A second may not;
If three, all the world knows.

63. When the eagle comes over
The ancient sea,
He gasps and gapes;
So is a man
Who comes among many
And has few advocates.

64. Every wise man
Should use his power
With discretion;
For he will find
When he comes among the bold,
That no one alone is bravest.

65. Every man should be
Watchful and wary
And cautious in trusting friends;
Of the words
That a man says to another
He often pays the penalty.

66. I came to many places
Much too early,
But too late to others;
The beer was drunk,
Or not ready:
The disliked seldom hit the moment.

67. Here and there I should
Have been invited
If I had needed a meal;
Or had hung two hams

At that true friend's
Where I had eaten only one.

68. Fire is best
Among the sons of men,
And the sight of the sun,
If a man can
Have his health,
With a life free from vice.

69. No man lacks everything,
Although his health is bad:
One is happy in his sons,
One in his kin,
One in abundant wealth,
One in his good works.

70. It is better to live,
Even to live miserably;
A living man can get a cow.
I saw fire consume
The rich man's property,
And death stood before his door.

71. The lame can ride on horseback,
The one-handed drive cattle;
The deaf, fight and be useful:
To be blind is better
Than to be burnt (on the pyre):
No one gets good from a corpse.

72. A son is better,
Even if born late,
After his father's death;
Memorial stones seldom

Stand by the road,
Unless raised by kinsman to kinsman.

73. The two are adversaries:
The tongue is the bane of the head:
Under every cloak
I expect a fist.

74. He whose fare is enough
Welcomes the night,
(the yards of a ship are short);
Uneasy are autumn nights;
Many are the weather's changes
In a week,
But more in a month.

75. He who knows nothing
Does not know
That many a one apes another.
One man is rich,
Another poor:
Let him not be thought blameworthy.

76. Your cattle shall die,
Your kindred shall die,
You yourself shall die;
But the fair fame
Of him who has earned it
Never dies.

77. Your cattle shall die,
Your kindred shall die,
You yourself shall die;
One thing I know

Which never dies:
The judgment on each one dead.

78. I saw full storehouses
At Fitjung's sons:
Now they bear the beggar's staff.
Such are riches,
As is the twinkling of an eye:
They are the most fickle of friends.

79. If a foolish man
Acquires wealth
Or a woman's love,
Pride grows within him
But never wisdom:
He goes on more and more arrogant.

80. Thus it comes to be,
If you question him of runes,
Those known to the high ones,
Which the great powers invented,
And which Fimbulthul (Mímir) painted
That he had best keep silent.

81. The day is to be praised at eve,
A woman after she is burnt (on the pyre),
A sword after it is proved,
A maid after she is married,
Ice after it has been crossed,
Beer after it is drunk.

82. One should chop wood in the wind,
Row out to sea in a breeze,
Talk with a girl in the dark,
The eyes of day are many.
Voyages are to be made in a ship,

But a shield is for protection,
A sword for striking,
But a damsel for a kiss.

83. One should drink beer by the fire,
Slide on the ice,
Buy a horse that is lean,
A sword that is rusty;
Feed a horse at home,
But a dog at the farm.

84. No one should put faith
In a maiden's words,
Nor in what a woman says;
For their hearts have been fashioned
On a turning wheel
And their breasts formed fickle.

85. In a creaking bow,
A burning flame,
A yawning wolf,
A chattering crow,
A grunting swine,
A rootless tree,
A waxing wave,
A boiling kettle.

86. A flying dart,
A falling wave,
A one-night's ice,
A coiled serpent,
A woman's pillow-talk,
Or a broken sword,

A bear's play
Or a royal child,

87. A sick calf,
A self-willed thrall,
A flattering *vala*,
A newly slain corpse,
A serene sky,
A laughing lord,
A barking dog,
And a harlot's grief,

88. An early sown field,
Let no one trust,
Nor prematurely in a son:
Weather rules the field
And wit the son,
Each of which is doubtful.

89. A brother's murderer,
Though met on the high road,
A half-burnt house,
An over swift horse
(a horse is useless
With a broken leg):
No man is so confiding
As to trust any of these.

90. Such is the love of women
Who meditate falsehood,
As if one drove unroughshod
On slippery ice,
A spirited two-year-old
And unbroken horse;
Or as in a raging storm

A helmless ship is beaten;
Or as if the lame were set to catch
A reindeer in the thawing mountain.

91. I now speak openly,
Because I know both sexes;
Men's minds are unstable towards women;
It is then we speak most fair,
When we think most falsely:
That deceives even the cautious.

92. He who would obtain a woman's love
Shall speak fair,
And offer money.
Praise the form
Of a fair damsel;
He who courts her, gets her.

93. At love no one should
Ever wonder
At another:
A joyous fair image
Often captivates the wise,
Which does not captivate the foolish.

94. Let no one wonder at
Another's folly,
It is the lot of many;
All-powerful desire
Makes of the sons of men,
Fools even of the wise.

95. The mind only knows
What lies near the heart,
That alone is conscious of our affections.
To a sensible man

No disease is worse
Than to not be content with himself.

96. I experienced that
When I sat in the reeds
Awaiting my delight.
That discreet maiden was
body and soul to me:
Nevertheless I do not have her.

97. I found Billing's lass (Rind)
On her bed,
The slumbering, sun-white maid.
A prince's joy
Seemed nothing to me,
If I could not live with that form.

98. "You must come, Ódin,
Yet closer to evening,
If you would win the maiden over;
All will be disastrous
Unless we alone
Should know of such misdeeds."

99. I returned,
Thinking to love
At her wise desire;
I thought
I should obtain
Her whole heart and love.

100. When I came next,
The warriors (Varnians) were
All awake,
With lights burning,

And bearing torches,
Thus was the path to pleasure closed.

101. But at the approach of morn,
When I came again,
All the household was sleeping;
I found the good
Damsel's dog alone,
Tied to the bed.

102. Many fair maids,
When rightly known,
Are fickle toward men:
I experienced that
When I strove to seduce
That discreet maiden:
That crafty maid
Heaped every kind
Of insolence upon me,
And naught I had of her.

103. Let a man be cheerful at home,
And generous toward a guest;
He should be of wise conduct,
Of good memory and ready speech;
If he desires much knowledge,
He must often discuss what is good.
He is called Fimbulfambi ("The Great Fool")
Who has little to say:
Such is the nature of the simple.

104. I sought the ancient Jötun (Fjálar),
Now I have returned:
Little I got there by silence;
In many words

I spoke to my advantage
In Suttung's halls.

105. On the golden seat
Gunnlöd gave me
A draught of the precious mead;
I later gave her a bad return
For her whole soul,
Her fervent love.

106. Rati's (Heimdall's) mouth
Made room for my passage,
And gnawed a passage through the stone;
The paths of the giants were
Above and below me,
I risked my head so rashly.

107. I reaped great advantage
From the well-changed image:
Few things fail the wise,
For Odroerir
Has been brought up
To men's earthly dwellings.

108. It is doubtful to me
That I could have come
From the Jötun's courts,
Had Gunnlöd not aided me;
I won the heart of that good woman,
Whom I took in my embrace.

109. On the following day
The Hrímthurses came
To learn of the high union,
In the hall of the high union;
They asked of Bölverk (Ódin),

Were he back among the gods,
Or had Suttung (Fjálar) destroyed him?

110. I believe Ódin
Gave a ring-oath,
Who will trust in his troth?
Suttung is deceived,
His sumble stolen,
And Gunnlöd cries for her lost kinsman!

111. It is time to talk
From the sage's seat.
I sat silently
By Urdabrunnr:
I saw and meditated,
I listened to men's words.
I heard runes spoken of,
And of divine things,
Nor were they silent on risting them,
Nor of sage counsels,
At the High One's hall,
In the High One's hall.
I thus heard say:

112. I counsel you, Loddfáfnir (Hödur),
To heed advice;
You will profit if you take it.
Do not rise at night,
Unless to explore,
Or would fare to the outhouse.

113. I counsel you, Loddfáfnir,
To heed advice;
You will profit if you take it.
You should not sleep

In the embrace of an enchantress—(Gullveig),
So she will not enclose you in her arms.

114. She will make it so
That you care little
For the *Thing* or prince's words;
Meal's and men's merriment
Will not please you,
And you will go to sleep sorrowful.

115. I counsel you, Loddfáfnir,
To heed advice;
You will profit if you take it.
Never entice
Another's wife—(Nanna)
To secret converse.

116. I counsel you, Loddfáfnir,
To heed advice;
You will profit if you take it.
If you have to travel
By mountain or sea,
Provide yourself with plenty of food.

117. I counsel you, Loddfáfnir,
To heed advice;
You will profit if you take it.
Never let
A bad man
Know your misfortunes;
For from a bad man
You will never receive repayment
For a kind heart.

118. I saw a wicked woman's
Words mortally

Wound a man;
A false tongue
Caused his death,
And most unrighteously.

119. I counsel you, Loddfáfnir,
To heed advice;
You will profit if you take it.
If you know you have a friend
Whom you can fully trust,
Go to visit him often;
For the way that no one treads
Is overgrown with brushwood
And high grass.

120. I counsel you, Loddfáfnir,
To heed advice;
You will profit if you take it.
Find a good man
To hold in friendship,
And learn to make yourself loved.

121. I counsel you, Loddfáfnir,
To heed advice;
You will profit if you take it.
Never be
First to quarrel
With your friend.
Care gnaws the heart
If you can disclose
Your whole mind to no one.

122. I counsel you, Loddfáfnir,
To heed advice;
You will profit if you take it.

You should never
Exchange words
With a weak-minded fool.

123. For you will never get
A return for good
From an ill-conditioned man;
But a good man will
Bring you favor
By his praise.

124. There is a mingling of affection,
Where one can tell
Another all his mind.
Everything is better
Than being with the deceitful.
He is not another's friend
Whoever says as he says.

125. I counsel you, Loddfáfnir,
To heed advice;
You will profit if you take it.
Even in three words
Do not quarrel with a worse man:
Often, the better yields,
When the worse strikes.

126. I counsel you, Loddfáfnir,
To heed advice,
You will profit if you take it.
Be not a shoemaker,
Nor a shaft maker,
Unless it is for yourself;
For a shoe if ill-made

Or a shaft if crooked,
Will call down evil on you.

127. I counsel you, Loddfáfnir,
To heed advice;
You will profit if you take it.
Wherever you hear of harm,
Regard that harm as your own;
And give your foes no peace.

128. I counsel you, Loddfáfnir,
To heed advice;
You will profit if you take it.
Never find joy
In evil,
But let good bring you pleasure.

129. I counsel you, Loddfáfnir,
To heed advice;
You will profit if you take it.
Do not look up
In a battle,
(The sons of men become
Like swine),
So men may not enchant you.

130. I counsel you, Loddfáfnir,
To heed advice;
You will profit if you take it.
If you induce a good woman
To pleasant converse,
You must promise fair,
And hold to it:
No one turns from good, if it can be got.

131. I counsel you, Loddfáfnir,
To heed advice;
You will profit if you take it.
I bid you to be wary,
But not over-wary;
Be most wary at drinking,
And with another's wife;
And thirdly,
That thieves do not trick you.

132. I counsel you, Loddfáfnir,
To heed advice;
You will profit if you take it.
Never treat
A guest or traveler
With insult or ridicule;
They who sit within
Often know little
Of what race they are who come.

133. The sons of men bear
Vices and virtues
Mingled in their breasts;
No one is so good
That no failing attends him,
Nor so bad as to be good for nothing.

134. I counsel you, Loddfáfnir,
To heed advice;
You will profit if you take it.
Never scorn
The gray-haired speaker,
Often the old speak good;
Often skillful counsels
Come from the shriveled skin,

Though it hang with the hides,
And flap with the pelts,
And is blown with the bellies.

135. I counsel you, Loddfáfnir,
To heed advice;
You will profit if you take it.
Do not berate a guest,
Nor push him away from your gate;
Treat the poor well,
They will speak well of you.

136. The bar is strong
That must be raised
To admit all.
Do give a penny,
Or they will call down on you
Every ill on your limbs.

137. I counsel you, Loddfáfnir,
To heed advice;
You will profit if you take it.
Wherever you drink beer,
Invoke the power of earth,
For earth is good against drink,
Fire cures ailments,
The oak for constipation,
A corn-ear for sorcery,
Elder for domestic strife.
Against the Heiptir invoke the moon,
The biter is good for bite-injuries;
But runes against calamity;
Let earth absorb fluid.

138. These songs, Loddfáfnir,
You will long lack;
Yet it may be good
If you understand them,
Profitable if you learn them.

139. I know that I hung
Nine nights
On the wind-tossed tree,
Wounded by my spear,
Given to Ódin,
Myself given to myself;
On that tree
Of which no one knows
From what root it springs.

140. No one gave me bread,
Nor a horn of drink,
I peered downward,
I took up the runes,
Wailing I learned them,
Then fell down thence.

141. I obtained nine *fimbul-songs*
From Bölthorn's (Ymir's), Bestla's father's,
Celebrated son (Mímir),
And I got a drink
Of the precious mead
Drawn from Odroerir.

142. Then I began to quicken,
And to become wise,
And to grow and to prosper;
Each word I sought
Resulted in a new word;

Each deed I sought
Resulted in a new deed.

143. You will find runes,
And explained characters,
Very powerful characters,
Very potent characters,
Which Fimbulthul (Mímir) drew,
And the oldest powers made,
And Ódin risted.

144. By Ódin for the Aesir,
By Dáinn for the Álfar,
And by Dvalin for the Dwarves,
Asvinr (Mímir) risted runes for the Jötuns,
Some I risted myself.

145. Know you how to rist them?
Know you how to interpret them?
Know you how to draw them?
Know you how to prove them?
Know you how to pray?
Know you how to offer?
Know you how to sacrifice?
Know you how to consume?

146. It is better not to pray
Than offer too much;
A gift ever looks for a return.
It is better not to send
Than sacrifice too much.
So Thund (Ódin) risted
Before the origin of men,

This he proclaimed
After he came home.

147. I know those songs
Which king's wives do not know,
Nor sons of men.
The first is called Help,
For it will help you
Against strifes and cares.

148. For the second I know,
What the sons of men require,
Who will live as healers.

149. For the third I know,
If I have great need
To restrain my foes,
I deaden the weapon's edge:
Neither my adversaries,
Nor arms nor wiles harm at all.

150. For the fourth I know,
If men place
Bonds on my limbs,
I sing so
That I can walk;
Fetters spring from my feet,
And chains from my hands.

151. For the fifth I know,
If I see a shot from a hostile hand,
A shaft flying amid the host,
It cannot fly so swift,
That I cannot stop it,
If only I get sight of it.

152. For the sixth I know,
If one wounds me
With a green tree's root,
Also if a man
Declares hatred to me,
Harm shall consume them sooner than me.

153. For the seventh I know,
If I see a lofty house
Blaze over those inside,
It shall not burn so furiously
That I cannot save it,
That song I can sing.

154. For the eighth I know,
What to all is
Useful to learn;
Where hatred grows
Among the sons of men—
I can soon set it right.

155. For the ninth I know,
If I stand in need
To save my ship in the water,
I can calm
The wind on the waves,
And lull the sea.

156. For the tenth I know,
If I see demons
Doing mischief in the air,
I can work so
That they will forsake

Their own forms
And their own minds.

157. For the eleventh I know,
If I am to lead those to battle,
Whom I have long held in friendship,
Then I sing under their shields,
And with success they go
Safely to the fight,
Safely from the fight,
Safely on every side they go.

158. For the twelfth I know,
If I see a hanged man's
Corpse in a tree,
Then I can so rist
And draw in runes,
So the man shall walk
And talk with me.

159. For the thirteenth I know,
If I sprinkle water
On a young man,
He shall not fall,
Though he comes into battle:
That man shall not sink before swords.

160. For the fourteenth I know,
If I have to name the gods,
Aesir and Álfar,
In the society of men,
I know them all well,
This few can do unskilled.

161. For the fifteenth I know,
What the dwarf Thjódreyrir sang

Before Delling's door:
Power to the Aesir,
Victory to the Álfar,
And wisdom to Hroptatýr (Ódin).

162. For the sixteenth I know,
If I wish to possess
A modest maiden's favor and affection,
I change the heart
Of the white-armed damsel,
And wholly turn her mind.

163. For the seventeenth I know,
That that young maiden
Will reluctantly avoid me.

164. For the eighteenth I know,
That which I never teach
To maid or wife of man,
(All is better
What one only knows:
This is the closing of the songs)
Save her alone
Who clasps me in her arms,
Or is my sister.

166. Now the High One's (Ódin's) songs
Are sung in the
High One's hall,
All are useful to the sons of men,
But are useless to giants' sons.
Hail to him who has sung them!
Hail to him who knows them!
May he profit who has learned them!
Hail to those who have heard them!

Catalog of Terms

The following is a list of names and words considered sacred in Ásatrú religion, which is intended to serve as a tool for newcomers to become more familiar with our terminology and occasionally express some ideas that will be treated in greater detail elsewhere. Because most of the entries are from the Old Norse (Norroen) language, their pronunciation is offered in parentheses using equivalent sounds in English. Words from other languages will be noted in their particular entry. The etymology will also be offered, when possible, to help in understanding their origin and purpose.

In Old Norse the first syllable of each word is always stressed, as will be seen in the pronunciations below. Stressed syllables will be capitalized in the parentheses. Rather than using the letters "þ" (pronounced "th" as in "thin") and "ð" (pronounced "th" as in father) these are generally replaced with "th" for "þ" and "d" for "ð". The letter "j" is always pronounced as a hard "y" and "f" generally sounds like "v" when it is not at the beginning of a word. The letter "g" is always pronounced hard as in "go", never soft as in "giant". Originally, "h" was pronounced like a "w" sound, as in "where", when placed before consonants, such as in Hladgud, Hnoss, and Hrönn. However, in later linguistic developments this sound was recognized as silent and often the "h" was dropped, so for our purposes here, and for simplicity's sake, it will be given the modern "h" sound, as in "help", before vowels and will be silent before consonants. "G" is also silent when placed before "n", such as in *"gnome"*.

Vowel Sounds

a as "a" in apt
á as "ah" in father
e as "eh" in echo
é as "ee" in see
i as "i" in hit
í as "ee" in see
o as "aw" in law

ó as "oh" in g<u>o</u>

ö as "uh" in b<u>oo</u>k

u as "u" in f<u>u</u>ll

ú as "oo" in f<u>oo</u>d

y as "e" in m<u>e</u> (short)

ý as "ee" in s<u>ee</u> (long)

æ as "ai" in h<u>ai</u>r (written "ae")

œ as "ur" in b<u>ur</u>n (written "oe")

au as "ou" in h<u>ou</u>se

ei as "ay" in p<u>ay</u>

ey as "ay" in p<u>ay</u>

er + ir as "er" in h<u>er</u>

or as "or" in f<u>or</u>

A

A. A. S.—"After Aldland's Sinking" (see "Aldland" below)—Abbreviated A.A.S., this means of observing the passage of years is the only one actually recorded in one of our sources, "*The Oera Linda Book*", whose validity has been the source of some controversy. It is based on the sinking of a sacred land once inhabited by the goddess Freyja and may be identical to Singastein (see). 2006 A.D. = 4199 A.A.S.

Aegir (AI-ger)—"The Frightening", "The Terrible". A sea-giant commissioned to hold a mead feast in his hall every year near the harvest. With his wife Rán he is father to nine giantesses who are personifications of the waves.

Aegishjalm (AI-gis-hyalm)—"Terror-Helm". Originally, this was a mythical helmet worn to inspire fear in one's foes, probably created by Ívaldi's sons as part of the Niflung hoard, then worn by the dragon Fáfnir, and then possibly by Hödur, who obtained it from Fáfnir's hoard, the "Niflung hoard". Later it became a system of symbols of protection, called Aegishjalmar.

Aesir (AI-ser)—"The Gods". The highest of the divine clans; primarily, though not solely, deities of valor and protection.

Aett (AIT, like "eight")—"Family", "Clan". This can be used primarily to designate the clan, as opposed to the "kyn", kin or immediate blood relatives.

Afi (Av-i)—"Grandfather". Husband of Amma and progenitor of the class of Karls or freeborn.

Afrád gjalda (AV-rahd GYAL-da)—"To pay Compensation". The act of righting one's wrongs towards another. Also called Gamban Gylda.

Ái (AH-i, like "eye")—"Great Grandfather". One of the divine artists who worked under Dvalin's, Mímir's son's, guidance. He is thus a "*dwarf*".

Ai (AH-i)—"Great Grandfather". Husband of Edda, the progenitor of the race of Thralls through the patronage of Heimdall.

Aldafödr (AL-da-fuhd-r)—"The Ancient Father". One of Ódin's many names. This signifies him as father of our folk and of the ages.

Aldagaut (AL-da-gout)—"The Ancient Goth". A name of Ódin, signifying him as father of our folk. "*Goth*" was originally an honorific title of the Teutonic people.

Aldland (ALD-land)—Old Frisian. "The Ancient Land". If this land is identical to Singastein it may have sunk because a celestial being (Svipdag) was slain on it. It is likely that this sinking represented the end of "the ancient time" (*ár alda*), the age of mythological events.

Álfar (AHL-var)—"Elves". The third of the Teutonic divine families, who are the Aesir, Vanir and Álfar. To this can be added the higher clan of Jötuns, born of Ymir's arms. The Álfar take on a lower status as demigods when they are born, but this can change. They are the sworn helpers of the gods, the greatest of nature artists and heroes. The males are called "Elf-Defenders" and the females "Dísir of Vegetation". There are several groups of Álfar, mainly divided into three primary factions. The foremost of these is the Ljósálfar or "Light-Elves", who deal with matters concerning the lighting of the sky. To this group belongs Delling, lord of the dawn, his son Dag ("Day") and the sun-dísir. Next is the Landvaettir, "Land-Wights", who protect the forests, streams, homes, etc. on Midgard. The name Álfar is not always bound to a single meaning, at least not in the later sources. There the name extends to the final division, Surt's sons, "The Svartálfar" or "Swarthy-Elves", and there Elves and Dwarves are sometimes confused with one another. These "Swarthy-Elves" are rebels against the gods, allied with the powers of frost.

Álfheim (AHLV-haym)—"Elf-Home". The land of the Álfar, located on the eastern edge of the Underworld (Jörmungrund). Frey, god of the harvest, received Álfheim as a "*tann fé*", a tooth-gift, and consequently became ruler over the Elves.

Álfhild (AHLV-hild)—"Battle-Elf". Originally the name of a sun-dís, probably called this because of her daily struggle with the wolf-giant Sköll.

Amalians (AM-al-i-anz)—"Descendants of Hamal". An ancient tribe celebrated among the Teutons, either identical to or closely connected with Mímir's sons, "The Brísings".

Amma (AM-a)—"Grandmother". The wife of Afi and ancestress of the class of Karls or freeborn.

Ámsvartnir (AHM-svart-ner)—"The Ever-Dark". The sea enveloped in eternal darkness, lying outside Náströnds, in the gulf where Lyngvi-Isle is located. This is where Loki, Fenrir and other sons of Muspel lie imprisoned until Ragnarök.

Ánarr (AH-nar)—"Second", "Other." Another name of Fjörgyn, who fathered the earth-goddess Frigga with Mímir's daughter, Nát. Ánarr-Fjörgyn is a Vana-god and in all probability is identical to Hoenir.

Andhrímnir (AND-reem-ner)—"Spirit-Rime". The cook of Valhall, possibly representing the element of air as part of the purest materials fed to the Einherjar. "Rime" is a sacred material of creation and fertility (compare the story of Audhumla, the cow who licked the rime to create the first god, Buri. It is likely that from this she was able to "impregnate" both Ymir and Buri through the milk from her teats).

Andlang (AND-lang)—"Outstretched". One of the nine heavens situated above one of the nine worlds, all of which have their own heaven. We actually cannot name all of the nine worlds, though we do know those of all nine heavens. Only Ásgard, Midgard and Jörmungrund can be named for certain as worlds. What many think of as "worlds" are actually districts of Jörmungrund (Álfheim, Vana-heim, Niflhel, etc.).

Andvari (AND-var-i)—"The Careful One". One of the dwarf-artists who worked in Dvalin's smithy and participated in the procession from Svarin's mound to the Aurvangaland. The hero-saga makes him a guardian over the trea-sures Völund left behind when he fled with his brothers to the Wolfdales.

Angerboda (AN-ger-baw-da)—"Grief-Boder". The name that Gullveig bore once she was exiled to the Ironwood, after she had been burnt her third time. She will remain there until Ragnarök with the wolf-progeny she bore with Loki.

Angeyja (AN-gay-ya)—"She Who Makes the Islands Closer". One of the giant maids that turn the World-Mill, "the mill of the skerries", which creates land from Jötuns' limbs. The others are Gjalp, Greip, Eistla, Eyrgjafa, Ulfrún, Imd, Atla and Jarnsaxa. They are called "Heimdall's nine mothers", because he is god of the pure fire, the friction-fire, brought forth by the grinding millstones.

Ansuz (AN-sooz)—(Gothic) "A god". The fourth rune of the 24 rune Elder "Futhark" or runic alphabet. It represents the gods and goddesses, causing it to be linked to ideals of the sacred in "The Runelaw".

Anzius (AN-zee-us)—(German) "A God". Used as a name of Heimdall as the god who brought culture to our people, though usually it is a generic term.

Ari (AR-i)—"Eagle". An eagle-giant who has his perch in Niflhel.

Árvak (AHR-vak)—"Early-Waker". One of Sunna's steeds who pulls the sun-chariot. The other is Alsvid.

Ás (AHS)—"A god". Like Ansuz, Anzius, which are alternate forms of this word, it is a general designation for a god. Plural "Aesir", feminine "Ásynja".

Ásatrú (AH-sa-troo)—"Faith in the Aesir". The name of the religion of our fore-fathers, recently established out of necessity. Also called Odinism, Theodism, Irminism, and Forn Sed.

Ásatrúar (AH-sa-troo-ar)—"Follower(s) of Ásatrú" (the term is both singular and plural). Designates a practitioner of the Ásatrú religion.

Ásgard (AHS-gard)—"Court of the Aesir". In its widest meaning, the world in Yggdrasil's upper branches where the Aesir live; in its strictest sense, the area inside Ásgard's walls, where Valhall and the other halls of the Aesir are found.

Ask (ASK)—"Ash". Mankind's progenitor, fashioned from an ash tree and given life by Ódin, Hoenir, and Lódur. This tree grew out of an acorn from Yggdrasil.

Ásmegir (AHS-mehg-er)—"Children of the Aesir". The beings dwelling Mímir's holy grove, including Baldur, Hödur, Lif, Leifthrasir, and their descendants, who shall be the parents of mankind in the coming world-age after Ragnarök.

Ásmund (AHS-mund)—"God-Gift". A king in ancient Svithjód, son of Svipdag and Freyja. One of the heroes in "the first great war".

Ásynja (AH-sen-ya)—"Goddess" or "Aesir Goddess". A goddess of the Aesir clan. It is said that the Ásynjur or Ásynjar have a hall in Ásgard, called Vingólf, which they share collectively.

Atla (AT-la)—"The Awful-Grim Maiden". One of the nine mothers of Heimdall who turns the World-Mill.

Auda (OUD-a)—"The Wealthy". A swan-maid and *dís* of vegetation. Also called Hervör Svanhvit, sister of Idun (Hervör Alvit), who was married to Slagfin-Gjúki. Possibly married to Forseti now.

Audhumla (OUD-hum-la)—"The Hornless Wealth-Cow". Primordial Aurochs created out of ice from Ginnungagap who fed Ymir with her teats and formed Buri by licking the ice or rime of the creation.

Aurboda (OUR-baw-da)—"Gold-Liquor". The giant Gymer's wife. Identical to Gullveig-Heid-Angerboda.

Aurgelmir (OUR-gehl-mer)—"Clay-Roarer". Another name of Ymir who rose up from the melted rime in the mud of Jörmungrund. This name is similar to another epithet of his: Leirbrimir = "Clay-Giant".

Aurglasir (OUR-glas-er)—"Mud-Glasir". A name for the part of Yggdrasil below ground, related to "Glasir" (see), which denotes its being covered by the sacred mud of the Underworld, which turns its roots white. See also Vedurglasir.

Aurvangaland (OUR-vang-a-land) or **Aurvanga sjöt** (OUR-vang-a SYUHT)—"The Land of the Clayey Plains". The primeval land of the Teutons, the southern most portion of the Scandinavian peninsula, modern day Skåne.

B

Baen (BAIN) pl. **Baenar** (BAIN-ar)—"Prayer". A reverent petition to the gods and goddesses. Ásatrúars pray standing with their arms outstretched to the sky.

Usually, this either follows of precedes some sort or offering, like a libation of mead.

Baldur (BAL-dur)—"The Bright", "The Glorious". The God of Summer, Justice, kindness and compassion, son of Ódin and Frigga. Husband of Nanna, the moon goddess. Baldur was killed by his brother Hödur after Loki tricked him into shooting an arrow made from mistletoe. He now lives in Breidablik, the hall in Mímir's grove, with other Ásmegir. He will lead the gods into the new era after Ragnarök.

Banings (BAN-ingz)—"The Destroyers", "The Corrupters". Loki's sons and clan folk.

Bára (BAHR-a)—"The Wave", "Billow". One of Aegir's nine daughters with Rán, personification of the wave. It is possible that they are mermaids or Haffrúar. The others are Himingloefa, Dúfa, Blódughadda, Hefring, Ud, Hrönn, Bylgja, and Kolga.

Barri (BAR-i)—"Pine Copse". The quiet grove, where Gerd agrees to meet Frey for their wedding.

Baugeid (BOUG-ayd)—"Ring Oath". The most solemn oaths, according to our traditions, are made on a sacred ring, to bind the person to them with the symbol of the circle. It is very likely that these rings were supposed to have a serpent motif to remind people of the punishments awaiting oath-breakers. These would go to Niflhel, the realm of the damned, to be immersed in the venom of serpents that cover the walls of the places of punishment.

Baugregin (BOUG-rehg-in)—"Artisan of Gold Rings". Another name of Mímir.

Beli (BEHL-i)—"The Bellower", "The Howler". Ruler of the giant clan to which Völund surrendered Frey and who received Freyja from Gullveig. Frey kills Beli with a hart's horn (a sword? cp. Sólarljód 78).

Beltaine (BEHL-tayn)—(Celtic) "Bel's Fires". This ancient May Day festival is as sacred to us as it is to our Celtic cousins. It had its Teutonic equivalent in Pfultag, Pulletag, or Pholtag—"Phol's Day". Phol (Fal) is another name of Baldur, identical to Bel of the Celts, which is fitting since he is the god of summer and this day marks the beginning of the season in his honor. It is celebrated on May ("Lencten") 1st-2nd.

Bergelmir (BER-gehl-mer)—A frost-giant, son of Thrudgelmir and grandson of Aurgelmir-Ymir. It is said that Bergelmir's flesh, like his fathers before him, is that which was used to make the present era's layer of soil.

Berkano (BER-kan-oh)—(Gothic) "Birch". This is the eighteenth rune of the Elder "futhark", generally associated with motherhood. The pictograph is thought to represent a pregnant woman's swollen breasts and belly. This is why it is connected to marriage and parenting in "The Runelaw".

Berling (BER-ling)—"The One Producing or Procreating". One of the four sons of Mímir, known particularly to have aided in the creation of Freyja's necklace, Brísingamen.

Berserker (BER-serk-er)—"Bear-Shirt Wearer". A warrior well known in the ancient North and feared by their enemies, for they would go into a violent battle frenzy that would make them seem invincible.

Bestla (BEHST-la)—"Bast-Cord" or "Tree-Bark". The primordial mother of the gods and first ancestress of the higher Jötun clan. With Bor she had the sons Ódin, Hoenir, and Lódur. She and her brother Mímir were born from the sweat of Ymir's arm, which was filled with the creative rime he had received through Audhumla's milk.

Beyla (BAY-la)—"Milkmaid". Wife of Frey's servant Byggvir, who tends the World-Mill's meal, made of the limbs of Jötuns, and spreads it over the earth. When Loki shows up at a feast at Aegir's and "blends the gods' mead with evil", Byggvir threatens to crush him in his mill. Loki calls Byggvir a chatterer in Frey's ear and an unjust divider of the mill's meal, and his wife a filthy wench.

Bifröst (BIV-ruhst)—"The Trembling Way". A bridge that connects Ásgard with the Underworld, Jörmungrund. It is erroneously thought to be a rainbow, or resemble a rainbow, when it is actually identical to The Milky Way.

Bifurr (BI-vur)—"Quaking One". A dwarf.

Bikki (BIK-i), also **Bekki** (BEHK-i)—"Foe", "Opponent". A name of Loki, when he was Gudhorm's advisor after being exiled from Ásgard.

Bil (BIL)—"Moment". Another name of Idun as the daughter of Ívaldi, sister of Hjúki-Slagfin, who brought the mead to the moon and was adopted as an "Ale-Giver" (Ölgefn) among the gods and goddesses.

Billing (BIL-ing)—"The Twin (of Delling?)". Lord of the sunset glow. Ruler of the Varnians who protect the Sun and Moon from the wolves that pursue them. He is Rind's father and Váli's grandfather.

Bilskirnir (BIL-sker-ner)—"The Bright-Shining". This is actually another name of Valhalla, probably given to it before the age of war came, during the peace era. Based on an expression by the Skald Gamli, Snorri Sturluson incorrectly assumed that Bilskirnir is Thór's hall.

Bjargrúnar (BYARG-roon-ar)—"Help Runes". A class of runes used particularly in the birthing of children. These would be "risted" or inscribed on the palms of the person delivering the child and on special birthing belts used to faciliate this.

Björt (BYUHRT)—"Splendor", "The Shining". One of Freyja's maidservant *dísir*.

Blíd (BLEED)—"The Blithe". One of Freyja's attending *dísir* who are her sisters and thus daughters of Njörd and Frigga.

Blík (BLEEK, like "Bleak")—"The Shining". One of Freyja's attending *dísir* who are her sisters and thus daughters of Njörd and Frigga.

Blind Bölvisí (BLIND like "Blend" BUHL-vis-ee)—Blind = "The Deceptive", Bölvisí = "The Cunning". Under this name Loki appears as an advisor to King Hadding, after his exile from Ásgard.

Blódablanda (BLOHD-a-bland-a)—"The Blood-Blending". The ancient rite where blood is mixed to form a family bond from a close friendship. This is done by first raising sod from the ground, then each cut themselves and let the blood mix while dripping onto the soil, the womb of Mother Earth, from which we came.

Blódeid (BLOHD-ayd)—"Blood oath". The most sacred oath. To take a blood-oath the oath-ring would be dipped into the liquid of the *blótbólli*, preferably the blood of a sacrificed animal, to solemnize it in the life essence of the slain creature.

Blódi (BLOH-di)—"Of the blood". One bound to another in the Blódablanda ceremony.

Blódughadda (BLOH-dug-ha-da)—"Bloody Haired". One of Aegir's nine daughters representing the waves.

Blódughofi (BLOH-dug-haw-vi)—"Bloody-Hoof". Frey's Horse.

Blót (BLOHT, like "bloat")—"Blood-Offering". A ceremonial sacrifice to the divine powers, mainly used as a generic term without actually denoting the need for blood. In such cases when "blood" or a life is sacrificed this is for the purpose of slaughtering animals for food. Blessing the meals we eat is a practice found in almost every religion. Some of the food is then offered to the presiding deities.

Blótbólli (BLOHT-bohl-i)—"Blót-bowl" or "Blood-bowl". A bowl in which a sacrificial liquid, such as the blood of a slaughtered animal or mead, is kept. During the *blót* an evergreen twig, called a *Hlauttein*, is dipped into this liquid, which is then sprinkled on the gathered to bless them.

Bodn (BAWD-n)—"Vessel." A name of Mímir's fountain, erroneously thought to be the name of a jar kept in Suttung's hall.

Bödvild (BUHD-vild)—"War-Maiden". One of Mímir's daughters with Sinmara. She is a night-*dís* and a sister of Nàt. Völund rapes her and from this union she has the son Vidga Völundsson, one of the heroes of the first great war.

Bókrúnar (BOHK-roon-ar)—"Book Runes". A class of runes, probably used in recording information. In ancient times birch bark was used as a form of paper. This bark was called "*bók*", from which we get the word "book".

Borr (BOR), also **Burr** (BUR)—"Son". Son of Buri and progenitor of the gods through his siring of Ódin, Hoenir, and Lódur with his wife, Bestla.

Borgar (BOR-gar)—"The Protector". The first judge-earl in Aurvangaland (Skåne), Halfdan's father. He is also called Skjöld and Jarl.

Bragarhorn (BRAG-ar-horn)—"Bragi's Horn". There is a holy Ásatrú observance called "*sumble*", which is a mead feast divided by several "rounds" or "horns" associated with specific actions. During the Bragarhorn each of the gathered boast of past deeds or swear to perform future deeds worthy of praise from the skalds.

Bragi (BRAG-i)—"The Poet". Son of Ódin and possibly Gunnlöd, married to Idun.

Breidablik (BRAY-da-blik)—"The Far-Shining". This is Baldur's abode in Mímir's grove, which he shares with the other Ásmegir until Ragnarök. His original home was Glitnir, which was handed down as an estate (*Odal*) to his son, Forseti.

Brimrúnar (BRIM-roon-ar)—"Sea Runes". A class of runes used to insure a safe passage at sea.

Brísingamen (BREE-sing-a-men)—"The Brísings Necklace". Freyja's necklace, said to be the most beautiful in all the worlds.

Brísings (BREE-singz)—"Fire Workers". Mímir's sons, also called Hildings, Harlungs, Brondings and Amalians.

Brokk (BRAWK)—"Ruminant". One of the sons of Mímir who created Brísingamen and other treasures for the gods. Identical to Dáin and Alfrik.

Brúni (BROON-i)—"Bushy-Browed" or "Brown-One". Another name of Völund.

Buri (BUR-i)—"Progenitor". Father of Bor and thus the primogenitor of the gods. It is likely that he gave birth to his son in the same way Ymir bore Mímir, and Bestla. He was licked from the primordial rime by Audhumla, who then fed him with her milk, also charged with the creative substance.

Byggver (BEG-ver)—"Corn-Spirit". Husband of Beyla and distributor of the World-Mill's meal as Frey's servant.

Býleist (BEE-layst)—"Whirlwind from the East". A storm-giant, brother of Loki and Helblindi.

Bylgja (BELG-ya)—"Billow". One of Aegir's nine daughters representing the waves.

Byrgir (BERG-er)—"Hider of Something." A mead reserve, most likely hidden by Surt or his son Suttung (Called Mjödvitnir "The Mead Wolf"). In the primeval age of peace, Surt (identical to Durin), was Mímir's trusted friend and ally. Then he turns against the gods and eventually causes the ruin of all creation at

Ragnarök. That he is particularly described as coveting the mead shows us that he most likely stole some of Mímir's mead, created Byrgir from this, then tried to conceal it. Later Ívaldi discovers it and has his children, Bil and Hjúki fetch it for him in the pail called Saeg, carried with the pole called Sumul. But the moon-god gets to them first and adopts them, which then causes Ívaldi to attack him, steal the mead, and take it to Surt in exchange for his daughter, Gunnlöd.

D

Dag (DAG)—"Day". Son of Delling and Nát who rides across the sky in his shining chariot pulled by his illuminating steed, Skinfaxi.

Dagaz (DAG-az)—(Gothic) "Day". The twenty-third rune of the Elder rune "futhark", representing Day as the marker of time and a symbol of universal order. For this reason it is connected to our place in this order in "The Runelaw".

Dáin (DAH-in)—"The Dead". This is a name of Brokk, designating him as a representative of death and the afterlife.

Danp (DANP, like "damp")—"Bellow's Blower". A primeval ruler, father to Skjöld-Borgar's wife and Halfdan's mother Drótt, who in her capacity as mother of the Teutonic regal family, received divine standing. Danp is probably the same as Budli, the progenitor of the Budlungs.

Delling (DEHL-ing)—"The Shining", "The Glittering". The Elf of the rosy dawn, outside of whose doors the dwarf Thjódreyrir sings songs of waking and blessings over the world each morning. He is the guardian of Breidablik, in Ódáinsakr, where nothing impure or evil may come. Delling sired Dag with Nát.

Dísir (DEES-er) singular **Dís**—"Goddesses". Female divinities of higher and lower birth. The name is chiefly used of the Norns and their female servants, the *fylgjur* and *hamingjur*.

Dísting (DEES-ting) or **Dísathing** (DEES-a-thing)—"Dís-Thing" or "Dísir-Thing" ("Goddess-Assembly"), also Dísablót—"Dísir-Blót". The midwinter sacrifice, an ancient agricultural festival focused on preparation for the year's coming work when tools of the trade are blessed (originally this was the plow, giving the celebration the alternate name "Charming of the Plow"). The festival is dedicated to the Dísir and their mistress, Urd, who also has the name Dís (Skaldskaparmál 75). It is also possible that Urd is identical to Gefjon (see), who is particularly connected to the plow. Dísting is celebrated on the full moon between January 21st and February 19th.

Dökkálfar (DUHK-ahl-var)—"Dark-Elves". The elves of the Underworld, most likely identical to the beings who punish the damned in Niflhel.

Dólgthrasir (DOHLG-thras-er)—"Longing for Battle". Identical to Dólgthvari (DOHLG-thvar-i) "Battle Stock". A dwarf.

Dóri (DOHR-i)—"Damager". One of the artists, working under Dvalin, who decorated Breidablik.

Drafn (DRAV-n)—"Wave". Identical to Bára, one of Aegir's nine daughters representing the waves.

Draug (DROUG)—"Outlaw", "One exiled". A mound-dweller or doppelganger living in a grave or grave-mound. Can be good or evil, depending on the nature of the person they were before death.

Draupnir (DROUP-ner)—"The Dropping". A ring forged by Mímir's sons for Ódin. Every ninth night it "drops" eight rings of equal value and weight. Also a dwarf-name.

Drómi (DROHM-i)—"Fetter". One of the fetters that Fenrir burst before he was bound with Gleipnir.

Drösull (DRUHS-ul)—"Steed" (cp. Yggdrasil). Identical to Skinfaxi, Dag's horse.

Drótt (DROHT)—"Folk-Mistress". Danp's daughter, Skjöld-Borgar's wife, Halfdan's mother. Identical to Erna and Tamfana, a goddess-name mentioned in Tacitus' *"Annals"*. According to the myth, before her marriage with Borgar, Drótt was married within the Hildings-Brísings clan and became mother to Hildiger, Halfdan's half-brother, who fell by Halfdan's sword.

Dúf (DOOV)—"The Sleepy". A Dwarf.

Dúfa (DOOV-a)—"The Diver". One of the nine daughters of Aegir who are the representatives of waves.

Durin (DUR-in) also **Durnir** (DUR-ner)—"Doorkeeper" or "Drowsy". The same as Surt, the personal subterranean fire, father of Suttung-Fjálar and progenitor of Suttung's sons. He was the gods' friend in time's morning and worked together with Mímir. It is likely that the two of them created the forms which Ódin, Hoenir, and Lódur gave life to, becoming Ask and Embla, the first humans or Teutons. Later he became the enemy of the gods and concealer of Byrgir's mead, which was stolen from Mímir's well. He takes part in Ragnarök, wielding the Völund sword, and causes the conflagration of the worlds.

Dvalin (DVAL-in)—"The Dormant One", "The One Sleeping". Mímir's son and one of the Underworld's most distinguished artists, identical to Sindri. He and Dáin were allowed to drink from their father's well of wisdom in time's morning, which therefore is called *Dvalins drykkr*, "Dvalin's drink". He spread the knowledge of runes among the dwarves, as Dáin did among the elves. He is one of the artists who forged Brísingamen and, in the hero-saga, the famous sword Tyrfing. Dvalin's daughters are human-loving *dísir*, who along with *dísir* of Ása-and Álf-birth choose mothers for the children that shall be born into the world and facilitate their birth. Under his command, Dvalin has a group of artists who decorated Breidablik, and who took part with the Swedes in the migration from Svarin's mound to Aurvargaland after the break between the gods and the subterranean smiths. In the mythology, Dvalin stands in close connection to Delling. His son Dag is called *Dvalins leika*, "Dvalin's Playmate", as is Sól. Dvalin's horse is called Módin. His name indicates that he is one of the seven sons of Mímir who were stuck with sleep-thorns and sleep in weapon—and treasure-filled halls, until Heimdall's trumpet wakes them to participate in the final battle.

Dvergar (DVEHRG-ar)—"Dwarves", "Artisans". The ancient smiths who created objects of fertility and vegetation. These were originally demigods and were not considered to be of diminutive stature. The terms "Dwarf" and "Elf" are used interchangeably in the lore, and it is probable that the Dwarves are a particular branch of the Álfar or Elves.

E

Edda (EHD-a)—"Great Grandmother". Mother of Thrall and ancestress of the race of Thralls. This word is also used to designate the two works which form the core of the Ásatrú tales and wisdom, though they have been tainted by Christian scribes. It is our objective to cleanse the Eddas of these biases, to present a body of lore by and for the people of our faith.

Eggthir (EHG-ther)—"Sword-Watcher". A kinsman of Gullveig who shares her exile in the Ironwood, where he tends her monster herds and guards the Völund sword, Gambantein, hidden there. He will turn the sword over to Surt's son, Suttung-Fjálar, when Ragnarök is impending.

Egil (EHG-il)—"Strife". The best of archers. He is Ívaldi's son, Völund's and Slagfin's brother, father of Svipdag-Ódr with his first wife, Gróa, and of Ull with his second wife, Sif. He was going to marry Signe-Alveig as a co-spouse with Sif, but was slain and robbed of her by Halfdan, who had done this before with Gróa. He adopted Röskva and Thjálfi. Also called Örvandill.

Ehwaz (EH-vaz)—(Gothic) "Horse". The nineteenth rune of the Elder futhark. Because of certain things said in the rune poems, it is connected by most scholars to ideas of friendship and loyalty, which is why it is connected to this in "The Runelaw".

Eihwaz (AY-vaz)—(Gothic) "Yew". The thirteenth rune of the Elder futhark, usually associated with death and dying, leading to its connection to respect for the dead in "The Runelaw".

Eikinskjaldi (AYK-in-skyald-i)—"One with the Oak Shield". A dwarf artist.

Eikthyrnir (AYK-ther-ner)—"Oak Stinger". The stag that stands on top of Valhalla, chewing Yggdrasil's leaves. From its antlers thunder clouds, laden with Vafurlogi, "quick fire" (lightning), are released. Thence all waters return to their source, Hvergelmir. The stag is called "Oak-Stinger" or "Oak-Antler" because oaks were believed to be the trees most often struck by lightning.

Einherjar (AYN-hehr-yar)—"Single Combatants". Warriors chosen among Midgard's heroes to live in either Ódin's Valhalla or Freyja's Sessrumnir. During the day they fight duels until all are dead, then are reborn to feast with the gods at night.

Eir (AYR, like "air")—"Help". Ásynja of healing, who belongs to the circle of Freyja's *dísir* and is probably Freyja's sister and a daughter of Njörd, like Frid, Blid, Björt, Hlíf, Hlífthrasa, Thjódvara, and Blík.

Eistla (AYST-la)—"Destroyer". One of Heimdall's nine mothers who turns the World-Mill.

Eitr (AYT-r)—"Poison, "Venom". The drink of the damned, which kills them a second time in Niflhel.

Elder (EHLD-er)—"Fire Kindler". One of the Aegir's servants.

Eldhrímnir (EHLD-reem-ner)—"Fire-Rime". The kettle in which Andhrimnir cooks the boar Saehrímnir, representing one of the pure "unearthly" elements used to feed the Einherjar.

Elhaz (EHL-haz)—(Gothic) "Defender". The fifteenth rune of the Elder futhark. It is also called Alciz (AL-keez) and Algiz (AL-giz), a name used by Tacitus to designate Baldur and Hödur as defenders of the folk. For this reason, it is connected to such ideas in "The Runelaw". Elhaz evokes participation in defensive behavior.

Élivagar (EEL-i-vag-ar)—"Stormy Rivers". The gulf, connecting rivers from the Hvergelmir fountain, by which Egil had his fortress, Ysetur. This bay, which separates Jötunheim from Midgard is also called Hrönn, Gandvik and Endil's (Örvandil's) meadow.

Elli (EHL-i)—"Old Age". A giantess. Personification of old age.

Ellilyf Ása (EHL-i-lev AH-sa)—"The gods' remedy against old age". A name for Idun's golden apples, which grow from the golden tree, Yggdrasil (Glasir). The fruits themselves merely have a youthful essence which, when sanctified by Hoenir, bring the divine gifts to children of expecting mothers. When sanctified by Idun, they keep the gods and goddesses young. It was probably Völund who gave his sister/lover the ability to do this.

Embla (EHM-bla)—"Mother". The first Teutonic woman, possibly formed by Mímir and Durin from a tree, then given life and the divine gifts by Ódin, Hoenir, and Lódur. The term Embla-Ask, used by Egil Skallagrimsson leads us to think that she was formed from an ash tree, like Ask. Hindu documents state the first man and woman were created from the same tree. The connection to the great ash tree, Yggdrasil, sustainer of all life, should not be forgotten here.

Erde (ER-deh)—"Earth". Another name of Frigga as the earth goddess.

Erik (ER-ik or AIR-ik) also **Eirik** (AY-rik)—"Honored Ruler". Another name of Svipdag, which he was called by when he became king of the North Teutonic tribes after Halfdan's death. His half-brother Gudhorm was called Jörmunrek "The Great Ruler", once he became a great king, and Gudhorm's half-brother, Hadding was called Thjódrek "Ruler of People". The ancient King Erik to whom the Swedes built a temple in the 9th century, once a revelation was proclaimed to them that the gods had given him a dignity of an Ása-god, is the mythology's Ód-Svipdag, Freyja's husband.

Ewa (EE-va)—(Old Frisian) "Even". The principle of balance in Ásatrú belief. I would like to paraphrase what is said of this in the *Oera Linda Bók*: *Ewa* is the standards that all people have impressed upon their spirit, so they might know what is right and wrong and with which they can judge their deeds and the deeds of others, as well as representing how well they were raised. It also means "water like", right and slick as waves which is not stirred by a heavy wind or anything else. If water is bothered, it becomes uneven, unright, but always is inclined to become even again, which lies in its essence. Likewise, the inclination to right and freedom lies in Frya's child (a person of Nordic descent, this is also found in "The Runelaw" under "Laguz"). *Ewa* and serenity are the marks of wisdom and righteousness, which all pious people should be trained in and all judges should have.

Eylimi (AY-lim-i)—Originally another name of the moon-god.

Eyrgjafa (AYR-gyav-a)—"She Who Creates Landbanks". One of Heimdell's nine mothers who turn the World-Mill. The meal of this mill is used to create land.

<h1 style="text-align:center">F</h1>

Fadir (FAD-er)—"Father". Husband of **Módir** (MOH-der). They are the progenitors of the noble families, the parents of Borgar-Jarl and Halfdan-Kon. Heimdall blessed their union, as he did the Thrall and Karl (Thane) classes, so all would be bound with a connection to the divine and to each other.

Fáfnir (FAHV-ner)—"The Embracer". A dragon, killed by Sigurd to obtain the Niflung hoard. In the mythology he is killed by Hödur to acquire this for the gods.

Fal (FAL)—"The Caretaker", "The Defender". Another name for Baldur, which is found also in Pholtag—"Fal's Day" (May 2nd) and Phol-mânôt—"Phol-month" or "Fal's month" (September). For this reason "Fal" could be a designation for September in our sacred calendar, symbolizing the end of summer as

Fal's Day, Beltaine, represents its beginning. This correlates with Baldur's birth and death.

Falhófnir (FAL-hohv-ner)—"Fal's Fetlocked" or "Shaggy Fetlock". Possibly Baldur-Fal's horse who creates fountains by stomping his hooves on the ground.

Fallow (FAL-oh)—(English). From German Brachmanoth—"Fallow Month". The name for June in the sacred Ásatrú calendar. Also called Selmanadr (Icelandic)—"Mountain Pasture Month", Sommermaaned (Danish)—"Summer Month", Aerra Litha (Anglo-Saxon)—"Before Litha".

Fárbauti (FAHR-bout-i)—"The One Inflicting Harm". A giant, father of Loki, Byleist, and Helblindi.

Fasta (FAST-a)—"The Loyal". The first folksmother, probably identical to Erna-Drótt.

Fehu (FEH-hu)—(Gothic) "Cattle", "Wealth". The first rune of the Elder futhark, symbolizing different aspects of wealth, which is why it is connected to this in "The Runelaw".

Fenja (FEHN-ya)—"Water-Maiden". A giant-maid associated with the turning of the World-Mill, or the lesser Grotti-Mill according to a later saga. She and her sister Menja turn the mill, and are also allied with Ívaldi's kin in the great Teutonic wars.

Fenrir (FEHN-rer)—"Fen-Dweller". The Fenris-wolf, son of Loki and Angerboda (Gullveig-Heid). He was bound by the gods with the fetter Gleipnir, an act which cost Týr his hand.

Fensalir (FEHN-sal-er)—"The Marsh Halls". Frigga's home in her land of birth, Vanaheim.

Fimafeng (FIM-a-vehng)—"The Handy". One of Aegir's servants, whom Loki beat to death when he heard that Fimafeng was a trustworthy and efficient servant.

Fimbulthul (FIM-bul-thul)—"The Great Teacher". Another name for Mímir.

Fimbulvetr (FIM-bul-veht-r)—"The Great Winter." There are two "Great Winters": the first took place long ago when Idun, Freyja, Frey, and other deities of vegetation were brought into the hands of the powers of frost, when Völund-Thjázi sent violent snow storms across the worlds as revenge for the loss of the Aesir's competition between Ívaldi's and Mímir's sons. The second will take place right before Ragnarök, when all the worlds will suffer terrible blizzards for three years continuously.

Foddik (FAW-dik)—(Old Frisian). "That Which Is Fed". A sacred, perpetual flame tended by seven women, called maids, for each day of the week. This flame would be kindled by the Naud-eldir "need fire", or "friction fire".

Fólkvang (FOHLK-vang)—"Plain of the Folk". Freyja's realm in Ásgard, where she keeps half of the Einherjar, the division of which is probably based on the descendants of Ód-Svipdag, her husband, going to her, and those of Halfdan, the Aesir's favorite, going to Valhalla.

Forn Sed (FORN SEHD)—"Ancient Customs", "Old Customs". The original designation used by our ancestors for Teutonic religion when it became necessary to do this in the face of the Christian Invasion.

Fornjót (FORN-yoht)—"The Ancient Being". A giant, killed by Thór. The storm and the destructive fire are represented as his sons.

Forseti (FOR-seht-i)—"The Presiding". Son of Baldur and Nanna and one of the *Ljónar*, divine judges. He possibly inherited Glitnir, the Thingstead of the gods, from his father. Identical to Mars Thingsus—"Mars (Týr) of the *Thing*", which would translate as "Thingtýr" (cp. Hroptatýr = Ódin). Thus he is the god of the *Thing*, said to "settle all disputes".

Fránangrsfors (FRAHN-ang-rs-fawrs)—"Fránang's Falls." A body of water where Loki, in salmon guise, was taken prisoner by the gods.

Freki (FREHK-i)—"The Greedy". One of Ódin's wolfhounds, also called Gífr, the other is Geri. This is also a name for a wolf in general.

Frey (FRAY)—"Lord", "The Dear". Son of Njörd and Frigga, brother of Freyja and god of agriculture and fertility.

Freyja (FRAY-ya)—"Lady", "The Dear". Daughter of Njörd and Frigga, sister of Frey and goddess of love and fecundity.

Freyjasdag (FRAY-yas-dag)—"Freyja's Day". The original name for "Friday", though it can also be dedicated to Frey (Freysdag) or Frigga (Friggasdag).

Fríd (FREED)—"The Fair", A *dís* of beauty in Freyja's surroundings. Probably one of her eight sisters and thus daughter of Njörd and Frigga.

Frid (FRID)—"Peace". An honored concept in Ásatrú religion.

Frigga (FRIG-a)—"The Beloved". Daughter of Fjörgynn and Nát. She is our Mother Earth who birthed ten children with her brother, Njörd (Frey, Freyja, Hlífthrasa, Fríd, Blíd, Björt, Eir, Thjódvara, Hlif and Blík). With Ódin, her husband, she had Thór, Baldur, and Hödur. She is the divine matriarch and Ásgard's queen.

Frosti (FRAWST-i)—"Frosty". Symbolic name of a participant in the procession, caused by the first Fimbulwinter, from Svarin's Mound to Aurvangaland.

Frosting (FROST-ing)—(English). From Icelandic *Fermanagh*—"Frost month". The name for November in the sacred Ásatrú calendar. Also called *Vintermåned* (Danish)—"Winter Month", *Herbistmanoth* (German)—"Autumn Month", and *Blotmanad* (Anglo-Saxon)—"Blood Month".

Fulla (FUL-a)—"Fullness". Maidservant of Frigga, who serves as her messenger, caretaker, and confidante. She is Frigga's sister, daughter of Hoenir-Fjörgynn, and *dís* of fertility. The Prose Edda states that she is a virgin and goes around with her hair flowing free and has a gold band around her head. This, compared with carvings found in Scandinavia, depicts a tradition where married women would have their hair braided or otherwise bound. Unmarried women would wear it loose, and adulteresses, according to Tacitus, had to keep it short.

Futhark (FU-thark)—The runic alphabet designated by the first six runes—Fehu, Uruz, Thurisaz, Ansuz, Raido and Kenaz. There are three futharks: the Elder futhark, consisting of 24 runes; the Younger futhark, consisting of 16 runes; and the Anglo-Saxon futhark, consisting of 33 runes.

Fylgja (FEL-gya), plural **Fylgjur** (FEL-gyur)—"Accompanier". Identical to the *hamingjur*, norns who are mankind's invisible companions and guardian spirits. Divided into three groups: *Mannsfylgja*—"Man's Companion", protecting individuals, *Kynsfylgja*—"Companion of Kin", protecting families, and *Aettars-*

fylgja—"Companion of the Race" or "Companion of the Clan", protecting larger groups of the Folk.

G

Galdr (GALD-r)—"Incantations". The intoning or singing of runic sounds or chants and the use of runes in spiritual practice in general. In opposition to the *Seid*, this is the holy art of the gods.

Gamban (GAM-ban)—"Compensation" or "Revenge". The means with which one cleanses themselves of a *nid*: through actual, direct amends. This can take the form of vengeance from the inflicted if it is not met.

Gambantein (GAM-ban-tayn)—"The Wand of Revenge" or "The Twig of Revenge". Völund's sword of revenge, the most powerful weapon ever created. It is said to be the first sword ever made, since Völund is called Fadir Morna "The Father of Swords". It has several attributes known in the ancient tales: it is said to fight by itself against the giant race, it can become like the tooth of an animal, it can be used like a torch and is said to have been hardened in dragon's blood. It was made by Völund, was taken from him by Mímir, then came into Svipdag's possession, who then gave it to Frey. Frey then gave it as a "bride price" for Gerd (as Svipdag may have done for Freyja), placing it into Gymir's and Gullveig's hands. Gullveig, with Eggthir, keeps the sword until Ragnarök, when they will give it to Fjálar-Suttung, who in turn will give it to Surt, who then brings forth the end of the worlds.

Gandr (GAND-r)—"Magic Implement". Originally something considered to be "magical" (i.e. sacred), but later came to designate a wand or staff used for ceremonial purposes.

Gandul (GAN-dul) also **Gondul** (GAWN-dul)—"The Entangler". A Valkyrie.

Gandvik (GAND-vik)—"The Magic Bay". Another name for the Élivagar.

Ganglati (GAN-glat-i)—"The Slow Moving". A man-servant of Niflhel's queen, Leikin.

Ganglöt (GAN-gluht)—"The Slow Moving". A maid-servant of Niflhel's queen, Leikin.

Gard (GARD)—"Court", "Yard". This word can be used to designate a sacred enclosure, in which our ceremonial areas may lie. A tradition states that such lands would be consecrated by walking along their borders holding the friction-fire (obviously in the form of a "ken", a sacred torch, see Kenaz). This rite can be used in making any place holy.

Gardrofa (GAR-draw-va)—"Fence Breaker". In the *Prose Edda*, the following episode, which probably occurred during the war between the Aesir and Vanir, is related: the Ásynja Gná, whom Frigga sent out an errand, has a horse who leaps through the air and water and is named Hofvarpnir. One time when she rode him, some Vanir asked who traveled there. Gná, replied that she rode on Hof-varpnir that Hamskerpir begat with Gardrofa.

Garm (GARM)—"Wolfhound". This is a name for mythic wolfhounds in general. It is also used specifically for the wolfhound that howls by the Gnipahellir (Gnipa-cave), when Ragnarök is imminent, and the bound evil forces break loose; or, it can designate the giant Hati, the moon's pursuer, called Mana-garm—"Moon-Garm".

Gastropnir (GAST-rawp-ner)—"Guest-Refuser". The wall around Ásgard. One story says that Ódin made the wall from Leirbrimir's (Ymir's) limbs, and another claims a giant was permitted to do this. There is evidence suggesting the former to be the mythological fact, though the giant plays a role in repairing the ancient wall.

Gebo (GEH-boh)—(Gothic) "Gift". The seventh rune of the Elder futhark, associated with gift-giving, which is why it is connected to charity and generosity in "The Runelaw".

Gefjon (GEHV-yawn) or **Gefjun** (GEHV-yun)—"Giver". She is a virgin and women who die unmarried come to her. Ódin says in the poem *Lokasenna* that she knows a family's fate as well as he does. This leads us to believe that she is identical to Urd, which may be confirmed by the fact that Urd is called Gefjon in the poem *Hrafnagaldr Odins*. Gefjon is said in the Prose Edda to take care of women who die unmarried. These women may be Urd's Dísir. Gefjon is said to have created Zealand with four giant-oxen. She owns a necklace, similar to Freyja's Brísingamen, which may have been given to her by Ódin. In ancient times oaths were sworn in her name. Icelanders during the middle ages compared

her to Diana or Minerva. She is also identical to Tacitus' Nyhellenia or Nehalle-
nia.

Gefn (GEHV-n)—"Giver". A name of Freyja.

Geirönul (GAYR-uhn-ul)—"Spear-Thrower". A Valkyrie.

Geirrod (GAY-rawd)—"Protection from Spears". A grant chieftain, father of
Gjálp and Greipp. He was slain by Thór during his war campaign into Jötunheim.

Geirskögul (GAYR-skuh-gul)—"Spear-Battle". A Valkyrie.

Geirvimul (GAYR-vim-ul)—"Spear-Teeming". A subterranean river, in whose
waves weapons roll. It's name connects to the spear as the most popular weapons
of the Teutons (see Tacitus' *Germania*)

Geitir (GAY-ter)—"Goat-Lord". Another name of the giant Gymir. Like the
giant-chieftain Beli ("Howler"), who is portrayed as having the head of a dog,
Gymir's appearance presumably is reminiscent, in one way or another, of a goat.

Gerd (GEHRD)—"Maker". Daughter of Gullveig and Gymir who became
Frey's wife through the aid of Skírnir-Svipdag. It is very likely that Gullveig
enchanted Frey with her evil *Seid*, so she could obtain Gambantein as Gerd's
"bride-price".

Geri (GEHR-i)—"Greedy". One of Ódin's wolfhounds. The other is Freki.

Gersemi (GEHR-sehm-i)—"Treasure", "The Ornamented". Daughter of Freyja
and Svipdag.

Gífr (GEEV-r)—"Greedy". Another name for Ódin's wolfhound, Freki. Also, a
group of magic beings that fly around in the air. In Ódin's Wild Jagd, "Wild
Hunt", he, Thór, Frigga and a host of Einherjar sometimes go out and cleanse
the air of them.

Gimlé (GIM-lee)—"Gem Roof", "Fire Shelter". The hall roofed with gold in
which the beings of the coming world-age shall dwell and enjoy eternal bliss. Possibly identical to Breidablik.

Ginnar (GIN-ar)—"Enticer". A dwarf.

Ginnregin (GIN-rehg-in)—"The Older Powers". A designation of the gods, especially it would seem, of the Vanir.

Ginnungagap (GIN-un-ga-gap)—"The Yawning Chasm". The empty abyss in Chaos, in which cold and warm waves met to create life and the worlds.

Giptar (GIPT-ar)—"Gifts". Identical to the *hamingjur* or *fylgjur*. They are also called heillir—"Givers of Health", audnur—"Givers of Wealth" and gáfur—"Givers of Faculties". They are our companions and assistants in life, who will act as witnesses for us at the Helthing, for the dead are mute.

Gipul (GIP-ul)—"Forward Rushing". A subterranean river.

Gisl (GIS-l) or **Gils** (GILS)—"Shining". One of the Aesir's horses.

Gjallarbru (GYAL-ar-bru)—"The Gjöll-Bridge". The gold-roofed bridge over the subterranean river Gjöll, guarded by the goddess Módgud.

Gjallarhorn (GYAL-ar-horn)—"The Resounding Horn". Heimdall's horn, probably a ram's horn, which is kept beneath Yggdrasil in the Underworld and will be used to announce Ragnarök.

Gjálp (GYAHLP)—"Roarer". Geirrod's daughter. At one time she was one of the giantesses turning the World-Mill, because she is accounted as one of the Heimdall's mothers. She was killed by Thór.

Gjöll (GYUHL)—"The Resounding" or "The Loud". One of the Underworld rivers that separates Hel from Niflhel, with the Élivagar. This is also the name for the boulder that holds Fenrir, bound by Gleipnir.

Glad (GLAD)—"The Shining". One of the Aesir's horses.

Gladsheim (GLADS-haym)—"The Home of Joy". The area inside of Ásgard where Valhalla stands.

Glaesisveller (GLAIS-is-vehl-er), also Glasisvellir (GLAS-is-vehl-er)—"The Glittering Fields". Mímir's kingdom in the Underworld in which Ódainsakr is located. The name is connected to Yggdrasil-Glasir, also known as Mimameid—"Mímir's-Tree".

Glasir (GLAS-er)—"The Resplendent". Another name for Yggdrasil, with its golden leaves and golden fruits, born from a golden seed. cp. Aurglasir, Vedurglasir.

Gleipnir (GLAYP-ner)—"Fetter". The fetter used to bind Fenrir said to be made from "the sound of a cat's footfall and the woman's beard, the mountain's roots and the bear's sinews and the fish's breath and the bird's spittle".

Glen (GLEHN)—"The Shining". Another name of Heimdall, who is husband to the mother Sól, not the daughter Sól.

Gler (GLEHR)—"The Shining". One of the Aesir's horses.

Glitner (GLIT-ner)—"The Shining Abode". The *Thingstead* of Ásgard. First it was Baldur's, then Forseti's home.

Gná (NAH)—"The Towering". The messenger of Frigga and an Ásynja. Originally, Gná was a common designation of a goddess or *dís*.

Gnipahellir (NIP-a-hehl-er)—"The Cave of the Precipitous Rock". Garm howls before the Gnipa-Cave, when Loki and Fenrir's bonds burst.

Gnitaheid (NIT-a-hayd)—"Gnita's Heath". The heath where Fáfnir brooded over the Völund treasure (Niflung hoard) when Hödur came to kill him.

Godard (GAWD-ard)—"Ones speaking the Godly Tongue". The collection of priests and priesteses in Ásatrú.

Godi (GAWD-i)—"One who speaks the Godly Tongue". A title used for a male priest in the Ásatrú faith.

Godin (GAWD-in)—"The Gods". Designating all the gods and goddesses.

Góin (GOH-in)—"Living Deep In Earth". The name of a serpent, probably symbolic, that gnaws Yggdrasil's roots with other serpents: Móin, Grábak, Grafvöllud, Ófnir, Svafnir and Nidhögg.

Göll (GUHL)—"The Noisy". A Valkyrie.

Grábak (GRAH-bak)—"Gray Back". A serpent that gnaws at Yggdrasil's roots.

Grafvitnir (GRAV-vit-ner)—"Grave-Wolf". Góin and Móin are called Grafvitner's sons. See above.

Grafvöllud (GRAV-vuhl-ud)—"Field Burrower". A serpent that gnaws at Yggdrasil's roots.

Grani (GRAN-i)—A horse ridden by Sigurd Fáfnirsbane in the later heroic saga. In the myth, Grani belonged to Brokk, Mímir's son, identical to Hjálprek-Elberich.

Greip (GRAYP, like "grape")—"She who seizes". A giantess. Gjalp's sister and Geirrod's daughter. At one time she was one of the maids who turn the World-Mill, since she is one of Heimdall's mothers. She is mother of Ívaldi's sons—Völund, Egil, and Slagfin.

Grepp (GREHP)—"Grasper". Three brothers with this name were members of Beli's clan when Frey and Freyja were in their power. The three Grepps were esteemed skalds among these giants.

Grerr (GREHR)—"Grower" A son of Mímir. One of the artists who created Freyja's necklace, Brísingamen.

Gríd (GREED)—"Greed", "Violence". A giantess, mother of the Ása-god Vídar with Ódin.

Grjótúnagard (GRYOHT-oon-a-gard)—"Stone Yard". Home of the giant Hrungnir.

Gróa (GROH-a)—"Giver of Growth". A *dís* of vegetation, daughter of the elf-ruler Sigtrygg. Sif's sister, Egil's and thereafter Halfdan's wife. Mother of Svipdag-Ód (with Egil), and Gudhorm (with Halfdan).

Grotti (GRAWT-i)—"Grinder". A name of the World-Mill and Frodi's Mill of the hero-sagas.

Gudhorm (GUD-horm)—"Esteemed by the Gods". Halfdan's and Gróa's son, Ód-Svipdag's, and Hadding's half-brother. Identical to Jörmunrek, Ermenrich.

Gullfaxi (GUL-vaks-i)—"Gold-Mane". The giant Hrungnir's horse, who came into the Aesir's possession after the giant's death, and was presented by Thór to his son Magni.

Gullinbursti (GUL-in-burst-i)—"Golden-Bristle". Frey's boar, an agricultural symbol. Also called Slidrugtanni and Hildisvin.

Gullinkambi (GUL-in-kam-bi)—"Golden-Comb." The cock in the World-Tree that wakes the Einherjar in Ásgard. Identical to Vidofnir and Salgofnir and a symbol of Lódur-Gevar as representative of the starry sky and atmosphere.

Gulltopp (GUL-tawp)—"Gold-tuft", "Golden Forelock". Heimdall's horse.

Gullveig (GUL-vayg)—"Gold-Drink" or "Gold-Intoxicant". Daughter of Hrímnir and Imd. The thrice born giantess, origin of the evil *Seid*. She was called Heid when she went around Midgard teaching her dangerous arts. She was called Aurboda when she was married to Gymir. She is now known as Angurboda while she dwells in the Ironwood, awaiting Ragnarök. As the thrice burnt and likewise living, she bore the name Hyrrokin, "the fire-smoked

Gungnir (GUNG-ner)—"Swaying One". Ódin's spear.

Gunn (GUN)—"Warrior Maiden". A Valkyrie.

Gunnar (GUN-ar)—"Warrior". One of Slagfin-Gjúki's sons.

Gunnlöd (GUN-lud)—"The Battle-Inviting". A giant maid, Suttung-Fjálar's daughter who helped Ódin steal the Byrgir mead from his father.

Gunnthráin (GUN-thrah-in)—"Warrior-Threatening". A subterranean river.

Gunnthró (GUN-throh)—A subterranean river.

Gydja (GED-ya)—"Priestess". A female priest of the Ásatrú religion.

Gýgr (GEE-ger)—"Ogress". The word for female Jötuns.

Gylfi (GEL-vi)—"King", "Prince". A Jötun transformed into a Swedish king in the *Prose Edda*. He supposedly gave Gefjon a "plowland" (the amount of land that can be plowed in one day), from which she carved out Zealand with the help of four giant oxen.

Gyllir (GEL-er)—"Golden". One of the Aesir's horses.

Gymir (GEM-er)—"Devourer". A giant ruler. Gullveig-Angerboda's husband. Gerd's father.

H

Hadarlag (HAD-ar-lag)—"Hödur's Metre". Hödur is one of the great musicians of our lore, which is why this verse-form is named after him. He and others, including Baldur, Bragi, Slagfin, Lódur, and Slagfin's son Gunnar, play on stringed instruments and can influence nature and people with their beautiful playing. The chief instrument was the lyre or harp.

Hadding (HAD-ing)—"The Hairy", "The Fair-Haired". Son of Halfdan and Alveig; Gudhorm's half-brother. His name alludes to his making a vow to not cut his hair until he avenged his father against Svipdag and regained his inheritance in his kingdom.

Haddingaland (HAD-ing-a-land)—"Hadding's Land". The fields of bliss in the Underworld, so-called because Hadding got to journey there and see their wonder, and because during the war between the Aesir and the Vanir, Hadding's fallen warriors got to stay there before they came to Valhalla.

Haffrú (HAV-froo)—"Mermaid", "Ocean-Maid" or **Hafherr** (HAV-hehr)—"Merman", "Ocean-Man". Designating the sea-creatures, similar to the Greek Merfolk. It is possible that Rán, Aegir's wife, is their queen. See also Marmennil.

Hafli (HAV-li)—"The Seizer". A warrior of giant-birth, Gudhorm's foster father and participant in his struggles.

Hagal (HAG-al)—"The Skillful". Skjöld-Borgar's friend, Hamal's father, Halfdan's foster-father.

Hagalaz (HAG-a-laz)—(Gothic) "Hail". The ninth rune of the Elder futhark. To farmers and other people hail represents disastrous weather, but its ice is also viewed as the active substance of creation, teaching us to recognize the neutrality of natural forces. This is why it is connected to such ideas in "The Runelaw".

Haki (HAK-i)—A giant.

Halfdan (HALV-dan)—"Half-Dane". Son of Skjöld-Borgar and Drótt, the first Teutonic king, regarded as Thór's son and given divine honors. He was married to Gróa, and was thus Svipdag's step-father, and with her had the son Gudhorm. Then he married Signe-Alveig, with whom he had Hadding. He robbed both of these women from Egil.

Hamal (HAM-al)—"Wether", "Ram". Son of Hagal. Halfdan's half-brother on Drótt's side. Hadding's confidante, foster-father, and war-general. Progenitor of the Amalian tribe. Identical to Hildebrand and Hildigir.

Hamdir (HAM-der)—"Hawk". One of Svanhild's brothers, the other is Sörli. They were stoned to death on Gudhorm's orders for trying to avenge the killing of their sister.

Hamingja (HAM-ing-ya), plural **Hamingjur** (HAM-ing-yur)—"Luck", "Guardian". Female protector assigned to us at birth, to witness for us at death. Identical to *fylgja*, *draumkona*, *norn*, *gipte*, and *dís*.

Hamr (HAM-r)—"Guise". An illusionary form that can be put on and taken off by those skilled in "magic". In all likelihood this represents the many "forms" one takes when they dream, especially in lucid state.

Hamskerpir (HAM-sker-per)—"Thin-Loined". The steed that sired Gná's horse Hofvarpnir with Gardrofa.

Handfastna (HAND-vast-na)—"Hand-Fasting". The name for the Ásatrú wedding ceremony, consisting of three divisions: 1) *Brudkaupa* "Bride-Purchasing" (also "Bride-Price"), where the vows are exchanged and the man brings the dowry for the woman. 2) *Brudöl* or *Bridale* "Bride-Ale", the wedding feast or "bridal". 3) *Háva rád* (HAH-va RAHD)—"The High Union", the consummation.

Hannar (HAN-ar)—"The Skillful". A dwarf.

Hárbard (HAHR-bard)—"Hoar-beard", "Gray-beard". A name of Ódin, which Loki once assumed in the poem *Hárbardsljod*.

Hardgrep (HARD-grehp)—"The Hard-Grasping". A giantess, Hadding's companion, daughter of Hadding's first foster-father (when he was hidden away), Vagnhöfdi.

Harvest (HAR-vest)—(English). Named after German Aranmanoth—"Reaping Month", "Harvest Month", used for August in the sacred Ásatrú calendar. Also called Konskurdarmanadr (Icelandic)—"Reaping Month", Homaaned (Danish)—"Hay Month", Weodmonad (Anglo-Saxon)—"Weed Month".

Hati (HAT-i)—"The Hateful". A wolf-giant. Son of Fenrir, who chases the moon (as Hati Managarm—"Moon-Garm") until Ragnarök, when he swallows it.

Haugbúi (HOUG-boo-i)—"Mound-Dweller". The alter-ego or doppelganger of a person, which remains in the grave, or grave-mound after death. Can be good or bad, depending on the disposition of the person before they died. Usually sleeps in the grave, but can wake up at night or be awakened by prayer or conjuration (the latter being part of the evil *Seid* art). They are generally considered to be benevolent, except when the animal elements (*lá* with *laeti*) consume it with animal instincts. Then they become hungry, but can never be sated, and lose all emotions and memory. They are killed by cutting off their head and piercing their heart with wood, like the Slavic vampires. They are driven out into the night by their ravenous hunger and will suck the blood of the living.

Haustblót (HOUST-bloht)—"Autumn Blót", "Harvest Blót". Three primary harvest festivals are known in our faith—Hleifblót, celebrating its beginning; Haustblót, celebrating its culmination; and Vetrablót, celebrating its end. This festival takes place on the Autumnal equinox.

Haying (HAY-ing)—(English). Named after German Hewimanoth—"Hay Month", used for July in the sacred Ásatrú calendar. Also called Heyannir (Icelandic)—"Hay Making", Ormemaaned (Danish) "Worm/Snake/Dragon Month", Aeftera Litha (Anglo-Saxon)—"After Litha".

Heathen Year—This is a means of marking the year, devised by Else Christensen. It is based upon the Zodiac sign of the Bull, corresponding to our sacred Aurochs, Audhumla herself. The era of the bull began in 4311B.C.E., making 2006 C.E. = 6317 Heathen Year (H.Y.).

Hefring (HEHV-ring)—"The Swelling Wave". One of Aegir's nine daughters who represent the waves.

Heid (HAYD)—"Witch". The name Gullveig bore when she roamed Midgard performing evil deeds and teaching her evil *Seid*.

Heidrun (HAYD-run)—"The Clear Stream". The she-goat that stands on top of Valhalla, chewing Yggdrasil's leaves. From her udders streams the mead, which fills a large vat, from which the Einherjar fill their drinking-horns. Like ours, this mead is not as powerful as the liquids from the three subterranean fountains.

Heimdall (HAYM-dal)—"The One who Shines Across the Worlds". God of the pure fire, the friction fire, and guardian of the worlds. Born of nine mothers, the nine giantesses who turn the World-Mill and created sparks from which he was born. Lódur-Mundilfori is the mill's caretaker and thus Heimdall's "father". He blessed the unions of the Teutonic classes, which leads to the appellation "Heimdall's sons" for our folk.

Heiptir (HAYP-ter)—"Supernatural Beings". Punishing spirits or beings of revenge, armed with thorn-roads. They avenge that which has not been avenged.

Hel (HEHL)—"The Concealer". 1) The kingdom of death, especially the fields of bliss. 2) Urd, the *dís* of fate and death. In Christian times, when the heathen kingdom of death was transformed into "Hell", Leikin, the being from Niflhel, received the name Hel in the *Prose Edda*, whereas in the *Poetic Edda*, Hel always signifies Urd or the subterranean kingdom of bliss where Urd's and Mímir's wells are located.

Helblindi (HEHL-blind-i)—"He Who Blinds With Death". A water-giant, Loki's brother.

Helför (HEHL-vuhr)—"The Journey to Hel". An ancient Ásatrú designation for a funeral. Nine days after the funeral is the deceased's Helthing trial, then people should pray for their access into Valhalla, Folkvang, or Hel's fields of bliss.

Helgenga (HEHL-gehng-a)—"One gone to Hel". Designation for the dead.

Helgrindar (HEHL-grind-ar)—"Hel-gates". Entrances to the Underworld.

Helskór (HEHL-skohr)—"Hel-Shoes". Special shoes blessed and placed on the feet of the dead, aiding them in their journey to the Helthing and signifying our respect for them.

Helsótt (HEHL-soht)—"Hel-sickness". A fatal illness given by Leikin, Urd-Hel's servant.

Helthing (HEHL-thing)—"Hel's Assembly", "*Thing* of the Dead". A contemporary designation for the *Thing* near Urd's fountain, where the dead are judged to determine where they will spend their afterlife.

Hengikjöpt (HEHNG-i-kyuhpt)—"Hanging-Chin". A giant who presented stones to Frodi for his Grotti-mill. A giantess is also known by this name.

Hepti (HEHPT-i) also **Heptifili** (HEHPT-i-vil-i)—A dwarf.

Herfjötur (HEHR-vyuht-ur)—"Host-Fetterer". A Valkyrie, who causes panic.

Hervör Alvit (HEHR-vuhr AL-vit)—"Host Warder" (Hervör) and "All-White" (Alvit). In the heroic sagas Idun appears partly under this name, and partly under the name Sigrdrífa.

Hild (HILD)—"Battle". A Valkyrie, closely connected to Hödur. Perhaps she is his wife.

Hildigun (HILD-i-gun)—"Battle-Warrior Maiden". A name used to differentiate the daughter Sunna from her mother, who is also called Sváva. She is Nanna's sister, and Máni's daughter. She was first married to Ívaldi, with whom she had the daughters Idun, Signe-Alveig, and Auda. Later she became Heimdall's wife.

Hildur (HILD-ur)—"Warrior". Progenitor of the Hildings.

Himinbjörg (HIM-in-byuhrg)—"Heaven's Defense". The stronghold by Bifröst's northern bridge-head defended by Heimdall.

Himingloefa (HIM-in-glur-va)—"The Sky-Clear". One of Aegir's nine daughters representing the waves.

Hjálmthrimul (HYAHLM-thrim-ul)—"Battle-Helm". A Valkyrie.

Hjörvard (HYUHR-vard)—"Sword Watcher". A name of Ódin as well as the giant Eggthir, who watches Gambantein until Ragnarök.

Hjúki (HYOOK-i)—"Returning to Health". Another name of Slagfin, Idun-Bil's brother who carried the Byrgir-mead to Máni, the moon-god, with his sister.

Hladgud Svanhvit (LAD-gud SVAN-vit)—Hladgud = "Necklace-Adorned Warrior-Maiden", Svanhvit = "The Swan-White". Another name of Auda, Ívaldi's daughter, Idun's sister, and Slagfin's swan-maid.

Hlaut (LOUT)—"Sacral Blood". To the ancients, blood was considered a holy substance because it is the life-force of all creatures, one of the gifts given to us by the gods. For this reason, the blood of slaughtered animals may sometimes be used in our ceremonies. This sacred liquid is then called "Hlaut". It is sometimes subsituted with mead.

Hlauttein (LOUT-tayn)—"Blood-Twig". An evergreen twig or branch, used like an aspergill, to bless the gathered with "Hlaut" or mead or even water. Ash would be the most holy tree for this purpose, as it corresponds to Yggdrasil.

Hleifblót (LAYV-bloht)—"Loaf-Blót", "Bread-Blót". This is a contemporary term reconstituting the Anglo-Saxon Lammas (hlafmaesse) "Loaf-Mass". It is a harvest festival formerly held in England on August 1st when bread baked from the season's first ripe grain was consecrated.

Hléssey (LEES-ay)—"Hler's Island" (Hlér = Aegir). The home of Aegir, where the feast of the gods takes place each year. It is also said of this island that Thór once fought with "berserk brides", giant maids who "confused the folk" (by sinking the island at sunrise, and raising it up again at sundown?). They sought to smash Thór's ship that he had dragged up on shore and placed on rollers. They attacked him with iron clubs and had driven Thjálfi off. The adventure must have occurred around the time when the North was being rebuilt after the fimbulwinter's end, and Thjálfi, protected and supported by Thór, repopulated the islands in the Scandinavian waters.

Hlidskjálf (LID-skyahlv)—"Gate-Tower". The Aesir's watchtower where they can view all the worlds, located in Valhalla ("Valaskjálf").

Hlíf (LEEV)—"The Protectress". One of the *dísir* in Freyja's company, probably one of her sisters.

Hlífthrasa (LEEV-thras-a)—"Protecting in Battle". One of the *dísir* in Freyja's company, probably one of her sisters.

Hlín (LEEN)—"The Protectress". Another name of Frigga and a name of one of her maidservants.

Hlökk (LUHK)—"Battle-Din". A Valkyrie.

Hlóra (LOH-ra)—"Loud". The *Prose Edda* has preserved traces of a myth, according to which Thór, like Týr, was entrusted to giants for rearing during the age of peace. The foster parents were named Vingnir and Hlóra, but they must have broken their obligations as foster parents and sought to deceive Thór, who would later become so dangerous to the giant world, because he killed them both at the age of 12. He must have carried his older hammer, the one made of stone, out of his foster parents' house, because in *Vafthrúdnismál* the hammer is said to be Vingnir's.

Hnefatafl (NEHV-a-tav-l)—"King's Tables". An ancient board game, forerunner of chess which is the game of the gods. They are said to have had one, made for them by the artists of nature, which can move its own pieces and act as an opponent.

Hnitbjörg (NIT-byuhrg)—"Fortification". Suttung-Fjálar's home in the "deepdales", Sökkdalir.

Hnoss (NAWS)—"Jewel". Daughter of Freyja and Svipdag.

Hoddgoda (HAWD-gawd-a)—"Hoard of the Gods". A treasure chamber in Mímir's kingdom, containing many of the gods' artifacts.

Hoddmímis Holt (HAWD-meem-is HAWLT)—"Treasure-Mímir's Grove". Mímir's grove in the Underworld, where Breidablik is located. Here is "where the fewest baleful runes are found" (*Grimnismál* 11). Also called Holt, Mimisholt, Ódáinsakr, and Ókólnir.

Hödur (HUHD-ur)—"Warrior". One of the Aesir, Ódin's son. He appeared in the hero-saga under the name Hedin. He has also been called Loddfáfnir, since he is the actual slayer of the giant-serpent Fáfnir. Inadvertently, and by Loki's manipulations, he killed his brother, Baldur. The myths did not portray him as blind, but as a remarkable sportsman and archer.

Hoenir (HUR-ner)—"Male bird". Ódin's brother who helped him create Midgard and the first humans. He is a patron of childbirth and children, who consecrates Yggdrasil's fruits for the purpose of delivering the divine gifts to the maternal womb. Symbolized by the stork and also called Lángifotr—"Long-Leg" and Aurkonung—"Marsh-King". He is identical to Vé.

Hof (HAWV)—"House", "Home". Used to designate a temple, which was originally the home of a priest or priestess. It can also be used generically, in the sense of a place of worship and is thus used interchangeably with "Vé" (see).

Hofgodi (HAWV-gawd-i)—"Priest of the Temple" or Hofgydja (HAWV-gedya)—"Temple Priestess". The title of those of the Ásatrú priesthood who deal with matters concerning the traditions and upkeep of the temple.

Hofvarpnir (HAWV-varp-ner)—"Hoof-Flourisher". The horse of Gná, son of Hamskerper and Gardrofa.

Högni (HUHG-ni)—Son of Gjúki-Slagfin, brother of Gunnar.

Hölmgang (HUHLM-gang)—"Island-Going". A duel, fought in isolation (traditionally on an island) to settle conflicts peacemakers of *Things* cannot resolve.

Holt (HAWLT)—"Grove". Mímir's grove in the Underworld. This word also designates the sacred graves where we honor our deities and celebrate our faith, also called a *lund*.

Hörg (HUHRG)—"Stone-Altar", "Standing Stones". An altar, called a *Stalli* when it isn't made of stone.

Hörn (HUHRN)—"Horn". A name of Freyja, given to her when she was among the Jötuns, after they enchanted her and bound her hair in a way that resembled horns.

Hörnbori (HUHRN-bor-i)—"He Who Bore Hörn's Hair". A dwarf, who probably loosened Freyja's hair from its binding.

Horning (HORN-ing)—(English). From the German Hornung—"Frozen Snow" or "Icicle". The term used for February in the sacred Ásatrú calendar. Also called Gói (Icelandic)—"Winter Month", Blidemaaned (Danish)—"Cheerful Month", and Solmanad (Anglo-Saxon)—"Sun-Month".

Hraesvelg (RAIS-vehlg)—"Corpse Swallower". An eagle-giant who creates violent storms.

Hraunn (ROUN) also **Hrönn** (RUHN)—"Billow", "Wave". Another name of the Élivagar and a name of one of Aegir's nine daughters who represent the waves.

Hreidmar (RAYD-mar)—Father of Fáfnir, Regin, and Otter.

Hrímfaxi (REEM-vaks-i)—"Rime-Mane". Nát's horse who grazes on the grasses of Jörmungrund, and the leaves of Yggdrasil, saturated in the sacred mead. From his bit a froth forms which becomes the morning-dew, which the bees collect and produce the honey we make our mead from.

Hrímgrímnir (REEM-greem-nir)—"Frost-Grímnir". A frost-giant, identical to Thrudgelmir. Grímnir is a name of Ódin, so this name designates Thrudgelmir as the chieftain of the Jötuns of Ymir's feet.

Hrímnir (REEM-ner)—"The Frost-Being", "Frost Giant". A frost-giant, identical to Bergelmir, Gullveig's father.

Hrímthurse (REEM-thurs)—"Frost-Giant", "Rime-Giant". One of the elder giant race including Ymir, Thrudgelmir, Bergelmir, etc. originated from the ice of Ginnungagap and having monstrous forms.

Hringhorn (RING-horn)—"Curved-Prow". Baldur's ship, which became his funeral pyre.

Hrist (RIST, like "wrist")—"Shaker". A Valkyrie.

Hródvitnir (ROHD-vit-ner)—"The Famous Wolf". A name of Fenrir, said to be Hati's father.

Hrossthjóf (RAWS-thyohv)—"Horse-Thief". A giant, Hrímnir's son, Gullveig-Heid's brother. According to Saxo, he must have prophecied to Ódin that he would father Baldur's avenger with Rind. The poem *Baldrs Draumar* states that Ódin rode down to the Underworld and woke a *vala* (seeress) buried there from the sleep of death who predicts the same. This suggests that the *vala* is Gullveig, Hrossthjóf's sister. In *Völuspá hin Skamma* (str. 4) it is said that "Heid and Hrossthjóf were of Hrímnir's race".

Hrungnir (RUNG-ner)—"The Noisy". A giant killed by Thór.

Hrym (REM)—"Frost". A storm-giant, one of the Jötuns' leaders in Ragnarök.

Hugi (HUG-i)—"Thought". The personification of thought, an illusion created by Fjálar that ran a race against Thjálfi which the latter could not possibly win.

Hugin (HUG-in)—"Thought". One of Ódin's ravens who flies around the world gathering information for him. The other is Munin.

Hugrúnar (HUG-roo-nar)—"Thought Runes". A group of runes containing wisdom and the skaldic art. This could be the foundation of a sacred Teutonic philosophy.

Huldreslaat (HUL-drehs-laht)—The music played by the Land-Wights, who are also called Huldrefolk.

Hun-War—The name of the war the giants waged against Ásgard, while the Vanir reigned there.

Hunting (HUNT-ing)—(English). From "Hunter's Moon", the name of the full moon or moon-cycle in October, giving the designation of this month in the sacred Ásatrú calendar. Also called Gormanadr (Icelandic)—"Slaughter Month", Saedemaaned (Danish)—"Sowing Month", Windemememanoth (German)—"Grape Gathering Month", Winterfylled (Anglo-Saxon)—"Winter's Filling".

Húsfreyja (HOOS-vray-ya)—"Lady of the House" (cp. German Hausfrau), "House-Freyja". The position of a woman within her home as its caretaker. It is an honored title of authority and nobility, marked by the keys of the home worn on her waist.

Hvergelmir (VERG-ehl-mer)—"The Roaring-Kettle". The well situated on Nidafjöll beneath the World-Mill which waters the northern root of Yggdrasil. Its sacred mead gives endurance.

Hymir (HE-mer)—A Jötun-chief, married to Týr's mother.

Hyndla (HEND-la)—"Bitch". Name of a giantess. *Hyndluljód* is the name of a genealogical poem consisting of heathen fragments with additions from the Christian era. Foremost among these additions is the poem's framing device, according to which Freyja seeks out the giant-maid Hyndla, who is well acquainted with mythic genealogy, to ask her to testify in an inheritance dispute between Freyja's lover Ottar (Ód-Svipdag) and one Angantýr.

Hyrr (HER)—"Realm of Delight". This is either a hall in Ásgard or is another name for Breidablik, situated in Ódainsakr, Mímir's holy realm.

I

Idavöllr (ID-a-vuhl-r)—"Plain of the Eddies". In time's morning the gods and the primeval artists worked together in the Ida-plains, crafting tools, forging, constructing, and building. In the renewal of the worlds, the gods will gather there around Baldur. Ida is another name of Slagfin, Ívaldi's son, who helped the gods in the primal era.

Idun (ID-un)—"The Rejuvenating", "The Dilligent". Daughter of Ívaldi and Sunna-Hildigun. She is Völund's sister and beloved, and probably in this capacity becomes mother of Thjázi-Völund's daughter Skadi. Later she became an Ásynja and wife of Bragi, and distributes the *Elliyf Ása*, Yggdrasil's apples consecrated by her powers alone, which keeps the gods young and immortal.

Ífing (EEV-ing)—Designation of the sea of air. In *Grimnismál*, it is said to be a river that never freezes and that separates the gods' land from that of the Jötuns.

Imbrecki (IM-brehk-i)—A son of Harlung, who was Halfdan's son, making Imbrecki Halfdan's grandson and nephew of Hadding and Gudhorm. Tricked by Loki, Gudhorm had him killed.

Imd (IMD)—"Embers (from the World-Mill)". One of Heimdall's nine mothers, a giantess who turns the World-Mill. She is also Gullveig's mother with Hrímnir.

Ingaevones (ING-ai-vohns)—"Ingi's Descendants". The Northern Teutons, more particularly the Swedes and Finns, opposed by the Danes of Halfdan's clan, the Skjöldungs.

Ingi (ING-i)—"Ing's (Frey's) kinsman" (Ing = "Fertility God"). Another name of Svipdag, who once ruled over Svithjód, the Northern Scandinavian domain.

Ingwaz (ING-vaz)—(Gothic) "Ing's Rune", "Ingi's Rune". The twenty-second rune of the Elder futhark. Connected as it is to Frey, god of fertility and sexuality, it is associated with these concepts in "The Runelaw".

Íri (EER-i)—A dwarf.

Irminism (ER-min-iz-m)—"The World-View". A branch of Teutonic religion particularly focused on German traditions and language.

Irminsul (ER-min-sul)—(Saxon) "The World-Pillar". A sacred icon representing Yggdrasil, the World-Tree.

Irpa (ER-pa)—"The Swarthy". When the swan-maids of the Ívaldi sons joined them in their rebellion against the gods, standing by them in the Ironwood, they "changed forms", became "she-wolves", who aided in Völund's revenge. As such they took part in the promotion of the first Fimbulwinter. It can be demonstrated that Irpa's sister, "Thorgerd Holgabrud", is identical to Sif, and thus Irpa is one of these swan-maids, probably Slagfin's beloved, Auda. Because of this she was later seen as a giantess producing hail storms.

Isa (EES-a)—(Gothic) "Ice" The eleventh rune of the Elder futhark, the ice rune. Ice is a symbol of strength and creative power, associating this rune with the ideas of discipline, which is why it is connected to such in "The Runelaw".

Ísarnkól (EES-arn-kohl)—"Ice-Cold Iron". A cooling technology placed by the gods between the shoulder blades of the sun horses Árvak and Alsvid.

Ívaldi (EE-val-di)—"The Mighty". An Elf-Chieftain. With Sunna-Hildigun, the daughter-goddess of the sun, he fathered the *dísir* of vegetation, the swan-maids Idun, Auda, and Signe-Alveig. With the giantess Greip he fathered the sons Völund, Egil, and Slagfin. With his sons, he was the oath-sworn watch by the Élivagar, until he took possession of the mead from the Byrgir well, which had been brought to the moon-god Máni, and thereby became an enemy of the gods. The hostility between the Aesir and their protegés on one side, and Ívaldi and his clan on the other continues through many generations: first Ívaldi himself falls in the struggle; then his sons Völund and Egil; then Egil's son Od-Svipdag and his son Ásmund. In the heroic sagas, where Ívaldi's clan appears under the name Niflungs and Gjúkungs, the struggle continues between them on one side and, on the other, the Amalians and Budlungs who belong to Halfdan's family, favored by the Aesir.

Jálk (YAHLK)—"Gelding". A name of Slagfin, who received a wound which may have castrated him when he had to fight his father Ívaldi in defense of his foster-father, Máni.

J

Jálk (YAHLK)—"Defender". A name that Ódin assumed when he visited Ásmund Svipdagsson. This name is also used by Baldur, and Ódin may have borrowed it from him.

Jari (YAR-i)—"Dispute". A dwarf.

Jarl (YARL)—"Earl", "Chief". Both a name of the second patriarch, Borgar-Skjöld, and the title given to Teutonic chieftains.

Járnsaxa (YAHRN-saks-a)—"She Who Crushes The Iron". A giantess who turns the World-Mill and is thus one of Heimdall's mothers. She is also the mother of Magni with Thór.

Járnvidjor (YAHRN-vid-yor)—"Maids of the Ironwood". Giantesses, kinswomen of Gullveig, that live in the Ironwood.

Járnvidr (YAHRN-vid-r)—"The Ironwood". Situated in the northernmost and easternmost regions of the Underworld, a forest filled with horrors and witchcraft, the haunt of Gullveig, Eggthir, Hati and the rest of "Fenrir's Kin", until Ragnarök. It is possible that in the primal age of peace it was called Gaglvidr, Galgvidr, which denotes a copper or bronze wood.

Jera (YEHR-a)—(Gothic) "Harvest", "Year". The twelfth rune of the Elder futhark, associated with agriculture and working the land, which is why it is connected to such ideas in "The Runelaw".

Jökul (YUHK-ul)—"Glacier". A frost-giant.

Jól (YOHL) also **Yule** (YOOL)—"Wheel". There are several concepts represented by this term. It is first and foremost a designation of the sacred spoked wheels representing different passages of time. The four-spoked wheel, also called the "Sunwheel" represents the solstices and equinoxes. The six-spoked wheel or Yule represents the year long "ages"—the primal age, golden age, silver age, copper age, iron age and the age of Ragnarök. The eight-spoked Yule, also called *achtwung*, represents the holy seasons and the holidays that mark them: Dísting, Ostara, Beltaine, Midsummer, Hleifblót, Haustblót, Vetrablót, and Yule. The Twelve-Spoked Yule represents the twelve months: Snowing, Horning, Lencten, Ostara, Shearing (also "Wynn"), Fallow, Haying, Harvest, Shedding (also "Fal"), Hunting, Frosting, and Yule. As you can see, Yule also signifies a holy day and a month. The holiday is a twelve day, thirteen night celebration beginning on the Winter Solstice (called Modresnacht, "Mother Night"), culminating on December 25th (called Weihnachten, "Holy Night") and ending at the New Year (called Zwölfte Nacht—"Twelfth Night"). The month represented by this term is obviously December, from the Danish *Julemaaned*—"Yule Month", also called *Hrút-manadr* (Icelandic)—"Ram Month" or "Hrútr's (Heimdall's) Month", *Heilagmanoth* (German)—"Holy Month", *Aerra Geola* (Anglo-Saxon)—"Before Yule".

Jólakaka (YOHL-a-kak-a)—"Yule-Cake". A sacred cake eaten at Yule, probably at the Weihnachten (see above), when the folk of today are honored. These cakes would be cut into the shape of pigs or boars, a sacred animal to this season.

Jólruni (YOHL-run-i)—"Yule-Boar". The three holy nights of Yule possibly represent honoring the past, present, and future. The Jólruni could thus embody this by being slaughtered at Modresnacht (when dead ancestors are paid tribute to), eaten at Weihnachten (when the folk is honored with a feast and gift exchanges), then its hide is used to make oaths for the coming year at the Zwölfte Nacht.

Jóltre (YUHL-treh)—"Yule-Tree". Our modern conception of the Yule-Tree, removed from the land and kept in the home, is a later tradition based on one that is ancient. In early times each home had a special "guardian tree" which was considered to have a strong bond with the family living there. In the winter, when the land becomes barren, the tree was decorated to mimic the more verdurous seasons of the year.

Jólvidr (YOHL-vid-r)—"Yule-Log". A log burned at the Modresnacht, honoring the return of the sun. It is kindled from the remains of the previous year's log and is usually of Oak or Ash.

Jörmungand (YUHR-mun-gand)—"The Great Gandr", "The Great Serpent". Son of Loki and Gullveig. He encircles the earth and is so large he has to bite his own tail to fit around it. He will fight with, and be killed by Thór at Ragnarök, but the Ásagod will die from his venom shortly thereafter.

Jörmungrund (YUHR-mun-grund)—"The Great-Ground". The Underworld.

Jöruvellir (YUHR-u-vehl-er)—"The Jara-Plains", "The Sandy-Plains". The Aurvangaland's border with the sea, where Ask and Embla were created.

Jötun (YUH-tun)—"Giant" or "Eater (from "Etin")". There are two Jötun clans—the higher born from Ymir's arms, descended from Mímir and Bestla; and the lower born from Ymir's feet, descended from Thrudgelmir. The former are divine and deserve divine honors, the latter are often enemies of the gods.

Jötunheim (YUH-tun-haym)—"Giant-Home". There are two: One in Midgard located in the far north and east, probably identical to the polar regions uninhabited by men. The other is in Niflhel, where the lower Jötuns go after death.

Julleuchter (YOOL-loik-ter)—(German) "Yule-Light". A candle holder or lamp, decorated with the six-spoked Yule and a heart (connected to Freyja) on each of its four sides. It would hold a flame of the foddik or Need-fire, making it a "ken", a sacred torch used for consecration and as an invocational beacon to the gods.

K

Kári (KAHR-i)—"The Wind". A Jötun. Son of Fornjót and brother of Aegir (water) and Logi (fire). Personification of violent winds.

Karl (KARL)—"Carl", "Freeman". Another name of Ódin and a name of the progenitor of "thanes" or freemen.

Kenaz (KEHN-az)—(Gothic) "Torch". The sixth rune of the Elder futhark, representing the sacred flame as well as the search for enlightenment, which is why it is associated with such ideas in "The Runelaw".

Kerlaugar (KEHR-loug-ar)—"Tub-Baths". Two rivers Thór must wade over to get to the Helthing near Urd's fountain.

Kíarr (KEE-ar) or **Kjarr** (KYAHR)—"Chieftain". Father of Sif and Gróa. Identical to Sigtrygg.

Kili—(KIL-i)—A dwarf.

Kolga (KAWL-ga)—"Raging Sea". One of the nine daughters of Aegir who are representatives of the waves.

Köll (KUHL)—"Cold". A giant killed by Egil.

Kon (KAWN)—"The Noble". Another name of Halfdan.

Körmt (KUHRMT)—"Protecting One". A river Thór must wade over to get to the Helthing near Urd's fountain.

Kvasir (KVA-ser)—"Fermented Drink". Personification of the mead, originally the name of Mímir's well. In a strophe by Einar Skalagram, poetry is called "Kvasir's blood". A narrative, composed in Christian times and found in the *Prose Edda* says that when the Aesir and Vanir made peace, it was sealed when they spat in a vat. As a sign of reconciliation, they created a man from the spittle, whom they named Kvasir, and who was extraordinarily wise, but fell victim to two dwarves, Fjálar and Galar, who slew him when he was their guest and let his blood run into a vat. They blended it with honey and, of that mixture, made the Skaldic mead. This pseudo-myth about the "sign of reconciliation", Kvasir, has its only basis in the half-strophe by Einar Skalaglam, which was misunderstood or deliberately misinterpreted by the creator of the pseudo-myth. That the dwarf Fjálar, Surt's son, (Suttung), is mentioned here probably has some connection to his theft of Mímir's mead to create the Byrgir fountain.

L

Lá (LAH)—"Blood". One of Lódur's gifts to humanity, originally given to the first Teutonic pair, Ask and Embla. Afterwards these gifts are impregnated within the fruits of Yggdrasil, then sent to expecting women. Our ancestors conceived the human body as made up of six elements, rather than two (matter and soul). These are Lódur's gifts—*Lá* with *Laeti*, "Blood with Motion" and Litr Goda, "The Image of the Gods"; Hoenir's gift—*Ódr* "soul", "ego", and Ódin's gift—*Önd* "spirit". Beyond the idea that *Lá* is the sacred life-force that keeps us going, it is also our genetics or family line, passed on through the generations.

Lading (LA-ding) or **Laeding** (LAI-ding)—A fetter with which Fenrir was bound, but he broke out of.

Laerád (LAI-rahd)—"Mead-Tree". Another name for Yggdrasil.

Laeti (LAI-ti)—"Motion". Combined with *Lá*, "blood", this designates the way a conscious being moves and acts, representing the animal elements as separated from the plant element we were created from. It is one of Lódur's gifts to our people.

Laguz (LAG-uz)—(Gothic) "Water". The twenty-first rune of the Elder futhark, the water rune, connected to the "Ewa" concept (see) and the ability to flow around obstacles in "The Runelaw".

Landtaka (LAND-tak-a)—"Land-Taking". A ceremony used when one settles or buys land, most especially attributed to Thjálfi, Egil's son and Thór's protégé, who is a god of settlements and sanctifying lands.

Landvaettir (LAND-vai-ter)—"Land Wights". A branch of the Álfar living in Midgard connected to the land in various ways. Some, like the Tomte, are connected to farms and homes, while others, like the Nix and Strömkarls are linked to forests and rivers.

Laufey (LOU-vay)—"Leaf-Isle". Loki's mother, called so as representative of the leaf-crown struck by the destructive fire produced from this, as his brother Helblindi was conceived from rain-torrents and water spouts of his father's hurricane and their brother Byleist became the tornado.

Leifnirs Eldar (LAYV-ners EHLD-ar)—"Leifnir's Flames" (Leifnir = Frey?). A wonderful potion that can allow one to free themselves from any fetter with their breath.

Leifthrasir (LAYV-thras-er) or **Lífthrasir** (LEEV-thras-er)—"Full of Life", "Desirous of Life". One of the Ásmegir, currently dwelling in Ódainsakr, Mímir's grove. He will be the progenitor of the next age's human race.

Leikin (LAY-kin)—"Plague". Loki's daughter, queen of the spirits of disease. In Christian times, she was confused with Hel (Urd, the dis of fate and death).

Leipt (LAYPT)—"Lightning". A river, flowing through Hel's fields of bliss, by whose clear and shining waters oaths are sworn.

Leita kynnis (LAY-ta KEN-is)—"Visiting Kinsmen". When one deceased is allowed entrance to Hel, the realms of bliss, they are first taken around, probably by their *hamingja*, to visit their ancestors and learn the history of their family and folk from those who experienced it firsthand. *Leita kynnis* designates this.

Lencten (LEHNK-tehn)—From German Lenzinmanoth—"Spring Month", also Middle English Lenten "spring". The name for March in the sacred Ásatrú calendar. Also called Einmanadr (Icelandic)—"The Month before Summer", Tormaaned (Danish)—"Winter Month", and Rhedmonad (Anglo-Saxon)—"Rhred's (Heimdall's?) Month".

Lettfetti (LEHT-feht-i)—"Light-Foot". One of the Aesir's horses.

Lidmeld (LID-mehld)—"Limb-grist". Mold from the world Grotti-mill, made from the bodies of Jötuns, used to create the fertile soil of the land.

Líf (LEEV)—"Life". One of the Ásmegir, the maiden preserved in Mímir's grove, Ódainsakr, who shall become the progenitress of the coming world-age's virtuous human race.

Likamí (LIK-am-ee)—"The Earthly Body". The natural elements which were formed or grown by Mímir (Modsognir) and Durin-Surt into human likenesses, then given life by Ódin, Hoenir, and Lódur.

Limar (LIM-ar)—"Limbs". Thorn-rods kept Lódur which the Heiptir use to drive nidings to Niflhel by beating their heals with them.

Limrúnar (LIM-roon-ar)—"Limb-Runes". A group of runes used in the healing art.

Lindbaugi (LIND-boug-i)—"Serpent-Rings". Possibly a designation for oath-rings in serpent-form, reminding those who take oaths of the punishment for breaking them. *Skaldskaparmál* 4, in a strophe by Bragi, calls a serpent "the ugly ring". Saxo (*Historia Danica* Book 8) mentions a ring in serpent form which strikes out and kills would-be thieves. These *Lindbaug*i are mentioned in *Völundarkvida* (verse 6).

Litr goda (LIT-r GAWD-a)—"Image of the Gods". A body of finer material existing within the *Likamí*, giving it shape and character which is visible to the eye. It is one of Lódur's gifts.

Ljónar (LYOHN-ar)—"Peacemakers". Also called *Jafnendr*—"Arbitrators". Among the gods these are Baldur, Hödur and Forseti, primarily. They are judges and work to "settle all disputes".

Ljósálfar (LYOHS-ahlv-ar)—"Light-Elves". The group of Álfar dealing exclusively with light, or the lighting of the sky, including Dag, Delling, both Sunnas, Billing and even Nát (Night is also called Ostara [see]).

Loddfáfnir (LAWD-vahv-ner)—"Slow-Fáfnir". Another name of Hödur. Many features from the story about Sigurd Fáfnirsbane's childhood adventures are collected from the myth about Hödur. In the song about Fáfnir, it says: "In ancient days, people believed that a dying man's word had great power, if he cursed his enemy by name". When he was mortally wounded by Sigurd, Fáfnir asked his young killer what his name was and for this reason Sigurd responded "Sluggish-beast" (*gaufugt dýr*, not "glorious beast" as it has heretofore been translated), this being an allusion to Fáfnir himself, who laid motionless on his treasure the greatest part of the day. Sigurd not only concealed his own name from the beginning, but chose one applicable to the questioner, so that the expected curse would fall back on him. In Thidrek's Saga of Bern, a hero, Heimir, appears who calls himself after a dragon whose bane he became. This explains why an Ása-youth appears in *Hávamál* with a peculiar dragon—or serpent-name. He found himself in Ódin's hall and received advice from him and warnings, whose content definitely refers to the myth about Hödur. That Hödur was known by the name Loddfáfnir has its basis in that he, depicted as a remarkable hunter, killed a dragon and called himself Loddfáfnir under the same circumstances as Sigurd called himself *gaufugt dýr*. Loddfáfnir has the double-meanings "rough serpent" and "sluggish serpent" and consequently comes very close to the meaning of gaufugt dýr. Also, in the song of Sigrdrífa, Hödur, not Sigurd, is the original hero.

Lódur (LOH-dur)—"Fire-Producer". Son of Bor, brother of Ódin and Hoenir, with whom he created Midgard and the Teutonic people. He is ward of the atmosphere and caretaker of the world Grotti-Mill. He is father of Máni and the mother Sunna (Sváva), who have the daughters Nanna and the daughter Sunna (Hildigun) together. Lódur is also called Vili, Mundilfori, and Gevar.

Lofn (LAWV-n)—"Permission", "Praise". An Ásynja, who is said to be good for lovers whose union is forbidden or otherwise impossible to invoke. She uses the influence she has with Ódin and Frigga to their benefit.

Logi (LAWG-i)—"Fire". The personification of fire in the service of destruction and as such belongs to Surt's household. He is a son of Fornjót and brother to Hlér (Water) and Kári (Wind).

Lögsömadr (LUHG-suh-mad-r)—"Law-Speaker". One who knows the tribal laws and can recite them at the *Thing* for ceremonial purposes and in settling disputes or discussing affairs.

Loki (LAWK-i)—"Fire", "Destroying Fire". Son of Farbauti and Laufey, adopted into Ásgard by Ódin. Father of Leikin, Fenrir, and Jörmungand with Gullveig, who joins him as the evil principle of the Teutonic Mythology. He is characterized by a psychological acumen and a sense of humor without parallel. The frightful and the comical are fused into one.

Lóni (LOHN-i)—"Lazy One". A dwarf.

Lopt (LAWPT)—"The Airy". Both a name of Loki and of Völund as the enemy of the gods, which is a synonym of his names Byr-"Storm" and Gust-"Wind".

Lyngvi (LENG-vi)—"Overgrown With Heather". The island in the Ámsvartnir sea where Loki, Fenrir and other "sons of the world-ruin" lie bound until Ragnarök.

M

Magni (MAG-ni)—"The Strong". Son of Thór and Jarnsaxa, brother of Módi and Thrud. He survives Ragnarök with Módi and together they inherit Thór's hammer.

Maid (MAID)—Designating a position in the tribe of virgin women who tend the sacred groves and temples and keep the foddik, or eternal flame, burning. They are devoted to Freyja, Gefjon, and Fulla.

Malrúnar (MAL-roon-ar)—"Speech-Runes". Runes that can give speech to the dead, especially when they come to the Helthing, where they are otherwise mute.

Máni (MAHN-i)—"Moon". Evidence points to the probability that Máni is identical to Lódur. However, it is known that Lódur-Mundilfori had a son named Máni who is a brother of Sunna. It may be that the son Máni is the consort of the elder Sunna and together they have the daughters Sunna-Hildigun and Nanna. As in other instances, it seems that both the father and the son may use the same name, like the two Sunnas, mother and daughter. Máni is lord of the Heiptir, and it is to him we pray to avoid their vengeful punishments.

Mánisdag (MAHN-is-dag)—"Máni's Day". Designates Monday in our reckoning of the weekdays.

Manna mjötud (MAN-a MYUH-tud)—"Fruits of Fate". Another name for the fruits of Yggdrasil after they have been consecrated for the wombs of expecting women. The deities involved in this process are Urd, Hoenir, Frigga, Freyja, and their attendants.

Mannaz (MAN-az)—(Gothic) "Man". The twentieth rune of the Elder futhark, associated with mankind and our people. Halfdan, the third Teutonic patriarch, is also called "Mannus", designating him as a father of the folk. Because of this, this rune is connected to ideals of our genetic inheritance in "The Runelaw".

Mannheim (MAN-haym)—"Man-Home". The part of the world where Ódin and the Aesir took refuge when the Vanir ruled in Ásgard.

Maringaborg (MAR-ing-a-borg) or **Maeringaburg** (MAI-ring-a-burg)—Hadding's home when he was in exile.

Marmennil (MAR-mehn-il)—"Merman" (see Haffrú). They are described as wise and prophetic, but silent. On more than one occasion, seafarers and fishermen have succeeded in capturing mermen, who then, after a promise of being released into the sea again, are able to foretell future events.

Mead (MEED)—ON Mjöd (MYUHD). The most sacred substance in our faith. It has six forms: the three from the Underworld fountains—Hvergelmir, which gives endurance; Mímisbrunn, which gives wisdom; Urdabrunn, which gives strength. The three mixed together is the "Veigar", which rejuvenates and clears the mind of painful memories. The mead of Ásgard comes from the leaves of Yggdrasil, which is watered by the Underworld fountains. Our mead comes from Hrímfaxi's dew and the bees who make honey from it.

Megingjörd (MEHG-ing-yuhrd)—"The Belt of Strength". Thór's belt which doubles his strength when he wears it.

Meili (MAYL-i)—"Gentle", "Mild". Another name of Baldur. Thór commends himself on one occasion as being Ódin's son and Meili's brother. In one of his epithets (foot-meili), the gentle Hoenir is compared with Baldur. The "rain of weapons" is called both "Meil-rain" and "Fal's rain", with reference to the "rain of weapons", in which Baldur stood when the gods shot, threw, and hewed at him.

Menglad (MEHN-glad) also masculine **Menglöd** (MEN-glod)—"Necklace-Lover", "Ornament-Lover". A name of Freyja, and of Frey in its masculine form. This epithet is also used in the plural (Menglödum) and then refers to them both.

Menja (MEHN-ya)—"Jewel-Maiden". Fenja's sister who turned the lesser Grotti-mill until it was destroyed. This has also been linked to damage done to the greater World-Mill during the Fimbulwinter, caused by these two giantesses.

Midgard (MID-gard)—"The Middle-Realm". The centermost portion of the earth-plate, surrounded by the ocean, in which humans reside. Earth.

Midsumarsblót (MID-sum-ars-bloht)—"Midsummer's Blót". The festival of the summer solstice, in honor of Baldur as god of the season and all the deities of light and warmth. A strophe in *Fjölsvinnsmál* (41) states that Freyja's *dísir* are offered to "every summer", which may refer to this celebration.

Mímameid (MEEM-a-mayd)—"Mímir's Tree". Another name of Yggdrasil.

Mímir (MEEM-er)—"The Thinker" or "Memory". Ymir's son, created from the sweat of his arms with Bestla. The ruler of Jörmungrund, the Underworld, keeper of Yggdrasil, guardian of the well of wisdom, the origin of spiritual cultivation, Ódin's maternal uncle, chief of the nature artists and primeval smiths. He was slain by the Vanir during their war with the Aesir.

Mímisholt (MEEM-is-hawlt)—"Mímir's Grove". Mímir's sacred grove in the Underworld.

Minnehorn (MIN-eh-horn)—"Memory-Horn". In the sacred mead-feast, known as *Sumble*, a "horn" or "round" in which ancestors are honored and toasted.

Mistiltein (MIST-il-tayn)—"Mistletoe", "Twig of Mistletoe". Besides the plant, this term designates the arrow forged by Völund for Loki, who gave it to Hödur, who unknowingly killed Baldur with it.

Mjöllnir (MYUHL-ner)—"The Crusher". The common name for both of the hammers with which Thór appears in the myths. The older hammer, called "Vingnir's Mjöllnir", was stone and had probably once belonged to Thór's foster-father, who was called Vingnir. The newer one, which was iron and was destroyed by Völund's sword, was forged by Sindri. This is probably one of the most sacred symbols of the Teutonic religion, recognized for its power against the forces of Chaos and its ability to consecrate anything. Because of this it is worn by most Ásatrúar as an amulet.

Módgud (MOHD-gud)—"Furious Battler". A subterranean *dís* who watches Gjallarbru, the bridge the dead cross to get to Hel.

Módi (MOHD-i)—"The Courageous". Thór's son, brother of Magni who inherits Mjöllnir with him after Ragnarök.

Módin (MOHD-in)—"The Courageous". Dvalin's horse.

Módir (MOH-der)—"Mother". Progenitress of the nobility, mother of Borgar-Jarl.

Móin (MOH-in)—"Moor-Animal". One of the serpents that gnaws at Yggdrasil's roots.

Mökkurkalfi (MUHK-ur-kalv-i)—"Cloud Calf". A clay-giant, created by the Jötuns to help Hrungnir in his battle against Thór. He was slain by Thjálfi.

Munvegar (MUN-vehg-ar)—"Paths of Pleasure". Roads in Urd's realm of bliss.

Moot (MOOT)—"Assembly". Another word for "*Thing*". Also called Folkmoot (cp. Danish *Folkething*). A gathering or meeting where the folk discuss important matters, settle disputes, and enjoy each other's company.

Morn (MORN, like "mourn")—"Agony of the Soul". A spirit of disease.

Munin (MUN-in)—"Memory". One of Ódin's ravens. The other is Hugin.

Muspel (MU-spehl)—"World-Ruin". The *Prose Edda* assumes that the southern part of Ginnungagap from which warmth comes is named Muspelsheim, and places Muspelsheim in contrast to Niflheim, the realm of primordial cold. This assumption is incorrect. The word *Muspel* signifies world-ruin, world-destruction, so "Muspel's sons" are the evil beings that accompany Loki on the ship Naglfar from the island Lyngvi in Ámsvartnir's sea to the battlefield where Ragnarök takes place.

Myrkvidr (MERK-vid-r)—"Dark-Wood", "Murk-Wood". Identical to the Jarnvidr, the Ironwood.

N

Nabbi (NAB-i)—A primeval artist, who forged the boar Gullinbursti with Dáin. Identical to Dvalin-Sindri, who is named beside Dáin-Brokk in other sources.

Nafnabinda (NAV-na-bind-a)—"Name Binding". The ritual of giving a name to a newly born child, performed by swaddling the babe in a cloth associated with its birth (black patchwork for low-born, red linen for freemen or thanes and white silk for nobility) and sprinkling it with water using a birch twig. Certain traditions even revolve around the giving of pseudonyms or nicknames later in life. In all such cases a gift always accompanies the giving of the name and such acts constitute an acceptance or adoption into one's clan or friendship.

Naglfar (NAG-l-var)—"Nail Ship". The ship built of dead men's nails, upon which Loki, Fenrir, and Loki's ("Muspel's") sons proceed to the battle of Ragnarök. The idea is that people should pay special care in their respects for the dead; we should wash them, comb their hair, trim their nails, and "pray for their happy sleep" (*Sigrdrífumal*). When this is not done it signifies the decline of morality and the coming of Ragnarök.

Nágrindar (NAH-grind-ar)—"Ná-Gates", "Corpse-Gates". The gates of Niflhel.

Náin (NAH-in)—A dwarf.

Náir (NAH-er)—"Corpses". Designating the *nidings* in Niflhel after they have died their second deaths and have not been allowed to drink of the rejuvenating "Veigar". This second death occurs when they reach the Nágrindar.

Nameday—This is a Catholic tradition which likely, as with most of their practices, has heathen origins. For them, it marks their day of baptismal, which for some reason is also associated with the giving of their "Christian" name. It should be noted that the catholic baptismal ceremony mimics the Odinic Nafnabinda, and not anything found in Biblical accounts. It is probable that this "Nameday" was an ancient Teutonic rite, similar to the modern birthday celebration. It was believed by the ancients that a child was not actually a living being with a soul (*Ódr*) until it was given a name.

Nanna (NA-na)—"The Brave One". A moon-dis, Máni's daughter, Sunna-Hildigun's sister, Bladur's wife. Among the Germans, she had the name Sinhtgunt, "she who battles her way forth during the night". In the song about Helgi Hundingsbane, which is a Christian imitation of the Baldur myth, Nanna is called Sváva, which was one of the names of her mother (Sunna-Sváva) in the myth. She is portrayed as a Valkyrie "who rides through air and water".

Náströnds (NAH-struhnds)—"Corpse-Shore". One of the places of punishment for the damned.

Nát (NAHT)—"Night". Mímir's daughter with Sinmara. The Mother of the Gods. She bore Njörd with Máni-Naglfari, Frigga with Hoenir-Fjörgynn, and Dag with Delling. She has sisters, night-*dísir*, who according to medieval sagas are twelve in number. One of them is Bödvild.

Naudeldir (NOUD-ehld-er)—"Need-Fire". The friction-fire, represented by Lódur and Heimdall as the purest of flames. Thjálfi and Thór once used it to stabilize and sanctify Götland, thus it is a tool used in consecrating land, among other things.

Naudiz (NOU-diz)—(Gothic) "Need", "Necessity". The tenth rune of the Elder futhark, the rune of need, associating it with such concepts in "The Runelaw".

Nauma (NOU-ma)—"Giantess" or "Woman". This name designates Idun in the poem *Hrafnagaldr Odins*, when she lives among her brothers, Ívaldi's sons. Völund, also called Thjázi, was one of these brothers, as well as her lover when she "dressed in a wolf-skin, changed disposition, delighted in guile, shifted her shape." Compare the names Irpa and Yrsa.

Neorxenavang (NE-or-zen-a-vang)—"Neri's Plain". Identical to Glaesisvellir. Mímir's domain in the Underworld. Mímir = Neri. An old Anglo-Saxon term for Paradise.

Nidafjöll (NID-a-vyuhl)—"Nidi's Mountain". The mountain range that separates Niflhel from Hel's realms of bliss, within Mímir's realm. Mímir = Nidi.

Nidhad (NID-had)—"The Underworld Being". Another name of Mímir, who once captured and imprisoned Völund.

Nidhögg (NID-huhg)—"The Underworld Serpent". An underworld dragon and one of the spirits who torment the damned. He gnaws at Yggdrasil's roots.

Niding (NID-ing)—"Criminal". One who has disgraced him or herself by commiting a "*nid*", a transgression of the sacred laws, which can only be countered by compensation.

Niding Pole—"Insult Pole". A pole raised to declare someone a *niding*, or to protest a disgraceful act. It traditionally either has a horse's head on it or an image of the accused in a lewd position.

Nidjar (NID-yar)—"Nidi's sons". The seven (in other traditions twelve) sons of Mímir who enclosed themselves in a citadel after their father's death and will sleep until Ragnarök. They are nature-artists and warriors.

Niflheim (NIV-l-haym)—"Mist-Home", "The World of Fog or Mist". The name for the land of cold in the far north of Jörmungrund, the Underworld. Its primordial frost blended with southern elements of warmth, nurtured by the well of wisdom, to create the first life forms and lands.

Niflhel (NIV-l-hehl)—"Mist-Hel". Identical to Niflheim, but the name of this realm after the primordial age of peace, when there arose a need for a place to house the damned. Here are the Hrímthurses, the spirits of disease, demons of torture, and monsters of all kinds. Over it all is its queen, Leikin, who serves as Urd's servant in respect to the punishments administered there.

Niflungs (NIV-lungs)—"Mist-Sons". A designation for Ívaldi's sons, Völund, Egil, and Slagfin.

Nisse (NIS-ee)—A branch of the Landvaettir.

Nixi (NIX-ee) or **Necks** (NECKS)—(German) "Water-Spirit". A branch of the Landvaettir, which can be heard striking their harps during storms at sea. A water-sprite, usually in human form or half-human and half-fish.

Njörd (NYUHRD)—"The Strong". A Vanagod, Frigga's half brother with whom she had Frey, Freyja and possibly also eight more daughters who are Freyja's maidservants (Blid, Frid, Björt, Hlíf, Hlífthrasa, Thjódvara, Eir and Blík). He is Máni's and Nát's son, and god of the sea, of wealth, commerce, and seafarers.

Njördsdag (NYUHRDS-dag)—"Njörd's Day". A contemporary designation of Saturday, "Saturn's Day", based on the fact that Njörd is equated with Saturn in the *Prose Edda* (Codex Wormianus) and that both Njörd and Saturn are associated with water, prosperity, and wealth. The island Tysneoen in Norway was once called *Njardarlog*—"Njörd's Bath", which we should compare to the Old Icelandic *Lagardag*—"Bath Day", used for Saturday.

Nóatún (NOH-a-toon)—"Ship-Yard". Njörd's native home in Vanaheim.

Nóri (NOHR-i)—A dwarf.

Nornir (NORN-er)—"Norns". Dísir of fate belonging to Mímir's clan. The foremost are Urd, Verdandi, and Skuld who weave the web of Wyrd, forming the destinies of all things. To the Norns also belong the *dísir* of birth, *fylgjur* or *hamingjur*, and Valkyrjur. Skuld is the leader of the Valkyrjur.

Nýall (NEE-ahl)—"New-All". A philosophy founded by Dr. Helgi Pjeturss in Iceland in the first part of the 20th century. It presents significant, scientific insights regarding the nature of dreams, human origins, the divine, afterlife, morality, etc.

Nýi (NEE)—"New Moon". A dwarf.

O

Ódáinsakr (OHD-ah-ins-ak-r)—"The Acre of the Not-Dead", "The Acre of Immortality". The land of the Ásmegir in Mímir's realm, where Baldur, Hödur, and Nanna reside.

Ódhroerir (OHD-rur-er)—"The Spirit-Rouser". One of the names of Mímir's well, which is also called Bodn, Són, and Kvasir.

Ódin (OH-din)—"The Inspiring". The chieftain of the gods. Son of Bor and Bestla, brother of Hoenir-Vé and Lódur-Vili, and father of Thór, Bragi, Baldur, Týr, Hödur, Vídar, and Váli. Married to Frigga. He is god of wisdom, music, poetry, victory, wind, inspiration, and so much more. He owns the horse Sleipnir, the spear Gungnir, the wolves Freki and Geri, the ravens Hugin and Munin, the ring Draupnir, and the hall Valhalla. He has over one hundred bynames and epithets.

Ódr (OHD-r) also **Ód** (OHD)—"Soul". Hoenir's gift to our folk, originally given to Ask and Embla and continued to be delivered to expecting women through the fruits of Yggdrasil. It forms the kernel of human personality, its ego, and its manifestations are understanding, memory, fancy, and will.

Ódr (OHD-r) also **Ód** (OHD)—"The One Endowed with Soul", "The Soulful". Another name of Svipdag, Freyja's husband.

Offóte (AW-voht-eh)—Hödur has a wolf-hound who came from the herds of the Jötun Offóte.

Ófnir (OHV-ner)—"The Entangler". One of the serpents who gnaws at Yggdrasil's roots. Also a name of Ódin.

Ókólnir (OH-kohl-ner)—"The Never-Cold Land". One of the names of Mímir's subterranean kingdom.

Ölgefjon (UHL-gehv-yawn)—"Ale-Giver". Another name of Gróa as a swan-maid, who are known specifically to be distributors of the mead, specifically Ásgard's mead pressed from Yggdrasil's leaves.

Ölgefn (UHL-gehv-n)—"Ale-Giver". Another name of Idun as a swan-maid.

Ölrún (UHL-roon)—"The One Knowing Ale-Runes". Another name of Sif as a swan-maid.

Ölrúnar (UHL-roon-ar)—"Ale-Runes". A group of runes used to bless and purify mead or ale. May also designate the brewer's art.

Önd (UHND)—"Spirit", "Breath". Ódin's gift to our folk, originally given to Ask and Embla and continued to be delivered to expecting women through Yggdrasil's fruits. It is that which forges our bond with the divine and allows us to participate in workings connected to them.

Ópi (OH-pi)—"Hysteria". A spirit of disease.

Óri (OH-ri)—"The Raging". A dwarf.

Örlög (UHR-luhg)—"Fate", "Original Law", "Primal Law". The force or principle, created by the Norns, which determines what is and what shall become.

Örlögthaettir (UHR-luhg-thai-ter)—"Threads of Fate". Threads created from the power of Urd's well which she feeds to her sister Verdandi, who weaves it into the Web of Wyrd, then Skuld cuts it with her sickle.

Örmt (UHRMT)—One of the rivers Thór has to wade through on his way to the Helthing by Urd's well.

Örvandil (UHR-van-dil)—"The One Busy with Arrows". Another name of Egil, Ívaldi's son.

Óskópnir (OH-skohp-ner)—The plain on which the battle of Ragnarök occurs. Also known as Vigrid's plain.

Ostara (AW-star-a)—(Old High German) "Goddess of the Eastern Dawn", "The Shining". Also called Eostre or Easter. Identical to Nát, goddess of night who brings the morning dews and greets her husband Delling, god of the dawn, each day. With him she had the son Dag ("Day"), which is a lovely poetic image:

Night bears the Day with Dawn. She has eleven sisters who are also *dísir* of night and at the same time of the dawn—the red-clad daughters of Mímir. Like the Hindu Ushas they can be called Ostaras after their leader. Ostara is also the name for the Spring Equinox in our festivals, as well as the name for the month of April in the sacred Ásatrú calendar, after the German Ostarmanoth—"Ostara's Month" and the Anglo-Saxon Eosturmonad—"Ostara's Month". It is also called Eggtid (Icelandic)—"Egg-Time" and Faaremaaned (Danish)—"Sheep-Month". Ostara-Nát is goddess of both the dawn of the day and of the year.

Othala (OH-thal-a)—(Gothic) "Property" (identical to "*Odal*"), "Estate". The twenty-fourth rune of the Elder futhark, associated with inheritance, which is why it is connected to such concepts in "The Runelaw".

Othali (AW-thal-i)—"Restless Anxiety". A spirit of disease.

Otter (AW-ter)—"Otter". Fáfnir's and Regin's brother, who enjoyed swimming in the form of an otter.

P

Perthro (PERTH-roh)—(Gothic) "Lot-Box", "Dice-Cup". The fourteenth rune of the Elder futhark, associated with oracles, connecting it to such concepts in "The Runelaw".

R

Rádgríd (RAHD-greed)—"Violent Counsel". A Valkyrie.

Rádsvid (RAHD-svid)—"Wise in Advice". A dwarf.

Ragnarök (RAG-na-ruhk)—"Twilight of the Gods". The doom of the world, the end of this world-age and its powers.

Raido (RIDE-oh, like "Ride"-O)—(Gothic) "Wagon", "Ride". The fifth rune of the Elder futhark, associated with traveling, which is why it is connected to such concepts in "The Runelaw".

Rán (RAHN)—"Robber". Aegir's wife, a sea-giantess, possibly a mermaid (*Haf-frú*). The waves, symbolized as nine sisters, are called her daughters (see Bára). That the drowned remained with Rán is an idea from the Christian middle ages. The mythic concept was that the drowned shared the fate of all the rest of the departed and came to the world of bliss or punishment. However, Rán's halls may have originally been considered to be an antechamber for the drowned on their way to Hel, where the giantess and her servants would tend to them.

Randgríd (RAND-greed)—"Shield Destroyer". A Valkyrie.

Randvér (RAND-veer)—"Shield-Warrior". A son of Gudhorm.

Ráni (RAHN-i)—Another name of Váli.

Ratatösk (RAT-a-tuhsk)—"Rati's Tooth" (Rati = "The Traveller" or "The Turner", Heimdall). Heimdall's fire-auger, symbolized as a squirrel (which is still a symbol of fire in folk-belief) in the poem *Grimnismál*, which runs from Yggdrasil's crown down to its root.

Regin (REH-gin)—"Powers". A name of the gods and primeval smiths that took part in the creation of the world. Also a name of Egil, who was among these "powers".

Reginleif (REH-gin-layv)—A valkyrie.

Rind (RIND, like "Rend")—The daughter of Billing, lord of the sunset glow. Mother of Váli, Baldur's avenger, with Ódin.

Röskva (RUHSK-va)—"The Maturing", "The One Bearing Fruit". Thjálfi's sister first adopted by Egil, then by Thór, as was her brother.

Róta (ROHT-a) or **Rósta** (ROHST-a)—"Creator of Confusion". A Valkyrie.

Rúnatal (ROON-a-tal)—"The Rune Poem". The part of the *Hávamál* dealing with Ódin's self-sacrifice to obtain the runes (verses 139-165). This contains all the elements of an initiation into manhood, which may have been mimicked by our ancestors. If this is the case, such an initiation could be named after the *Rúnatal*.

Rund (RUND)—A Valkyrie.

Rune (ROON)—"Secret". A sacred group of various symbols with many spiritual and practical uses, as well as charms and teachings related to all sorts of topics. The runes act as guides and lessons in matters dealing with aiding others and gaining success in any endeavor. They also act as prayers and songs to the gods and goddesses.

Runic Era—This is a dating system based on one of the earliest runic finds, although since its formulation earlier artifacts have been discovered. The mythological concept is that this would signify the time when the gods brought us the runes. This find was dated back to 250 B.C.E., making 2006 C.E. = 2256 R.E.

Rusila (RUS-il-a)—Ívaldi's mother, queen of the Álfar and an ancient queen of the Swedes (Sviones), also said to be a mermaid. She is identical to the German Rusla and Rütze.

S

Saehrímnir (SAI-reem-ner)—"Sea-Rime". The boar of Valhalla, said to be slain and reborn each day. It probably symbolizes the purest elements fed to the Einherjar.

Saegr (SAIG-r)—"Effervescent Juice". The pail of Byrgir's mead taken with Bil and Hjúki to the moon.

Sága (SAH-ga)—Some have assumed that the Norse Mythology gave history its own goddess on the basis of the name *Saga*, which was thought to be identical with saga, narrative, legend, history. The goddess-name *Saga* however is *Sága* in its Icelandic form and associated with Saegr, the name of the pail in which Bil and Hjúki bore Byrgir's mead when they were taken aloft by the moon. Thereafter Bil became an Ásynja, and she is identical to Idun. She and Sága are one and the same. Concerning Sága, it is said that "she and Ódin gladly drink from golden goblets, in Sökkvabekk, while cool waves swish over". Sökkvabek (the sinking ship; *bekk*r is one of the Old Norse poetry's ship-designations) is a poetic name of the moon, which as cargo bears Byrgir's mead and was "Ódin's wineship". The cool billows that swish over Sökkvabek belong to the sea of air. Thus, if not directly the Ásynja of history, Sága is nevertheless the Ásynja of the skaldic mead and skaldic inspiration, and because historic events are especially commemorated through the skaldic art, the name Sága can continue to be used in that sense.

Sangrid (SAN-grid)—A Valkyrie.

Seid (SAYD)—"Sorcery". The black-art, founded by Gullveig. It is characterized by mind-control, poisoning, conjuration, and necromancy. It was banned by the gods after the Aesir/Vanir war, declared to be harmful to our folk.

Sela (SEHL-a)—"Woman". A giantess, sister of the giant Köll. Both were killed by Egil.

Shearing (SHEER-ing)—(English). The name for May in the sacred Ásatrú calendar. It could also be called Wynn "Joy" after the rune Wunjo and the German Winnemanoth—"Joy Month". Also called Sólmanadr (Icelandic)—"Sun Month", Mejmaaned (Danish)—"Blossom Month", and Thrimilcmonad (Anglo-Saxon)—"Month of Three Milkings".

Shedding (SHEHD-ing)—(English). The name for September in the sacred Ásatrú calendar. It can also be called "Fal", from the German Pholmânôt "Phol's Month" or "Fal's Month". Fal is identical to Baldur. Also called Haustmanadr (Icelandic)—"Autumn Month", Fiskemaaned (Danish)—"Fish Month", Witumanoth (German)—"Wood Month", and Halegmonad (Anglo-Saxon)—"Holy Month".

Sid (SID)—"The Slow". A subterranean river.

Sif (SIV)—"The Dís of Affinity". Daughter of Sigtrygg, a swan-maid, a *dís* of vegetation, Gróa's sister and Egil's second wife, who bore the archer and skier Ull with him. She was later adopted into Ásgard as an Ásynja, for after Egil's death she became Thór's wife. She is probably identical to Thórgerd Hölgabrud and Yrsa.

Sigmund (SIG-mund)—"Victory-Gift". Another name of Ódin, Hödur's father. In the heroic poems, Sigurd Fáfnirsbane, whose story contains many elements of Hödur's myth, has the father Sigmund.

Sigrdrífa (SIG-r-dreev-a)—"Giver of Victory". In Ynglingasaga, Vanlande, a variant of Völund, has the maid Driva, the same as Sigrdrífa, as his lover. In the myth Völund's lover was Idun. Thus in the heroic poems it is originally Idun who bears the name Sigrdrífa.

Sigrún (SIG-roon)—"She Who Knows the Victory Runes" (cp. Ölrún). Under this name, both of Halfdan's wives Gróa and Alveig are combined into a single personality in the heroic poem about Helgi Hundingsbane, which gathers elements from the myth about Halfdan.

Sigrúnar (SIG-roon-ar)—"Victory Runes". A group of runes that grant victory in battle or in endeavors.

Sigtrygg (SIG-treg)—"Victory-True". Gróa's and Sif's father, killed by Halfdan. Identical to Kíar.

Sigyn (SIG-en)—"Victory". A giantess, Loki's wife who holds a bowl over his face to keep a serpent's venom from pouring on his face. The venom-spewing snake is a typical punishment for nidings, which the gods imposed upon Loki for his crimes. When Sigyn empties the bowl his face is exposed and his extreme torment is said to cause earthquakes.

Silfrintop (SILV-rin-tawp)—"Silver Forelock". One of the Aesir's horses.

Simul (SIM-ul) or **Sumul** (SUM-ul)—"Brewing Ale", "Mead". A designation of the pole on which Bil and Hjúki bore the pail Saegr with Byrgir's mead. Connected to the word "*sumble*" (see).

Sindri (SIN-dri)—"Cinders". A name of one of Mímir's most talented artist sons, identical to Dvalin. This is also the name of the hall or smithy where Mímir's sons work, near Nidafjöll.

Singastein (SING-a-stayn)—"The Ornament Rock". Identical to Vagasker and Aldland, this is where Freyja stood by Svipdag during his time of exile. It is the skerry where Heimdall and Loki fought for Brísingamen.

Sinir (SIN-er)—"Strong-of-Sinew". One of the Aesir's horses.

Sinmara (SIN-mar-a)—"Sinew-Maimer". Mímir's wife, mother of Nát, Bödvild and other Night-*dísir*, the Ostaras. This is actually an epithet referring to Mímir-Nidhad's queen ordering Völund's hamstrings to be severed.

Sjöfn (SYUHV-n)—"Love". An Ásynja belonging to Freyja's circle. She is concerned with turning men and women's minds to love.

Skadi (SKAD-i)—"Shadow", "Scathe". Völund's daughter with Idun, a skier and huntress. Became an Ásynja and married Njörd. Lived with Ódin in Mannheim when he was exiled from Ásgard.

Skald (SKALD or SKAHLD)—"Narrator", "Divinely Inspired". A bard or poet who tells the old tales in verse form or sings the sacred songs.

Skaevad (SKAI-vad)—"The Hurrying". One of the Aesir's horses.

Skef (SKEHV)—"Sheaf". Another name of Heimdall, who came to the shores of the Aurvangaland with a sheaf of grain and the tools of agriculture.

Skeggjöld (SKEHG-yuhld)—"Battle-Axe". A Valkyrie.

Skeidbrimir (SKAYD-brim-er)—"Fast-Galloper". One of the Aesir's horses.

Skídbladnir (SKEED-blad-ner)—"The Thin-Planked". The ship Ívaldi's sons made for Frey before the breech between them and the gods. It can travel on land, sea, or air, and can be folded up to fit in one's pocket, but is otherwise so large it can fit all the gods and their equipment within it.

Skilfings (SKIL-vings)—"Skelf's (Skef's, Heimdall's) Descendants". Identical to the Ynglings.

Skinfaxi (SKIN-vaks-i)—"Shining Mane". Sól-Sunna's horse.

Skírnir (SKEER-ner)—"The Shining One". Another name of Od-Svipdag.

Skjöld (SKYUHLD)—"Shield", "The Protector". Son of Fadir and Módir. Moreover a son of Skef-Heimdall and his successor as chief in Aurvangaland. Married to Drótt and father of Halfdan. He was the first earl and judge and was consequently the first king's father and progenitor of the Skjöldungs. He is also called Borgar, Rig II, Dómar, Berchter and Berig.

Skjöldungs (SKYUHLD-ungs)—"Skjöld's Descendants". The first royal line, progenitors of the Danish nobility who found their capital in Lund, which they may have originated from.

Sköll (SKUHL)—"Mockery". A wolf-giant. Fenrir's son who chases Sunna (Sváva, the mother) on her path through the sky. He will swallow her and the sun at Ragnarök.

Skrýmir (SKREE-mer)—"Big Fellow" or "Boaster". Another name of Surt.

Skuld (SKULD)—"Debt", "Spinster". One of the high Nornir, Urd and Ver-dandi's sister. She is leader of the Valkyries who are a branch of the lesser Norns.

Slagfin (SLAG-vin)—"The Finn of Stringed Instruments". Son of Ívaldi and Greip, brother of Egil and Völund, Auda's (Hlagud Svanhvit's) husband, progen-itor of the Gjúkungs. Also called Idi, Hjúki, Thakkrad or Dankrat, Irung, Ald-rian, Jálk, Hengest, and Gjúki.

Sleipnir (SLAYP-ner)—"The Runner". Ódin's eight-legged horse, son of Svadil-fari and Loki in mare-guise.

Slíd (SLEED)—"The Fearsome". A subterranean river, that flows from Hvergelmir through Niflhel.

Slídrugtanni (SLEED-rug-tan-i)—"Razor-Tooth". Frey's golden boar, also called Gullinbursti.

Snö (SNUH)—"Snow". A giant. One of the symbols of the Fimbulvetr. Accord-ing to Saxo the Longobards migrated from Svithjód when "King Snow" ruled there.

Snoer (SNUR)—"Daughter-in-Law". Wife of Karl and progenitress of the class of Karls or Thanes.

Snótra (SNOHT-ra)—"The Prudent". An Ásynja, said to be wise and to have beautiful manners. She may be identical to Idun (who is called Snót in Haust-laung).

Snowing (SNOW-ing)—(English) "Snowing". Probably named after the "Snow-moon", the full moon or moon-cycle in January, giving the designation of this month in the sacred Ásatrú calendar. Also called Thorri (Icelandic) or Thor-ramánadr—"Black Frost Month", Tormånad (Swedish)—"Thór's Month", Glugmaaned (Danish)—"Window Month", Wintarmonath (German)—"Win-ter Month", and Aeftera Geola (Anglo-Saxon)—"After Yule".

Sökkdalir (SUHK-dal-er)—"Deep-Dales". Surt's realm situated in the depths of the Underworld.

Sökkvabekk (SUHK-va-behk)—"Sinking Ship". The name of the moon during its descent.

Sól (SOHL, like "soul")—"Sun". Two Vanadísir, mother and daughter possess this name. The mother is also called Sváva and the daughter Hildigun. The latter shall drive the sun-car after the renewal of the world. She is Máni's daughter with the elder Sól. They are also called Sunna, Álfrödull, Álfhild, and Álfsól.

Són (SOHN)—"Blood". One of the names of Mímir's well, which gave the author of the *Prose Edda* cause to make Kvasir into a "conciliator" between the Aesir and Vanir. In the myth, Mímir himself attempts to reconcile the divine clans and is slain by the Vanir. This story may have something to do with Surt's theft of the Byrgir mead, originally from Mímir's well.

Sörli (SUHR-li)—Brother of Hamdir who was slain by Gudhorm in an attempt to avenge their sister Svanhild's death.

Sowilo (SOH-vil-oh)—(Gothic) "Sun", "Victory". The sixteenth rune of the Elder futhark, connected to the sun and to victory. This could also be a rune of Baldur as god of summer and one of the *Ljónar*—"peacemakers", which is why this rune is associated with such concepts in "The Runelaw".

Spá (SPAH)—"Prophecy". Foreseeing the future, divination.

Stada (STA-da)—"Stance", "Position". Used to designate a Nordic form of postures similar to the Hindu yoga.

Stafur (STAV-ur)—"Stave". The ideogram of an Odinic symbol.

Stallahringur (STAL-a-ring-ur)—"Stalli-Ring", "Altar-Ring". A ring usually worn by a member of the Godard on the right arm as a symbol of authority. During ceremonies or blótar (*blóts*) the ring is attached to the *Stalli* or *Hörg* by a string or chain, so oaths can be made on it. Such a ring was probably designed with a serpent-motif to remind those who make oaths on it of the punishments for breaking them.

Stalli (STAL-i)—"Altar". An indoor or temple-altar, whereas a *Hörg* is an outside or grove-altar.

Strömkarl (STRUHM-karl)—"River-Sprite". A branch of the Landvaettir associated with rivers and waterfalls, whose lyre can be heard on summer nights.

Sumble (SUM-bleh)—"Mead-Feast". A sacred drinking feast consisting of several rounds or "horns", including the Minnehorn "Memory-Horn", where ancestors are honored, and the Bragahorn "Bragi's Horn" where deeds are boasted of or oaths are made to partake in future exploits.

Surt (SURT)—"The Swarthy". Representative of the subterranean fire. In the beginning, he was the gods' friend and Mímir's co-worker; thereafter he is their enemy. Father of Fjálar-Suttung and chieftain of Suttung's sons. The last possessor of the Völund sword, which, when used by Jötun-hands, causes the subterranean fires to burst loose, bringing forth the world-conflagration. He is also called Durin, Durnir, Svarthöfdi and Sökkmimir.

Suttung (SUT-ung)—"Surt's Son". Identical to Fjálar. Also called Mjödvitnir "Mead-Wolf", because he was probably the one who originally stole some of Mímir's mead to create the Byrgir fountain. He is Gunnlöd's father. Right before Ragnarök he fetches the Völund sword from Eggthir in the Ironwood to bring it to his father.

Svadilfari (SVAD-il-var-i)—The sire of Ódin's horse with Loki.

Svalin (SVAL-in)—"Cooler". The shield held before "the shining god", possibly Heimdall, to protect Sól-Sunna from the sun's heat as she drives the sun-car across the sky.

Svárang (SVAHR-ang)—"The Heavy Oppressor". A personification of the Fimbulvetr. The Scandinavian tribes that this "terrible winter" drove southward toward Aurvangaland are called Svárang's sons in *Hárbardsljod*. Thór and Halfdan battle them, first to stop them at the bay and afterwards to compel them to return to their forefather's land, greening again, until they finally sue for peace. There, Thór is described as defending a "river" (the bay south of Aurvangaland) against them and it is said that they cast stones over the river at him, united with elves, as these tribes were then, and giants, which later in the myth are the actual, but not the only stone-throwers (even Thór and Halfdan cast stone-blocks, after their usual weapons fail them). The supposition lies at hand that the erratic stone-blocks found south of the bay and the Baltic were explained in heathen times as thrown there during the Fimbulvetr by "Svarang's Sons".

Svarins Haugr (SVAR-ins HOUG-r)—"Svarin's Mound". The starting point for the Swedes' and their allies' campaign against Aurvangaland. Saxo mentions Svarin as a tributary king under Svithjód's king Sigtrygg, Gróa's father, and gives him seven real and seven illegitimate brothers who, like him, fall in the campaign against Halfdan. One may suppose that all of these brothers were progenitors of the royal families of the peoples of Svealand and Götland in the myth. It is also possible that some of the huge grave-mounds near Uppsala caused the myth in its northern form to identify the Scandinavian migration's starting point as a grave-mound.

Svartálfar (SVART-ahlv-ar)—"Swarthy-Elves". The elves who joined Surt-Durin after his rebellion against Mímir. In this sense the name could also mean "Surt's Elves". Compare Surt's name Svarthöfdi "Chieftain of the Swarthy", "Head of the Swarthy".

Svartálfheim (SVART-ahlv-haym)—"Home of the Swarthy-Elves". Identical to Surt's Sökkdalir.

Sváva (SVAH-va)—"Sleeper". The mother Sunna, who has the daughters Sunna and Nanna with Máni. This is also a name of Nanna herself.

Svidur (SVID-ur) or **Svidrir** (SVID-rer)—"The Swede". Another name of Ívaldi, as Sweden's champion, which Ódin adopted when he appeared in Ívaldi's guise and robbed Suttung of Byrgir's mead. It is said that "Sweden" or "Svithjód" derives its name from him.

Svipdag (SVIP-dag)—"The Glimmering Day". Egil's and Gróa's son. Freyja's rescuer and husband. King of the North Teutons, the mythology's favorite hero. Also called Ód, Ottar, Otharus, (in Saxo some of the myth of Hotherus is taken from his), Erik, Skírnir, and Hermod.

Svipul (SVIP-ul)—"Battle". A Valkyrie.

Svithjód (SVI-thyohd)—"Sweden", "Land of the Sviones", "Svidur's Land". Since very ancient times this name has encompassed much greater regions than Svealand (Sweden) proper. In the myth Svithjód's Northern Empire has been regarded as stretching to the mythic Élivagar (Gandvik), which is the boundary water between Jötunheim and Midgard, in the north. It also encompassed the land of the Skridfinns (Ski-finns), Ívaldi-Svidur is the king of Svealand and the Skridfinns at the same time. And with reference to the "chalet", Geirvandil's chalet, Ysetur, that he and his son Egil had by the Élivagar, the king of the Ynglings has been called "defender of the chalet" by Thjódólf. In Tacitus' time, in the first century A.D., the Sviones in the south were regarded as the ruling people on the Scandinavian peninsula.

Svöl (SVUHL)—"The Cool". A subterranean river.

Sylg (SELG)—"Swallower". A subterranean river.

Syn (SEN)—"Denial". An Ásynja. She is said to guard the doors of Valhalla and shuts them against those who are not to enter. She is invoked by defendants in trials. She must therefore have some position at the Helthing.

Sýr (SEER)—"Sow". A name of Freyja, given to her by the Jötuns when she was in their power.

T

Tannfé (TAN-vee)—"Tooth-Gift". A gift given to a child when they cut their first tooth.

Tanngnjostur (TAN-nyawst-ur)—"Tooth-Gnasher". One of Thór's goats that pulls his chariot. The goats can be killed, eaten, and then resurrected when consecrated by Mjöllnir.

Tanngrisnir (TAN-gris-ner)—"Tooth Grinder". One of Thór's goats that pull his chariot.

Theodism (THYOD-iz-m)—"Folk-Belief". A branch of Teutonic religion particularly focused on Saxon traditions and language.

Thing (THING)—"Assembly". A formal gathering where important matters are discussed and debated, disputes are settled, and legal issues resolved. The Ásatrú tribal council.

Thjálfi (THYALV-i)—"Child of the Dyke or Delve". First Egil's and Gróa's, then Thór's foster son and companion, Röskva's brother. Colonist of the Scandinavian islands after Fimbulvetr.

Thjázi (THYAHZ-i) or **Thjátsi** (THYAHTS-i)—"The Giant". Another name of Völund, which the Norse sources prefer to use concerning him after he changes his nature, becomes the author of the Fimbulvetr, chieftain of the giants, as well as the gods' and Midgard's most dangerous enemy. Other characters, such as Surt-Durin, Idun-Nauma and Auda-Irpa, experienced similar name changes when they turned away from the gods. This may suggest a sanctity in their original names, perhaps given to them by the gods or their representatives, which they later rejected.

Thjódnuma (THYOHD-nu-ma)—"Sweeping People Away". A subterranean river.

Thjódreyrir (THYOHD-ray-rer)—"Waker of the People". The dwarf that sings songs of blessing outside of Delling's door at dawn.

Thjóvara (THYOHD-vart-a)—"Folk-Warner". One of Freyja's attendant *dísir*, possibly her sister as well.

Thökk (THUHK)—"Thanks" or "Grattitude". The being in female guise who refused to "cry Baldur out of Hel". Most likely Loki.

Thór (THOHR)—"The Thunderer". Son of Ódin and Frigga. God of thunder, the farmers' benefactor, protector of Midgard. He wields the hammer Mjöllnir against Jötuns, as well as wears the belt of strength, Megingjörd and a pair of gloves which aid in his use of the hammer. He is Sif's husband, Magni, Módi and Thrud's father, Ull's stepfather and Thjálfi and Röskva's foster father. He is also called Indridi, Hlorridi, Veor, Vingthór, Björn, Asabragi, Sannung, Atli, Himin-soli.

Thórgerd Hölgabrúd (THOHR-gerd HUHLG-a-brood)—"Thór's-Gerd Holy-Bride" or "Thór's-Gerd Loki's (Halogi's)-Bride". According to a Christian saga, Hakon Hladajarl worshipped two *dísir*, Thórgerd and Irpa, daughters of the saga-king Hölgi in Halogaland. If the story has any basis, these *dísir* probably belonged to the earl's mythic family-tree that went back to Skadi and Völund. It is likely that Thórgerd is Sif, Völund's half-sister, who became "Thór's-Gerd", his wife, his "holy bride". If "Loki's Bride" is meant here, this may have some connection to statements in *Harbardsljód* and *Lokasenna*, where Loki claims to have been Sif's lover. That Thórgerd and Irpa appear as giantesses in some sources may relate to their role as the swan-maids of Ívaldi's sons, who joined their kinsmen as lovers and took part in the development of Fimbulvetr. This Irpa, "The Swarthy", Thórgerd's sister, would be Auda, Sif's sister.

Thorri (THOR-i)—"Black-Frost". A frost-giant.

Thórsdag (THOHRS-dag)—"Thór's Day". The original designation of Thursday.

Thráin (THRAH-in) or **Thróin** (THROH-in)—"The Threatening". A dwarf.

Thrall (THRAL)—"Thrall". Name of both the lowest class in ancient Teutonic society and its founder, son of Ái and Edda, husband of Thír.

Thríma (THREE-ma)—"Battle". A Valkyrie.

Thrúd (THROOD)—"The Mighty". A Valkyrie, Thór's daughter.

Thrúdgelmir (THROOD-gehl-mer)—"Mighty-Roarer". A frost-giant, Ymir's son, born from his father's feet. Progenitor of the Hrímthurses, the lower-class of Jötuns.

Thrúdheim (THROOD-haym)—"Home of the Mighty", "Thrúd's Home". Also called Thrúdvang—"Plains of the Mighty", "Thrúd's Plains". Thór's native home.

Thrym (THREM)—"The Noisy". The Jötun who once stole Thór's stone hammer and asked for Freyja's hand for its return.

Thrymgjöll (THREM-gyuhl)—"The Loud-Grating". The gate made by Ívaldi's sons for Gastropnir, the Ásgard-wall.

Thrymheim (THREM-haym)—"Noise-Home". Völund's and Skadi's land in greater Svithjód.

Thurisaz (THUR-i-saz)—(Gothic) "Thurse" or "Thorn". The third rune of the Elder futhark, associated with the Jötuns or Thurses as the great conflicting force against the gods, which Thór battles courageously, without fear and without complaint. Because of this it is associated with such concepts in "The Runelaw".

Thurs (THURS)—"Giant". A designation of the low-born Jötuns of Ymir's feet.

Thviti (THVIT-i)—"Cut Into the Ground". When the gods bound Fenris with the fetter called Gleipnir they took the attachment fastened to it, called Gelgja ("stake"), and drawing it through a great boulder called Gjöll drove the stone deep down into the earth. Then they took a huge rock called Thviti and sank it still deeper into the earth, and used this stone as a fastening peg.

Tíva (TEE-va)—"Father-Sky". This is a name of Ódin representing him as the most ancient god of the wind and the sky. His name Vôdana, Wotan is identical to the Hindu Vâta, their god of the sky. Tíva is the same as Ziu, Zio, Tiwaz, Tiw, and Týr, a name Ódin's son inherited from him.

Tívi (TEE-vi) pl. **Tívar** (TEE-var)—"Sky-Beings", "Sky Gods". A name for the gods of higher rank, the Aesir and Vanir. Other common god-designations are hapt and band.

Tiwaz (TEE-vaz)—(Gothic) "Týr" (Ódin's son). The seventeenth rune of the Elder futhark. In order to protect the gods' honor when they bound the wolf Fenrir, Týr sacrificed his hand as a pledge. Such an act defines the honorable disposition of the gods. Seeing as this pledge is connected to oaths given to Fenrir, such concepts are associated with this rune in "The Runelaw".

Tjausulur (TYOUS-ul-ur)—"Constant Restlessness". Spirits of disease in Niflhel.

Tomte (TAWM-teh)—"House-Elf". A branch of the Landvaettir connected to homes and farms. Traditionally, at Yule, bowls of milk are left out to pay for their services. They protect the home and help out in family chores when they can.

Topi (TAWP-i)—"Insanity". A spirit of disease in Niflhel.

Tramar (TRAM-ar)—"Evil Witches". Demons and sorceresses who cause suffering and torment.

Trollkundur (TRAWL-kund-ur)—"Troll Women". Identical to the Tramar, also called Tunridor—"Riders of Darkness" and the Kveldridur—"Horsewomen of Torture or Death" or "Night Riders". They ride on black steeds bringing suffering to the innocent.

Týr (TEER like "tear")—"The God", "Sky-God". Ódin's son, not the original Sky-Father, but who inherited his name. His mother was a giantess. He is the god of war and warriors, said in the *Prose Edda* to not be a peacemaker, thus he is also not the god of the Thing or of justice.

Týrsdag (TEERS-dag)—"Týr's Day". The original designation of Tuesday.

U

Udr (UD-r)—"The Wave". One of the nine daughters of Aegir who represent the waves.

Ulfrun (ULV-run)—"Wolf-Runner", "She Who Rides a Wolf". One of Heim-dall's nine mothers who turns the World-Mill.

Úlfdalir (OOLV-dal-er)—"The Wolfdales". The haven of Ívaldi's sons after their breach with the gods. Either within or identical to the Ironwood.

Ull (UL)—"The Glorious". Son of Sif and Örvandil-Egil, Thór's step-son. He is god of the winter hunt along with his goddess cousin Skadi. He once held Ódin's throne when the Ása-father was exiled by the Vanir from Ásgard. He is Svipdag's half-brother and trusted companion.

Uni (UN-i)—A dwarf. One of Dvalin's artists.

Uppregin (UP-rehg-in)—"The Upper Powers". Divinities living in the Under-world who have duties to perform in "the upper heavens": Nát, Dag, Sól, and Máni.

Úrarhorn (OOR-ar-horn)—"Aurochs Horn". The drinking-horn, a vessel held sacred in Ásatrú used in drinking mead at *blóts*, sumbles, etc.

Urd (URD)—"Fate", "That-which-is". The foremost Norn who feeds the *örlögthaettir* "threads of fate" from her well to her sister Verdandi so they can be woven into the Web of Wyrd. She is the *dís* of fate and death, ruler over Hel and the Helthing near her fountain. She is also called Hel, who is not Loki's daughter (Leikin).

Urdabrunn (URD-a-brun)—"Urd's Well". The southernmost of the subterra-nean fountains whose mead gives strength.

Úri (OOR-i)—A dwarf. One of Dvalin's artists.

Uruz (OOR-ooz)—(Gothic) "Aurochs", also Úr (OOR)—"Primal", "Original". The second rune of the Elder futhark. Because the word can be etymologically linked with *örlög* (*urlagnen* "the original laws"), this rune represents this concept in "The Runelaw".

Útgard (OOT-gard)—"The Outer Realm". Identical to Surt's Sökkdalir, which is his exile outside the lands of the gods.

Útgard-Loki (OOT-gard LAWK-i)—"Loki of the Outer-Realm". Identical to Surt.

V

Vadgelmir (VAD-gehl-mer)—"Roaring Water". A subterranean river that liars must wade through with dire consequences.

Vaferlögur (VAV-er-luhg-ur)—"Quick-Fires", "The Bickering Flames". Flames surrounding fortresses as protection, with lightning bolts that also strike targets, including the earth. They originate in the Vafer-laden clouds which Thór, among others, can strike to emit these "flames". They are said to be "smart" and never miss their mark, and were implemental in the slaying of Völund-Thjázi.

Váfthrúdnir (VAHV-throod-ner)—"Strong in Entangling (with Questions)". An old, very wise Jötun that Ódin, under the name Gagnrad, sought out to compete with in a contest of wisdom. When Gagnrad finally asks him what Ódin whispered in Baldur's ear, the giant must admit his own defeat.

Vagasker (VAG-ask-er)—"Ocean-Skerry". Identical to Singastein and Aldland, where Freyja stood by Svipdag in his exile, where Heimdall and Loki battled for Brísingamen, and where Hadding was cursed by Freyja for killing her husband, which probably caused the island to sink.

Vagnhöfdi (VAG-n-huhv-di)—"Wagon Chieftain". A warrior of giant-birth, Hadding's foster father, Hardgrep's father. Also called Vagn "Wagon" and Kjálki "sled".

Vala (VAL-a) or **Völva** (VUHLV-a)—"Seeress". Whether a practitioner of the holy *Galdr* or the evil *Seid*, this term designates a female diviner.

Valaskjálf (VAL-a-skyahlv)—"Hall of the Chosen". Possibly identical to Valhalla, even though Valaskjálf's roof is said to be "thatched with silver" and Valhalla is roofed with golden shields.

Valhalla (VAL-hal-a)—"Hall of the Chosen". Ódin's hall in the domain of Ásgard called Gladsheim, where his half of the Einherjar are kept. The Old Norse "*Valr*", which is found in the compounds Valfödr, Valkyrja, Valhalla, etc. does not mean "the slain", but rather "one chosen for the destiny that awaits them in another world". It therefore represents those heroes *chosen* for the glory of Valhalla, not those required to die in battle for this.

Váli (VAHL-i)—"Warrior". An Asa-god, son of Ódin and Rind, who killed Hödur to avenge Baldur's death.

Valkyrjur (VAL-ker-yur) singular **Valkyrja** (VAL-ker-ya)—"Choosers of the Chosen". Norns, who at Ódin's or Freyja's command, select warriors on the battlefield to die by weapons and convey them through the Underworld to Ásgard. They also lead warriors who have died from causes other than violent on the paths to Valhalla. Once there they serve the mead to those who have become Einherjar.

Vanadís (VAN-a-dees)—"Vanir Goddess". A designation of Freyja, but can be used to signify any *dís* of the Vanir clan, like Vanagod, Ása-god or Ásynja for other deities.

Vanaheim (VAN-a-haym)—"Vanir-Home". The land of the Vanir on the Underworld's (Jörmungrund's) western rim.

Vanir (VAN-er)—"Fertility Gods". Next to the Aesir they are the foremost tribe of divinities, whose function is primarily focused on the natural order and regulation of the mechanisms of the worlds. They are also deities of peace and love, invoked often in such matters concerning them.

Vár (VAHR)—"Vow". An Ásynja, goddess of promises, whose name is invoked at the Handfastna, the marriage ceremony. She sees to it that these oaths are kept and punishes those who break them.

Varna vidr (VARN-na VID-r)—"Forest of the Defenders". The home of the Varnians where the Sun and Sunna are protected each night.

Varnians (VAR-ni-ans) or **Varns** (VARNS)—"The Defenders". Warriors of the sunset glow, Billing's retinue that watch over Sól-Sunna's rest.

Varr (VAR)—"Cautious". A dwarf, one of Dvalin's artists.

Vartari (VAR-tar-i)—"Lip-Tearer". A thong with which Brokk used to sew up Loki's lips after the competition of the artists.

Vé (VEE)—"The Holy (Place)". The area where a sacred act is performed, consecrated and dedicated to the gods. That this would be named after Ódin's brother, Hoenir-Vé, is fitting because he is said to be the priest of the gods who "chooses the lot-wood". It may sound strange that the gods would have a priest, but only if you do not understand the true nature of sacrifice among the ancients. Rather than simply an act of piety, offerings made to the divine, by anyone, empower them and help them in performing their wonderful feats. Ódin once sacrificed himself to himself and the gods are said in *Völuspá* to have set up temples and altars to sacrifice to each other in time's morning. The term Vé signifies a sanctuary, and can refer to our sacred temples or groves, and is thus related to *Hof.*

Vébond (VEE-bawnd)—"Bond of the Holy Place". The barriers of the *Vé*, ropes strung around the sacred stead to mark the consecrated area.

Vedrfölnir (VEHD-r-vuhl-ner)—"The Weather Bleached". A hawk perched upon the eyes of an eagle perched in Yggdrasil's branches. The eagle is said to be very knowledgeable, and is probably Ódin himself.

Vedurglasir (VEHD-ur-glas-er)—"Weather-Glasir". Designates Yggdrasil, or more particularly its "wind-swept" crown.

Vegdrasil (VEHG-dra-sil)—A dwarf, one of Dvalin's artists.

Veigar (VAY-gar)—"The Liquids". The blended meads of the Underworld fountains. Also called Dýrar Veigar—"Precious Liquids" and Skirar Veigar—"Clear Liquids", "Pure Liquids".

Veraldar nagli (VER-ald-ar NAG-li)—"The World-Nail". An ancient Teutonic name for the North Star, once believed to be the fixed point all the other stars revolve around. It was thus considered the central pillar of the World-Mill, said to cause the stars to turn, among other things.

Verdandi (VER-dan-di)—"That-Which-is-Becoming". Urd and Skuld's sister, one of the three great Norns who weaves the *Örlögthaettir* "threads of fate" into the Web of Wyrd.

Vetrablót (VET-ra-bloht)—"Winter Blót", "Winter Sacrifice". Also called "Winter Nights", it is the festival marking the end of the harvest when food is stocked for winter. It takes place on the Njördsdag (Saturday) between Hunting 11th and 17th and lasts three nights. This may be the time when the Álfablót—"Elf-Blót" takes place.

Vídar (VEE-dar)—"The Far-Ruler". An Ása-god, Ódin's son with the giantess Gríd. He will avenge Ódin's death at Ragnarök after Fenrir swallows the Ásafather. He "will stride forward and place one foot on the lower jaw of the wolf. On this foot he will be wearing the shoe which has been in the making since the beginning of time, it consists of the strips of leather men pare off at the toes and heels of their shoes, and for this reason people who want to help the Aesir must throw away these strips (as a sacrifice). Vídar will take the wolf's upper jaw in one hand and tear his throat asunder and that will be the wolf's death". (Gylfaginning).

Vídbláin (VEED-blah-in)—"The Wide-Blue". One of the heavens.

Vidga Völundson (VID-ga VUHL-und-son)—Son of Völund and the night-dís Bödvild. A hero fighting on the side of the Ívaldi-clan.

Vídofnir (VEED-awv-ner)—"The Wide Open". The golden cock, identical to Gullinkambi and Salgofnir. A symbol of the starry heaven and the atmosphere, and possibly of Lódur-Gevar, the ward of the atmosphere.

Vidólf (VID-ohlv)—"Forest Wolf". A giant and sorcerer. Origin of the evil valas and possibly one of Gullveig's fathers (remember she was born three times and reborn three times, probably to different parents).

Vígríd (VEEG-reed)—"The Battlefield". Thought to be identical to Vídi (VEED-i)—"The Wide-Land", which is Vídar's home. It is the field where the Ragnarök battle will be fought, said to be 120 leagues in every direction, located in Jörmungrund.

Vígthríma (VEEG-three-ma)—"Thunder-Strife". The battle Thór and Ódin and other lightning wielders fight against the Jötuns of destructive lightning. Defines a violent thunderstorm and its ending.

Vili (VIL-i)—"Will", "The Willful". This name can also mean "desire", "longing". It is an epithet of Ódin's brother Lódur who is god of friction and the friction-fire who gave us sexual desire through his divine gifts (which is why such desire is connected to "animal" instincts, Lódur's *lá* with *laeti* represents the animal component in humans).

Vilmeid (VIL-mayd)—"Soothsayer". A Jötun sorcerer.

Vindheim (VIND-haym)—"Wind-Home". The World, as far as the winds blow.

Vindsval (VIND-sval)—"Wind-Cold". A symbolic designation of winter's father. Compare the epithets Vindkald—"Wind-Cold", Varkald—"Springcold", and Fjölkald—"Verycold", with which Svipdag in Fjölsvinnsmál characterizes himself, his father Egil, and his grandfather Ívaldi.

Vingnir (VING-ner)—A giant, Thór's foster father, killed by him. Thór obtained his first hammer from him, made of stone.

Vingólf (VIN-gohlv)—"Wine-Hall". The hall of the Ásynjur in Ásgard. Because of conflicting reports found in the *Prose Edda* concerning the use of this hall, it may have originally been a generic term for a divine stead which was made into a proper name.

Vinland (VIN-land)—"Wine-Land". The name given to North America by the Vikings due to the large amount of grapes they discovered. Commonly used today by Ásatrúars to designate this.

Vitki (VIT-ki)—"Seer", "Magician". A male diviner or practitioner of the holy *Galdr* or evil *Seid*.

Völund (VUHL-und)—"The Woe-Minded". An Elf-Cheiftain and primeval artist, thereafter the king of the giants and "earth's worst foe". Ívaldi's son, Egil and Slagfin's brother, Idun's half-brother. His name occurs among different Teutonic peoples in different forms. The oldest written forms documented are Valund and Veland. Others are Valland, Vallandi, Vanlande, Galen, Wayland, Wieland, Verland, Völund, and Velint. Völund is an epithet, limited to the Icelandic literature, which plays on words, meaning "woe-minded", "woe-disposed". In other Nordic lands, he was never called this, and yet in the 1200s, the form Völund was not even commonly adopted in Iceland. The myth about three artist-brothers who are first the gods' friends and decorated the earth with vegetation and the gods' halls with ornaments, but thereafter, on account of a contest between them and another primeval artists (Sindri), became the gods' enemies and sought to destroy the world, is, as far as the investigation into this matter can now determine, the first epic element in the Teutonic mythology. It is of proto Indo-European origin and is rediscovered in the Rigveda, the collection of Hindu sacred hymns. Völund has the following names: Thjázi, Ajo, Anun, Önund, Rögnir, Brúnni, Ásolf, Varg, Fjallgyldir, Hlébard, Byr, Gust and Lopt.

Vón (VOHN)—"Expectation". The river that flows from the fettered Fenrir's mouth.

Vör (VUHR)—"Awareness". An Ásynja, said to be so wise and searching that nothing can be concealed from her.

W

Walpurgisnacht (VAHL-puhr-gis-nahkt)—(German) "Walpurgis' Night". Walpurgis means "Dís of the Mountain of the Slain" (cp. Reginsmál where Ódin is called "Man of the Mountain") and is probably identical to Frigga. This celebration takes place on Ostara (April) 30th as the Beltaine eve. Frigga is Baldur's mother and probably the original "May Queen" who was represented by veiled women with her masked husband Ódin (Grímnir—"The Masked One"). The procession of Nerthus in Tacitus' *Germania* is probably connected to this rite.

Weregild (WUR-gild or VUR-gild)—(German) "Man-Payment". An ancient tradition of offering amends for killing someone as part of afrád gjalda or gamban gylda.

Wodensdag (VOH-dens-dag)—("Woden" is German). "Woden's Day", also Ódinsdag—"Ódin's Day". The original designation of Wednesday.

Wralda (RALD-a)—(Old Frisian) "Old Man", "God of the World" ("World" comes from "Were-ald", meaning either "man-age" or "old-man"). Ódin as the creator of Midgard.

Wunjo (VOON-yoh)—(Gothic) "Joy". The eighth rune of the Elder futhark, associated with joy and happiness, which is why it is connected to such concepts in "The Runelaw".

Wyrd (WEERD or VEERD, identical to "weird")—(Old English) "Fate", "Destiny". Both a variant spelling of "Urd" and the concept of fate in Ásatrú philosophy.

Y

Ydalir (E-dal-er)—"The Dales of the Bow". A land lying south of the Élivagar, where Egil's fortress is located. The land is the inheritance (*odal*) of Egil's son, Ull.

Yggdrasil (EG-dras-il)—"Ygg's (Ódin's) steed". The World-Tree born of a golden seed, with golden leaves and golden fruit. Its trunk and branches are probably silver or "as white as the membrane called the skin that lies around the inside of an eggshell". Yggdrasil is also called Mímameid—"Mímir's Tree", since Mímir guards the middlemost root; Laerád or Hrár vidr—"Mead-Tree", since it is nourished by the meads of the three wells of life in the Underworld; Mjötvidr—"Fate-Tree"; Glasir—"The Resplendent", Aurglasir—"Mud-Glasir", and Vedurglasir—"Weather-Glasir". It is often called "Yggdrasil's Ash".

Ylfings (EL-vings)—"Ylf's Descendants". A mythic royal family, closely related to the Hildings.

Ylg (ELG)—"Swelling". A subterranean river.

Ymir (EM-er)—"Roarer". The primordial Jötun, formed from the rime of Ginnungagap once it was melted by heat. From the sweat of his arms, filled with Audhumla's fertile sustenance, he sired Mímir and Bestla. From his feet came Thrudgelmir. He was slain by Bor's sons, possibly for killing Audhumla. His body was used to decorate Midgard.

Ynglings (ENG-lings)—"Yng's Descendants". Identical to the Skilfings, a Swedish noble tribe of mythic origin, consisting of two clans, ultimately fused: Ívaldi's clan (the actual and oldest Ynglings, "Niflungs") and Skjöld-Borgar's clan (Skjöldungs).

Yngvi (ENG-vi)—"Prince", "Warrior". This name is used by Frey, Heimdall and Svipdag.

Yrsa (ER-sa)—"She-Wolf". After careful consideration it can be proven that many of the elements of the story of Hrólf Kraki were taken from that of Ull. In Hrólf's saga his mother is Yrsa, who is therefore identical to Sif. In Saxo Sif has the name Kraka (Craca), which may have some connection to Hrólf's surname.

Ysetur (E-seht-ur)—"The Chalet of the Bow". The fortress in Ydalir by the Élivagar where the gods had their outpost against the Jötuns, entrusted to Ívaldi and his sons. The fortress is also called "Geirvandil's or Geirvadil's (Ívaldi's) Chalet". It became Ull's home after Ívaldi's sons rebelled against the gods and died.

Sources

The Agricola and Germania by Cornelius Tacitus, tr. by H. Mattingly, revised by S.A. Handford, Penguin, 1970.

Altnordisches Etymologisches Wörterbuch by Jan De Vries, Leiden 1962.

The Ancient Fires of Midgard, by Andrea Haugen, 1999.

Annals of Imperial Rome by Cornelius Tacitus. Penguin Classics, revised 1956.

Astrobiology by Thorsteinn Gudjonsson. Bioradii Books 1976.

The Bhagavad Gita tr. by Ramananda Prasad. International Gita Society, 2001.

Dictionary of Northern Mythology by Rudolf Simek. Cambridge 1993.

Dreams are the Keys to the Cosmos by Thorsteinn Gudjonsson. Bioradii Books 1982.

Germanic Heathenry by James Hjuka Coulter. 1st Books Library 2003.

Heimskringla by Snorri Sturluson, tr. by Lee M. Hollander. University of Texas Press, revised 1991.

The History of the Danes by Saxo Grammaticus, tr. by Peter Fisher. Boydell & Brewer, 2002.

A History of Sweden by Lars O. Lagerquist. Swedish Institute, 2002.

A History of the Vikings by Gwyn Jones. Oxford University Press, 1984.

Investigations into Germanic Mythology by Viktor Rydberg, Vol. I, translated in three parts as *Teutonic Mythology* by Rasmus Anderson, Norroena, 1907.

Investigations into Germanic Mythology by Viktor Rydberg, Vol. II, translated in two parts by William P. Reaves, iUniverse 2004 & 2006.

Iron John by Robert Bly. Reed Business Information, Inc. 1990.

King James Bible—World Bible Publishers.

Norse Mythology by Rasmus Anderson, Knight + Leonard, 1875.

The Oera Linda Book tr. By Frank H. Pierce, 1983.

Our Fathers' Godsaga by Viktor Rydberg, tr. by William P. Reaves, iUniverse, 2003 (www.iUniverse.com). This text provided many of the entries and information for "The Catalog of Terms" in this book.

The Poetic Edda tr. by Henry Adams Bellows. Dover Publications, 2004.

The Poetic Edda tr. by Lee M. Hollander, University of Texas Press, 1990.

The Prose Edda by Snorri Sturluson, tr. by Anthony Faulkes. Everyman, 2003.

The Prose Edda by Snorri Sturluson, tr. by Jean I. Young. University of California Press.

The Prose Edda by Snorri Sturluson, tr. By Jesse Byock, Penguin, 2005.

The Holy Qur'an tr. by A. Yusuf Ali. Tahrike Tarsile Qur'an, 1999.

Raiðo: The Runica Journey by Jennifer Smith, Tara Hill Designs, 1993.

The Rigveda tr. by Ralph T. H. Griffith. Motilal Banarsidass, 1992.

Rituals of Ásatrú vol. I-III by Stephen McNallen, Ásatrú Free Assembly.

Edda Sæmundar Hinns Frôða (The Poetic Edda) tr. by Benjamin Thorpe. Trübner & Co. (1866).

If you have any questions or comments please contact us at: info@norroena.org

or visit our website: www.norroena.org

978-0-595-38964-3
0-595-38964-3

Made in the USA
Middletown, DE
05 April 2019